Recreation Trends and Markets:
The 21st Century

John R. Kelly
University of Illinois at Urbana-Champaign

Rodney B. Warnick
University of Massachusetts at Amherst

#43323562

ISBN: 1-57167-435-7

Library of Congress Catalog Card Number: 99-68599

Cover Design: Charles L. Peters

Interior Design: Janet Wahlfeldt

Cover Photos: Photo Disc

Sagamore Publishing, Inc.

P.O. Box 647

Champaign, IL 61824-0647

Web Site: http//www.sagamorepub.com

With all due appreciation of my supportive wife, Ruth Kelly, and my wonderful daughters, Professors Susan Kelly and Janice Kelly, I would dedicate my efforts on this volume to a remarkable number of former students and younger colleagues who have been so appreciative and supportive of me and my work through the years. You have really helped.

Jack Kelly

I wish to dedicate this book to Deb, my wife, and Ben and Matt, my sons and Mahlon and Dot, my parents, who have all supported me through the years in thought, word, prayers, and special assistance to make this book and the collection of the data possible. Each has given up time and been patient with me over the writing and analysis period. I have been so fortunate to have such a supportive family. This book is a symbol of that support.

I also owe a great deal of gratitude to the faculty, staff, and students I have come in contact with over the years at Frostburg State, the University of Montana, Penn State University and the University of Massachusetts. For those who helped me during those years to become a better researcher, teacher and scholar, I extend my heartfelt "Thanks."

Rod Warnick

Contents

Contents

Contents

This project first began with a practical request. A park and recreation district had to decide what to do with a school building they had acquired. Their fundamental question was simple: What kinds of activities would attract the most participants, not just next year but in the next ten years? What were the current trends in recreation participation?

In the years that have followed, similar questions have been raised by other providers of recreation and leisure resources. Corporations have wanted to understand better the participation basis for their products and services and especially their key market segments. Trade associations have asked for assistance in augmenting their expenditure data with analysis of participation trends. Recreation markets, unlike many business enterprises, depend entirely on what people choose to do because they enjoy it. Participation trends are critical.

At first, in the preparation of the 1987 project it became evident that there was no reliable analysis of consistent studies of a wide spectrum of recreation participation. There was, however, an unexploited resource in the yearly market surveys done for the purposes of media planning and advertising. This data became the basis of the 1987 *Recreation Trends toward the Year 2000* book (Kelly, 1987). In recent years there have been numerous requests for an update of that book. Both the market data and analytical methods, however, have been expanded and improved to make this book much more comprehensive than the earlier one. Many new activities were added to the surveys while the participation patterns for more established activities changed.

There are a number of related practical issues: public recreation providers have to decide on facilities and personnel; business entrepreneurs need to identify markets for products and programs before they make significant investments; resource managers must decide on the best mix of access, sites, and amenities. Answers to all these questions are based on recreation participation.

What are people doing as recreation? Do such factors as age, gender, income, regional location, and education identify those most likely to engage in particular activities? Is participation in an activity growing, shrinking, or remaining relatively stable, and, most important for those deciding on investments, what are likely future trends?

There is, of course, no shortage of speculation about such questions. Often comparing data with quite different bases, promoters and journalists uncritically extol new trends or even the latest "craze." Almost without exception, such promotions have no reliable trend data, no figures on comparable activities, and no clear identification of just who is involved in the activity. What is unfortunate is that too often significant investments are made based on unsubstantiated and usually false claims.

As will be explained in the first chapter of this book, looking ahead just isn't quite that easy. Data sources are inconsistent. Population changes may be conflicting rather than additive. Recreation trends are embedded in habits, lifestyles, resource opportunities, and economic and social contexts. Trends are seldom linear or mono-dimensional. In fact, one surprise was that among all the data and publications there has been very little about trends, especially for periods of over a few years.

This book does not incorporate every possible source of information or resolve all inconsistencies. It does bring together in an analytical framework participation data previously available only by subscription. Also, it provides a picture of national trends. Such an analysis can be valuable background for specific decisions. It is, of course, no substitute for analysis of the particular market area for a program or facility. Nor does it replace a sound understanding of the meanings and contexts of recreation engagement. There has been a tremendous growth in research-based knowledge that expands and corrects much that had been taken for granted in the 1960s and 1970s.

Nevertheless, this book is unique. It brings together previously unavailable information and analysis in a compact form. It may be read for its overall analysis of recreation trends. It may be used as a reference when particular activities are of interest. It may be employed by students and scholars as the springboard for critical discussion. For recreation planners and entrepreneurs, it offers a context for the analysis of specific communities and markets. It is, then, intended to be practical, a book to be passed around the office and committee rather than decorate the bookshelf.

The analyses of activities are in summary form. The authors have access to much fuller data and have completed more complex analyses for most of the activities, about a one foot stack of tables, graphs, and summaries. For consulting based on such material, we may be contacted by e-mail (Addresses: warnick@hrta.umass.edu and jr-kelly@uiuc.edu) or through our universities.

We are grateful to the publishing company for encouraging and supporting this book. Joe Bannon kept insisting that it was needed in the field. Primarily we are grateful to the Simmons Market Research Bureau, Inc. of New York for their generosity in making their past data available to ours and other universities. They have been most gracious and helpful. While the interpretation of these data is ours, the data source is the property of SMRB. We are also grateful for the assistance of the University of Massachusetts business and reference librarians, Jill Ausel, Mike Davis, and Associate Library Director Gordon F. Fretwell, who were critical in maintaining, updating, and acquiring the volumes of the Simmons Market Research Bureau's *Study of Media and Markets* over the years (1975-1996). For many years the data were contained in over 40 bound volumes. Now the data are available in an interactive CD format that will make possible a number of new opportunities for the future use of this valuable data source. We are also grateful for newer sources of data. In particular, we acknowledge the cooperation and assistance of Richard Lipsey of Sporting Goods Research Network (SGRnet) of Princeton, New Jersey, for help in tracing newer niche activities. Another and quite different approach to trend analysis for resource-based outdoor recreation has been compiled by H. Ken Cordell and associates for the U.S. Forest Service and recently published by Sagamore Publishing *(Outdoor Recreation in American Life: A National Assessment of Demand and Supply Trends,* 1999).

John R. Kelly
Professor emeritus
University of Illinois at Urbana-Champaign

Rodney B. Warnick
Professor
University of Massachusetts at Amherst

Chapter 1

Looking Ahead

In 1863 Jules Verne published a novel depicting Paris in the 20th century. It was suppressed because of its dismal scenario and only recently discovered locked away in a safe. Verne envisioned people getting around in vehicles controlled with steering wheels and gas pedals and powered by gas motors. This was 26 years before the invention of the internal combustion engine. He also predicted a "photographic telegraph," the modern fax, and the electric chair for executions. Life, however, was miserable because the "demon of money" drove people from higher values to consumption.

There will be no such incredible flights of fancy in this book. Neither the authors nor our sources have any special insight into the future. In fact, we are skeptical of those who make such claims. The one sure thing about the future is that it is uncertain. We can never know with certainty just what tomorrow will bring in any aspect of our lives. The paradox of planning is that we usually base our plans on continuity and recognize at the same time that change is inevitable and inexorable. Nothing will be quite the same next year, including ourselves. Yet we plan and invest on the assumption that the basic institutional contexts of life will remain much the same as they are today.

That paradox of looking ahead will shadow every dimension of our project. We will be taking the best information about both continuity and change that is currently available. We will examine the sources critically and compare their implications. We will formulate projections about recreation participation based on the analysis of long- and short-term trends as well as on changes in the population. We will put all this in an overall context of models and meanings. And then, when all this is completed, we will be reminded that some of the assumed continuities are problematic and some of the changes less than certain. Moreover, all the factors we will include in the analysis are interrelated so that a few small miscalculations could be compounded into sizable error. Let's look at two recent examples:

(1) It was fashionable in the 1950s and 60s to forecast a fast approaching "leisure age" in which the former domination of productive work would give way to lifestyles with more free time and emphasis on nonwork activity. In fact, the future of leisure was defined as a problem by many who were sure that demand would overwhelm resources and that many workers would be unprepared to use this abundant time constructively. Projections even included exponentially increased needs for recreation professionals and resources by 1980.

What happened? First, the projections were based on the long-term reduction in average weekly hours of employment since the 1880s. That trend continued through the immediate post-World War II years and then leveled at about 40 hours per week (Schor, 1991). Since 1960, economic cycles more often have led to unemployment than to a general reduction of the work week. Second, every level of the American economy including finance and production is now integrated into a global system in which advances in one nation are dependent on advances in others. Third, the projection presumed continued rapid growth in the American economy, a projection

Chapter 1

Looking Ahead

rendered inaccurate in the 1970s and 80s by international competition and leveling rates of productivity. Fourth, the "average workweek" does not represent the wide variation found among those outside the factory, especially in the growing service sector of the economy. Fifth, other factors are involved in time use, such as the increased time devoted to work and maintenance travel in growing metropolitan complexes. All time not spent on the job is not devoted to leisure (Robinson and Godbey, 1997). Sixth, most of the gains in nonwork time were absorbed by at-home activity, especially television, rather than by organized recreation. Seventh, there was a great increase of women in the paid workforce, especially mothers who experience a "time crunch" from multiple roles of responsibility. And there were other factors. The point is that any simple extrapolation from one trend to complex social change is almost certain to be rendered invalid by factors that crisscross the field of social action.

(2) Today we are told over and over that we are far along in the transition from a "production economy" to an "information society." The personal computers on which we write are only one element of this allegedly profound change. The computer and its communications technologies now facilitate a rapid exchange of information on all levels and for myriad purposes. When adopted, computers with complex software programs and linkages to a worldwide web permit all sorts of new ways of problem-solving and communication. Without undertaking an exhaustive analysis, however, we can sketch a number of reasons why even this "revolution" has limits. First, of course, is cost. Most of the world can't afford the technology, however dramatically prices decrease.

Second, implementation of any technology has multiple costs, not only in equipment but in personnel preparation. It is one thing to fold a useful technology into an economic system to increase efficiency. It is quite another to reformulate the nature of the system—how problems are defined and solutions are conceptualized. So far the "computer revolution" is more a dramatic adaptation of new technology to old problems. As such, the revolution will depend on the extent to which it is judged to be cost-efficient. Corporations are finding that the hardware costs are only the beginning. In a global competitive economy, technologies, however dramatic, will be implemented successfully only when they yield a market advantage.

Third, the world economy still requires heavy industry, agriculture, housing, and a variety of social services as well as electronic goods. Information is crucial, but information about what? For example, electronics has had an enormous impact on global financial transactions, but information is NOT investment capital. In fact, capital is required to support the information industry.

Fourth, the boom, recession, and redevelopment of the electronic games industry illustrates that any technology, even in leisure, must tie into established investments, lifestyles, value systems, and skills. Electronic games will not replace physical exertion, aesthetic involvement, or social interaction as significant elements of leisure styles. Technologies by themselves cannot completely transform complex cultures. The point is that electronic information processing is one significant factor in economic and social change, but it is not THE factor that will transform the productive needs of a world economy, the social patterns of reproduction and nurture, the personal values placed on community and bio-social self-development, or even an old-format activity such as reading. So far the costs of equipment, going on-line at a distance, and of the information itself, to say nothing of acquiring the skills of understanding and operation, have restricted financial network users to a relatively limited group that can profit from their scope and speed. This group, however, is expanding as a larger proportion of the younger population acquires the technical and financial resources to utilize its possibilities.

Fifth, the ramifications of a multi-use technology such as electronic communications can do more than merely add an activity to the current list. Rather, for the adept, the information technology can produce a better-informed participant in countless activities, with tourism only currently the most marketed example. Further, games are already taking new forms. For example, fantasy games allow for interactive networks to play games as individuals and teams in formats and competitions that can span continents and oceans. The expansion and varieties of such games are often time-intensive and will have an impact on other activities. A pervasive technology can, over a period of a decade or more, alter the formats of such activities as fantasy games but also draw from the time and financial resources previously dedicated to other activities.

If we are now at least a little suspicious of those projections that base radical social transformations on a single factor, economic or technological, then are there viable alternatives?

Why Projections Are Useful

We cannot avoid trying to fathom the future because we plan and invest. If municipal managers are planning land use and recreation facility development in a growing area, how do they choose among the alternatives? Once space is dedicated, personnel are hired, and buildings are equipped, it is costly to initiate activities other than those in the plan. Is racquetball going to replace tennis? Will aerobic dance fade as a fascinating fad for educated young women or will it retain a significant participant group? Will the time-intensive nature of golf and the high cost of urban land limit its participation? Will more and more exercise activity retreat to the home and to flexible times rather than be with scheduled groups? Will new neighborhoods have lots of children requiring playgrounds or post-parental adults seeking walking paths? What are the best locations for various kinds of resources provided by either the market or public sectors?

Answers to such questions require developing two projections: (1) Who will be living in the area? That is, what are the demographic projections? (2) What will their recreation participation patterns and priorities be? To avoid being trapped by a concrete set of provisions later found to be unsuited to potential users, recreation planning calls for looking ahead as clearly and completely as possible. The trend patterns of growth and decline of older activities over periods of decades can yield many clues to the probable future trends for new or developing activities.

In both the market and public sectors of the society, the matter of investment must also be considered. Financial investment for space and equipment, personnel investment for hiring and training, and organizational investment for the development of programs and products all require decisions based on projections of future return. Bringing a new product on line, for example, involves conceptualization, design, modeling, testing, evaluation, product design and tooling, marketing, distribution, and the assignment of all the factors of production to the complex process. If the potential market is based on some sort of recreation participation, then a projection of latent demand, alternatives, direct and indirect competition, and the basis of trends is absolutely necessary to minimize loss.

Why Projections Are Dangerous

If we had absolutely reliable and comparable data on participation trends and the precise composition of user groups, such projections would be relatively simple and trustworthy. At least that would be the case if all trends were linear—simply extending current rates of growth or decline. Reality, however, is more complex.

Trends may not be linear. Rather, recreation activities are much like other products. Market analyses have discovered a "product life cycle." New market products have an phases of introduction, growth, peak, decline, and either the stability of a plateau or failure. There have been similar patterns for activities. This "activity life cycle" (Kelly, 1985) indicates that most activities follow a pattern of growth, peak, decline, and either plateau or virtual disappearance. Only a relatively long-term trend analysis can distinguish between stable or growing activities and those that are declining or may even be fads. Some activities grow rapidly and then retreat to become niche activities with about 1 or 2 percent of the population participating regularly. Projections based on only a few years are deceptive unless placed into a fuller context. Some activities may even have temporary growth spurts in response to events such as Olympic television exposure. Further, there are multiple factors in such a cycle, including the breadth and depth of the market, costs, conflict with lifestyles and value systems, and fit with other activities. The most dangerous use of projections is to assume continued growth of any activity. All markets have limits.

Analysis of the major market segment for video arcades, for example, showed a concentration of preteen and teen males, a very limited and volatile market. Further, the weapons-aiming electronics technology on which the early games were based was limited in the kinds of skills required. Even more important, the number of regular game players among other market segments, especially adults, was quite limited. A marked peak and decline was predicted based on identified limitations of the activity *and* the demonstrated participation segments. Later renewal of the markets was based on the expansion of the home computer market, new hardware capacities and software programs, and increased marketing. Technology can create a second wave of market expansion, but this, too, will have its cycle. In short, along with the technology itself, the composition of participants, the activity, resource costs and requirements, and the social contexts all must be analyzed to begin to develop reliable projections. That is the sort of approach that will be employed in this book.

Principles of Analysis

The projections offered here are based on several premises. None are esoteric, but all involve more than just extending trend lines. The analyses here involve participation rates, the numbers of participants, the volume of participation days, identified market segments, and selected demographic factors. Changing patterns were reviewed and interpreted in a multifaceted context.

First, recreation activities are not an independent sector of life. Rather, leisure, which incorporates organized recreation, is connected with all other dimensions of life. The life domains of family, work, and community all have elements of leisure woven through their hours and days, off-task activities engaged in primarily for the experience. Leisure is a context for the development and expression of intimate relationships, especially those of romance and the family. All sorts of off-task episodes and interactions color life in the office, store, or plant. Expressive actions are combined with developmental aims in church, child- and youth-serving organizations, playground, and school. The entire institutional fabric of the community and society is related to recreation choices, resources, and meanings.

Second, recreation choices and activities are limited by the institutional arrangements of the society. Schedules of time available for non-work activity are shaped by work requirements. Economic resources depend on the reward system of the economy and one's place in that system. Public resources for recreation are based on political priorities as well as the state of the economy. Market investment in recreational resources depends on anticipation of profit. The kinds of activities that are encouraged or restricted are based on the value systems that are reinforced by religious and secular institutions. The contexts of recreation are opened and closed by the social, economic, and political systems.

Third, hopes, aims, desires, and values are learned in those systems. Further, they vary with cultural background and the particular institutional contexts of nurture and associations. The roles taken as students, workers, family members, and so on change through the life course. What others expect of us and what we expect of ourselves, as well as the available opportunities and resources, all change as we move from childhood through youth and adult roles to the final periods of life. Students are not just younger than retirees; they live in an entirely different set of circumstances.

Fourth, recreation is a significant part of general lifestyles. Those lifestyles differ according to ethnic and educational background, gender and sexual orientation, by region of the country, and age-indexed period of the life course. Leisure is central to the lifestyle of teens, integrated with nurture for young parents, tied to resources and self-definitions for pre-retirement adults, and sometimes more central again for retirees. Leisure tends to be integrated into overall lifestyle rather than separate from it.

Fifth, leisure styles, as one dimension of lifestyles, also show both variety and coherence. Most adults have a "core" of leisure engagement in immediate and accessible activities such as television, reading, informal interaction with important others who are available in the household or other regular contexts, and other at-home activities. Beyond this core, most seek a "balance" of activity appropriate to the life period: activities that are engaged or relaxed, strenuous or restful, social or solitary, demanding or disengaged, exploratory or familiar in contexts that offer a variety of social and environmental elements. That balance tends to change through the life course as the core remains relatively stable.

Sixth, the availability of resources is an important factor in participation. A family moving from Florida to Minnesota may switch from waterskiing to snow skiing. Team sports that are fostered in school are often abandoned as soon as school is left behind. Damming a stream and creating a lake will draw nearby residents into new forms of water activities. To reverse the traditional market dictum, supply creates demand. Provisions in new locations create demand as their activities draw participation.

Seventh, in the market sector, investment in products, resources, or services may be based on already existing participation. Such identified markets and their segments may be the basis of an overall plan. Just as often, however, there is the assumption that supply will create demand. In order to locate and supply a viable market, the business plan projects changes in recreation patterns, at least in the market area. For established activities, trend and market analysis can be invaluable. When new participation is projected, the risk is much higher.

These seven principles suggest that recreation participation is shaped by a society's socioeconomic context as well as by access to resources and opportunities. Further, both personal aims and social contexts change as individuals and households move through the life course. Insofar as recreation choices are nested in overall lifestyles, there is no definitive dimension of individual or social action that is irrelevant to those choices.

Sources of Trend Projections

These principles suggest that in looking ahead it is necessary to decide which factors are most influential and likely to shape both opportunities and choices. The contexts are as important as data on participation itself. At the very least we need to know something about shifts in resource provisions as well as significant economic and population trends. In Chapter 2, we will attempt to develop a framework for such analysis.

There are also complications, however, with our information sources on recreation participation itself:

(1) There are long-term figures that concentrate on expenditures rather than on participation. Even when those figures are adjusted for inflation, the categories are not based on participation in any specific activities, nor are the data strictly comparable from one decade to another. As a consequence, only the most general conclusions about types of recreation-related purchases can be drawn. Further, research has indicated that there is no reliable correlation between expenditures on equipment and actual participation (Kelly, 1973). Further, ownership of equipment is not an accurate index of participation.

(2) Despite an irregular series of national surveys on outdoor recreation participation, they are not comparable. Original data have been lost. Data collection techniques were not consistent. Samples vary from one study to another as do the activities studied, measures of frequency, and demographic measures. Recent attempts to gain consistency are too short-term and limited in their scope of activities.

(3) Other surveys such as the A. C. Nielsen series on sports and recreation are limited to clearly-identified activities with marketing relevance. The consistency of that series with a national sample was violated by its irregularity and eventual cancellation after 1982.

(4) The best current source of data comes from national marketing surveys that are completed each year for over 15,000 households and in recent years exceeded 23,000 to 25,000 households. They provide useful participation data for two decades. Employed here is the Simmons Market Research Bureau's annual *Study of Media and Markets* (SMS). The samples and measures of participation are generally consistent. New activities such as health club participation, fitness walking, and mountain biking are added as they become recognized as significant participation ventures on the parts of Americans. The primary purpose of the recreation portions of the studies is

to connect life patterns with media planning and advertising promotion by the sponsoring businesses. From these market studies, we can assess participation trends for the activities they include.

Because of the limitations in data sources, the analysis must be divided between long- and short-term trends. For the long-term, only the most dramatic shifts can be identified with any confidence. In the short-term of the last decade, however, the statistical basis for trend analysis is relatively precise.

Looking ahead, on the other hand, involves extrapolation of trends from the long- and short-term data, placing those trends in a context of relevant demographic and social shifts, and then weighing the most relevant factors. The limitations, then, are only partly due to the data sources. There are also limitations of analytical perspectives. For example, since no one can forecast the state of the economy with any confidence, dramatic changes in the amounts and distribution of disposable income are problematic. Yet, with many kinds of cost-intensive recreation, especially where travel is involved, economic conditions are a major factor in future participation.

Cohort Differences

One other limitation should be recognized at the outset. We know that the rates of participation in almost any activity are different today for those aged 60 to 69 than for those in that age category 20 years ago. In the same way, those who will be 60 to 69 in 20 years, and are now 40 to 49, can be expected to have different rates of physical, cultural, and travel-based recreation than those now aged 60 to 69. These differences are based on what is termed "cohort" analysis, which focuses on age groups born in the same years, moving through life experiencing the same historical events of the same ages, and entering each new life course period together. As with the military metaphor, they "march together as a cohort" through life. Cohort analysis presumes that each cohort reaching an age period will differ from those preceding in some ways and be similar in others.

Each cohort has different experiences in different periods of their lives: wars, depressions and recessions, and cultural changes. The current retirement cohort was raised without the stimulation and distraction of television, far and away the most common leisure activity for the past four decades. They experienced three wars, for some as combatants and for some as critics and resisters. They were raised by parents who had to deal with a major economic depression. Many analyses suggest that cohorts differ in significant ways.

The most identified cohort is the "Baby Boom" generation born between 1946 and 1964 and now in their forties and fifties. The extraordinary size of this cohort has attracted considerable market attention and now is the focus of concern as they approach retirement and Social Security support. One exhaustive analysis (Strauss and Howe, 1991) suggests that the "Boomers" differ from the previous "GI" and "Silent" generations by being less attached to social discipline and more attached to establishing new value systems of self-development and self-esteem. Their leisure would, then, be more self-oriented and less conventional than older cohorts. Members of the next cohort, "Generation X," are still defining themselves in a period of change and insecurity indexed by divorce, income differences, and value uncertainty.

Each cohort has its own history. For example, up to the last decade, each has higher levels of education and different economic opportunities. They also have different cultures based on their historical contexts and events. The point is that each generation will be different than earlier ones *at every age*. For example, the preoccupation with body image of the "Boomers" produced an entire recreation industry mistakenly labeled "fitness." The future of this industry depends not only on a continuation of that preoccupation as "Boomers" age, but also the orientation of the next cohorts as they are in the prime "fitness" market age periods.

Misleading Models

Quite a number of individuals and centers have established reputations as "futurists." They purport to tell us how the future will be different from the present, usually in a catchy and dramatic fashion. While some are far more sophisticated than others, many projections are misleading due to the adoption of unbalanced models.

The first misleading model is based on technological determinism. It is temptingly simple to latch onto a new technology and project a revised future based on its potential influence. Such projections ignore factors of cost, skill acquisition, satisfaction, diversity of leisure motivations and meanings, social contexts, and access based on economic and social resources. The simple fact is that most technologies are never implemented to their fullest potential. They must be cost-effective, consistent with established skills and values, complementary to other dimensions of life, available, and satisfying in some way.

Technology is one factor in social change. In some arenas, such as mass media and home entertainment, this half-century has seen radical technological change. Even in such areas as intimate sexual interaction, contraceptive technologies have had powerful impacts. These impacts were effective because they were consistent with established behavior patterns, value systems, and other technologies. The point is that new technologies are adopted—or not—because of many factors. Technologies may make social change possible, but they do not create inevitable outcomes.

The second misleading model involves gaining attention more than analytical error. The fact is that change is exciting, and continuity is dull. No futurologist will get headlines by proclaiming that the leisure patterns of child-rearing parents have changed very little in the last 30 years. To get attention, it is more provocative to announce that working mothers no longer have time to play with their children. True or not, such statements are picked up and repeated until they become the "common wisdom" of the news media. For example, "everybody knows" that the "fitness revolution" has transformed American lifestyles. The truth is that most Americans don't exercise regularly and are measurably unfit, which has been the case ever since the Industrial Revolution and urbanization.

Several professional "trend watchers" have attracted considerable attention and revenue with their packaging of scenarios of the future. They employ a variety of methods, but there are some consistencies among them. First, they usually presuppose that whatever can be done will be done. They recognize few limitations, even in a world in which most people are still poor. Second, their data tend to be journalistic. They seldom have any systematic analysis of consistent and representative data sources. Rather, they latch onto stories of new and different activities, behavior patterns, and toys with little analysis of how many people are really doing it and who they are. Third, they invent clever labels for whatever "trend" it is they are selling at the moment. Fourth, they seldom have any principles of evaluation; anything that sounds good may be true. Fifth, they charge large lecture and consulting fees.

In our analysis, considerable emphasis will be placed on continuities, however unsexy this may be. The best predictor of future behavior remains past behavior. Changes are more often gradual than abrupt, more likely to be subtle than dramatic. There are very few real social "revolutions," even in a relatively changeable area such as leisure. For example, we have placed unexpected spikes of participation into statistical contexts of "moving averages" as well as historical perspectives. We also examined six different types of trend patterns for 10 years beyond 1996 to analyze fits to historic trends. While too complex for our summary reports, they were background for the projections offered and discussed throughout the book's chapters.

Summary

The best summary, then, is simply that looking ahead is complicated. It requires identifying and evaluating a number of interrelated factors. This art, not a science, always deals in likelihoods rather than sureties, in relativities rather than absolutes. In the next chapter, we will examine some of the contextual factors that influence changes and continuities in recreation participation. Then we will take the best recreation trend data available, analyze their contexts and meanings, and develop estimates for the future. To some extent, they will be guesses; but they are systematic and grounded guesses.

References

Kelly, John R. 1973. "Three Measures of Leisure Activity." *Journal of Leisure Research* 5: 56–65.

Kelly, John R. 1985. *Recreation Business*. New York: John Wiley.

Robinson, John, and Geoffrey Godbey. 1997. *Time for Life: The Surprising Ways Americans Use Their Time*. College Park, PA: The Pennsylvania State University Press.

Schor, Juliet. 1991. *The Overworked American*. New York: Basic Books.

Strauss, W. and N. Howe. 1991. *Generations: The History of America's Future*. New York: Morrow.

Chapter 2

A Framework for Projections

The contexts in which leisure styles are developed, resources are allocated to recreation, and decisions are made to participate are constantly changing. Every change, however, is not significant for the analysis of recreation patterns and trends. In this chapter, we will examine some demographic, economic, and social trends that are particularly pertinent to recreation resources and choices. We will also enlarge a bit on the cohort model in order to identify salient market segments for recreation. This chapter, then, is background for the examination of activity trends and projections that will follow.

Demographic Trends: Who Will Be There?

Recreation participation in types of activities as well as frequency and style varies by age, gender, education level, region, ethnicity, and financial resources. Therefore, changes in the composition of a population will have impacts on recreation demand. Demographic trends since the 1980s include shifts important to the identification of recreation markets.

The Graying of America

The long-term trend is toward an older population. At the beginning of the century, less than 4 percent of the population was 65 or older. By 1980, there were over 11 percent in this "retirement period," with the percentage expected to exceed 20 percent by the year 2030. The Bureau of the Census estimates that the 65 and over population will increase from 34 million in the year 2000 to 70 million in 2030. Of course, this gain reflects the cohort aging of the "Baby Boomers." For most of 20th century, the increase came from the reduction in death rates in lower age categories. Now the age group with the greatest rate of increase is the "old old," those over age 75.

This older population is different from previous cohorts. They are less likely to be poor or in ill health. They have higher education levels and incomes. The death rates of males are now falling as rapidly as those of women (Farley, 1995). About 25 percent are poor or near poor, about the same as the total population over age 25. Low-wage workers totally dependent on Social Security for retirement income are, however, never far from poverty despite their assured income.

A second cause of the shift in age-group proportions has been the result of the long-term decline in fertility. Smaller families shift the percentages upward. Now the decline in middle-age and later-age mortality is increasing the absolute members of the over 65 age group. That increase is disproportionately composed of women over age 75.

Fertility and Family Size

The long-term rate of fertility, that is, the number of children per adult woman, has declined for the entire century. Only a brief surge following World War II interrupted this decline. The rate was halved in the 19th century and halved again between 1900 and 1980 (Fuchs, 1983). Several factors are intensifying that long-term trend. Delayed marriage for women, women's rising education levels and labor force participation, and early-marriage divorce rates have reduced the number of children desired. There are fewer husband/wife households, fewer women leaving the work force for child-bearing and child rearing, and more women remaining unmarried (Masnick and Bane, 1980). The conditions for childbearing combine with the higher costs of child rearing to reduce the number of children desired. Every cohort except the "Baby Boom" crop is smaller than the one preceding. The Census Bureau now projects 19 million children under five in the year 2000 and a small increase to 22 million in 2030.

Household Composition

There is more diversity in living arrangements of adults and their children. The number of children living with two parents has declined, but in 1990 more than 7 out of 10 children lived with a father and mother (Farley, 1995). Children raised by single parents are disadvantaged economically despite the decrease in family size and the educational gains of the parents. The poverty rate for women raising children without husbands is 63 percent for whites and 73 percent for African Americans. The major change is the greater likelihood that women will be employed outside the home when they have young children at home.

The makeup of households is also changing in consistent ways. Since 1980, widow-headed households decreased from 36 to 34.4 million. Female-headed households with children will increase from 5.4 to 7 million; the divorced from 6.2 to 8.8 million, half of whom will have children living at home. Households headed by married couples will decline from 42 to 36 percent. Since 1960, about double the proportion of households are headed by single adults. The increases are most dramatic for women, especially the never-married, the formerly-married with and without children, and older widows.

This means that in the coming decades, at least half of American children will have some period of childhood in single-parent families. They will have fewer brothers and sisters, usually one or none. The breaking and reconstituting of family units into blended families with periods of transition will be a common experience at all levels of society. Further, more and more adults will reach later periods of life without a marriage intact and with a history of family instability and marital dissolution.

Other Demographic Trends

A number of other trends are expected to continue:

- The overall size of the population of the United States will remain relatively stable, increasing about 8 percent from 2000 to 2025. The periods of major growth due to immigration and fertility are over.
- Half or more of the growth will be due to immigration. Major sources of new citizens are Latin America and southern Asia. While language and other differences appear to slow the rates of assimilation, adoption of majority patterns through school and workforce learning requirements are already underway, especially for second and third generation immigrants.
- The geographical area of most rapid growth has been the South and Southwest, with 90 percent of the total growth occurring in the 1970s. A reduction of employment opportunity growth in those areas, along with factors such as water limitations in the Southwest, are slowing this trend.
- The "Baby Boom" cohort, 40 percent larger than the preceding cohort, will continue to age as a population "bulge." In the 1990s their leading edge entered the pre-retirement age period of those who have "launched" their

children and who have maximum discretionary income. In the year 2000, projections are for 26 million age 18 to 24, 37 million 25 to 34, 44.6 million 35 to 44, 37 million 45 to 54, and 24 million 55 to 64.

- Education levels are higher for every succeeding population cohort. Of those entering the work force now, 70 percent have some college education, while the majority of those beginning work a half-century ago had nine years or less of schooling. Increasingly, some post-high school education is a threshold requirement for employment that is not marginal, unstable, or subject to replacement at minimum hourly wages.

Summary

The American population in the 21st century will consist of smaller families, more households headed by single adults, more unstable marriages, higher education levels, and greater population segments in retirement and "old old" periods of the life course. An anomaly is the "Boomer" cohort born between the end of World War II and 1960, after which the long-term fertility decline was re-established. The population of the United States is no longer increasing due to fertility, with each infant and childhood cohort being larger than the one before. Even a temporary increase in childbearing by the "Boomers" who delayed starting families will be dampened by marriage instability, women's participation in the labor force, and the desire for fewer children.

Economic Trends: Income and Employment

A number of economic factors will have significant effects on recreation participation. While it is impossible to forecast the cycles and waves of economic expansion and recession, to specify the sectors of the economy most likely to prosper during any period, or to project income and inflation trends for the next decade, certain contextual elements seem well-established.

First, the scope of economic enterprise and organization is now global rather than national. Finance, production, and distribution now involve world as well as national markets. Corporations are international even when based in a domestic economy. International corporate mergers, as in automotives, are more common. Therefore, the presumed relative strength of the American economy as separate from world markets, production costs, and capital investments is no longer valid. Communication and capital exchange is global and essentially instantaneous.

Second, the long-term trend for the American economy is a decline in rates of productivity growth. Formerly dominant positions of major industries such as in automotives, steel, heavy construction equipment, and electric-power devices have been lost and are unlikely to be regained. The impacts for the magnitude and distribution of income in the United States have already been significant and promise to continue.

Third, labor-intensive production is being shifted to regions with relatively low wages. This shift, along with the loss of world markets, has moved more and more employment out of production and into the service sectors of the economy. Human services, health care, retailing, and other non-production employment account for almost all the growth in employment since 1970. For domestic economic health to continue and to support the consumer and service economies, markets for those goods financed and produced by American firms and yielding a return on American investment must be maintained and expanded.

The percentage of income spent on recreation remained fairly consistent, an average of about 6.5 percent, until the 1990s when it has gradually increased about 1.5 percent. That percentage is higher for those with greater discretionary income and lower for those with less. The distribution and the total magnitude of income have an impact on recreation participation that are costly, namely, on leisure consumption. Much of the expansion in recreation expenditures since 1950 has been correlated with a growing economy. If the world market and productivity factors move the American economy into a low-growth period, then the demand for cost-intensive recreation will grow slowly as well. There are, however, two economic dimensions for which the trends are clearer than the global. They are the distribution of income and patterns of employment.

Income and Wealth: Who Has It?

American society is marked by great disparities in income and wealth. Entry-level and low-threshold service sector jobs pay minimum wage. Even for those with year-round employment, income before taxes will total only about $12,000 to $14,000. At the other end are positions in finance, medical specialties, and management, with incomes of from $100,000 to $500,000 per year. A great many are running short of money for food and rent each month, while others are primarily concerned about investments that minimize taxation rates.

The 1980s slowed the growth in average earnings and increased inequality as the less-educated suffered declines. Those declines in "real" incomes spread to older white-collar workers in the 1990s. The gender gap in incomes was reduced, but remains significant. Declines in real wages were greatest for nonwhites and those without college education. The poverty rates became most marked for mother-child families, particularly minorities (Farley, 1995).

Methods of calculation vary. However, a conservative estimate from the Bureau of the Census in 1993 was that the 20 percent of the population with the highest incomes received over half the total income and the lowest 20 percent about one percent. Another estimate is that the highest five percent possess 90 percent of the total wealth. Trends, according to the Congressional Joint Committee, indicate that the disparities are increasing. The middle 20 percent's share of income has declined along with the lowest 40 percent. More and more of the so-called "middle class" are slipping in real incomes and share of wealth. Most disturbing is the fact that children are now the population segment most likely to live in poverty. The aging, however, are more likely to have adequate retirement incomes.

The result is that the lowest end in earnings, up to 20 percent, has no "discretionary" income at all. At the other end, 10 percent have enough to be able to allocate significant amounts on leisure. In between are the 70 percent who are able to spend modest amounts directly on leisure, $500 to $5,000 per year, but for whom cost is always a major factor in participation. Unemployment and minimum wage jobs for the bottom 30 percent suggest that the marginal and sub-marginal household percentage may be increasing. If so, then recreation markets will be expanded at the upper end, but reduced for the lower 60 percent of the population.

Whatever the more specific shifts, the overall distribution remains one of great differences. Those differences will affect participation in all kinds of recreation that come at high cost, especially those requiring travel or access to expensive resources. Only an overall increase in real income, not likely in the global economy, or a dramatic shift in the pattern of distribution, not likely in the political climate, will alter the significance of income for recreation demand.

Employment Trends: Who Works and When?

The trend toward service-sector employment already introduced has occurred in a period of reduced markets for the products of heavy industry, general economic growth despite a series of cycles, and an increase in consumer markets based on rising incomes for major segments of the population. As a consequence, almost all new jobs have been in retailing and services with parallel reductions in some heavy industry and labor-intensive production. Some analyses suggest that the major exportable products of the American economy are now technical knowledge and investment capital, both of which are income producing.

The service sector has been more likely than production to employ women in occupations such as retail clerks, nurses, teachers, and other kinds of direct person-to-person work. Further, those have generally been lower-paid occupations contributing to the fact that women have on average been paid only 70 percent as much as men for jobs requiring equal preparation. The growth in service employment has been one factor in the increase of women in the labor force, but not the only one.

First, the trend is long-term. Female employment increased from 15 percent for those aged 25 to 44 in 1890 to 60 percent in 1990 with a steady rate of increase at about 3 percent per decade to 1950 and 9 percent for the 50s, 60s, and 70s (Fuchs, 1983). The 60 percent proportion included married women with preschool children and rose to 75 percent for those with school-age children.

Second, the trend is related to other changes, such as the rising divorce rate and the need for more women to be self-supporting. Since 1950, however, the greatest increase has been among women with children living at home.

Third, the "women's movement" has stressed economic opportunities for women. However, the ideologies of the movement followed rather than led the changes. Greater attention to women's opportunities has been concurrent with increased requirements for women's income to support households and to shifts in the kinds of employment available.

Projections for households headed by two adults are that dual incomes will rise from 45 percent in 1980 and 65 percent in 1990 to over 80 percent by the turn of the century. The trend is based on the patterns of women now in their 20s and 30s and the expectations of those now in school.

It is important to note that most employed women report that their motivation is primarily economic; they need the income for household support. This is especially the case for female-headed households. The trend toward employment is connected with the decreased likelihood of a single marriage that lasts until "death parts." Further, most female employment is at the lower end of the income spectrum. There are many more female K-Mart clerks than rising executives.

Related to the trends toward service-sector and female employment is the dramatic increase in irregular and "off-time" work schedules. More and more jobs, especially those in retailing and human services, are in establishments that operate seven days a week and often 24 hours a day. This means that a high proportion of the work force does not work from 8 to 5 Monday through Friday. The consequence is that the demand for recreation opportunities may be less confined to traditional week-ends, evenings, and vacations. Flex time work schedules, accelerated by information technology, also make recreation schedules more variable.

A second impact is the scarcity of time. All studies show that employed women with children living at home have the least discretionary time of any segment of the population (Schor, 1991; Robinson and Godbey, 1997). They must find their leisure in relatively compact and convenient periods and are least able to designate regular weekly periods for activity apart from employment, household maintenance, rest, and nurture and child care.

On the other hand, despite the economic necessity of most women's employ-ment, two-income families have higher levels of discretionary income. Although much of that income may go into providing the time and household work substitutes that make employment possible, some may remain for recreation. For some two-income households, time is more scarce than income. This scarcity places more emphasis on quality in recreation choices.

One other employment trend is just beginning to be recognized. It is that labor force rates for men aged 55 to 64 are declining. The rate, as high as 85 percent in 1965, has fallen to about 67 percent. Some of this reduction is by choice. Some is the result of industrial layoffs in "sunset" industries. Some results from reductions of higher-salaried managers in businesses striving for more cost-efficiency or engaged in corpo-rate mergers. Whatever the factors, it appears that unemployment among the former "pre-retirement" age group, though sometimes masked as "early retirement," is be-coming more common.

Summary

The two main trends in employment are the shift to service-sector employment and the increased participation of women. Both are based on fundamental economic trends related to the place of the American economy in world markets and economic organi-zation of production. While the rates of change may decrease, the direction of the trends seems well-established. The implications for recreation demand are based on income distribution as well as schedule constraints and household demands on women.

Social Factors in Recreation Projections

Life is not made up of discrete factors, each of which makes an independent impact on individuals and groups. Rather, every change is nested in some others and has effects that are mediated through the culture and institutions of a social system. For example, as the cost of housing increases and residence sizes are reduced, the space available for both group interaction and for privacy in the prime leisure location, the home, is cut back. At the same time, more space may be dedicated to larger invest-ments in electronic home entertainment. Some of this loss is mitigated by smaller family size, a concurrent trend. Nevertheless, economic factors of housing cost and income are interrelated with income, family size, and in-home technologies to change leisure styles.

Leisure and Lifestyles

Leisure styles are a part of "life styles." Those lifestyles are related to cultural and educational background, financial resources, climate and geography, occupational schedules and social expectations, type of community, value orientations, and social status. Within identified lifestyles, any change has impacts on everything else. What we choose is based on what we have learned, experienced, valued, considered appropriate and possible, and have found to be approved by others. Leisure styles are embedded in larger contexts, especially those of immediate communities of families and friends.

Nevertheless, there have been a number of attempts to characterize lifestyles that are useful in understanding social and economic interrelationships. Before identifying a number of continuities and changes in leisure styles, it would seem useful to introduce examples of more inclusive lifestyle typologies.

Some of the typologies are primarily psychological in their analysis. Most have some sort of progression from inadequacy to full functioning. Abraham Maslow's (1954) progressions were based on the accomplishment of tasks along a continuum from fundamental survival and security through social belonging and esteem to self-actualizing and creative action. Leisure becomes particularly important as a context for the activity that goes beyond survival and of seeking a place in society to self-creating activity. Erich Fromm (1955) combined developmental psychology and economic orientations in his typology of those who progress through stages of hoarding and exploitative marketing to truly productive lives in community with others. David Riesman (1950) produced a typology based on where people look for the values and images with which they identify. The "inner-directed" were contrasted with the "outer-directed," as well as with those oriented primarily to tradition or those who are fundamentally autonomous.

All of these typologies have implications for what individuals will seek in their recreation—their styles and motivations, as well as locales and kinds of activity. Few analysts, however, have focused on leisure and recreation in developing their typologies. Focus has tended to be on economic roles and interpersonal relationships. More recently, leisure has been included in a few lifestyle typologies:

(1) The simplest is based on a study of adults aged 40 and above in a Midwestern community (Kelly, 1987). The typology is based on the concept of "life investment." The domains in which people invest their resources, find their identities, and from which they receive support characterize different orientations to life. The largest number of the adult sample was found to be "balanced investors" who directed their resources and commitments toward at least two of the three life domains of work, family, and leisure. For them, leisure was not a separate segment of life, but was integrated into a balanced set of investments that had considerable continuity through the life course. The second significant group was "family-focused." For them, both work and leisure tended to be instrumental, valued as they contributed to the development and expression of family relationships. The other two types of significance reflected a lack of access to satisfying relationships and opportunities. They were limited or deprived of opportunity through the life course. Somewhat surprisingly, primary focus on either leisure or work to the exclusion of other domains was extremely rare among those over-40 adults. One primary difference between the

17

"balanced investors" and the "family-focused" was in leisure. The "balanced investors" were most likely to value their leisure investments as an integral and important domain of life rather than primarily as a context for family interaction.

(2) A second typology that includes leisure as a basis of distinction is derived from the Values and Lifestyles Program (VALS) of the Stanford Research Institute International (Mitchell, 1983). This market segmentation typology is based on a national sample and brings together dimensions of work, family and intimacy, community, leisure, and value orientations, along with access to economic and social resources. The first division consists of those who are "need-driven" and struggle with scarcity. Those with greater resources are divided between the inner-directed and the outer-directed with the proposed possibility of an integrated style.

Factors in the categorization include period in the life course, educational background, economic position and resources, and psychological predispositions, as well as social and political values. A summary of the nine styles follows:

The Need-Driven:

- Survivors who are older, poor, fearful, and preoccupied with getting through the day and week (4 percent).
- Sustainers on the edge of poverty who have strategies for making it despite being economically and socially marginal (7 percent).

The Inner-Directed:

- "I-am-me" self-centered and self-preoccupied youth who exemplify the dilemma of wanting both individuality and acceptance from their peers. This transitional group is quite leisure-oriented on their way to more adult styles (5 percent).
- Experiential younger adults who are oriented toward personal growth and development and for whom leisure is central to their values (7 percent).

The Outer-Directed:

- Belongers who are aging, traditional, conventional, and oriented toward family values. Such "middle-mass" Americans constitute 35 percent of the adult population.
- Emulators who are younger and ambitious and trying to achieve a place in the system. They use leisure for acceptance (9 percent).
- Achievers who believe they have made it in social and economic positions or who are well on the way. Leisure may be secondary to status roles (22 percent).
- Finally, there is the possibility of an "integrated" lifestyle of relatively mature and autonomous adults who direct their lives according to flexible images, relate in accepting ways to others, and whose lives are integrated in development appropriate to the period in their life course. The integrated are estimated to be only about 2 percent of the adult population.

The VALS research group has employed this typology to distinguish market segments for a variety of goods and services. They believe that such a typology is more useful than the usual demographic profiles in identifying those who make certain market choices and why they make those choices. At least they offer an approach to understanding how age, economic standing, and social status are indices of lifestyles that combine several dimensions. Leisure choices and investments are integrated dimensions of these lifestyles, rather than a segmented and residual set of behaviors.

Market Segmentation

Market segmentation need not deny such inclusive lifestyle typologies to identify different leisure and recreation styles. Important differences are based on the more traditional factors of age, gender, family status, and economic resources. For example, recreation market segments can be distinguished by socioeconomic categories such as the following:

Stable Market Segments:

- High-end consumers whose incomes and assets enable them to afford major expenditures for whatever leisure they value most. Their travel is expensive and extensive. They are the major market for high-cost items such as prestige resorts, exclusively located second homes, and big-ticket deluxe travel.

- Blue collar workers are now augmented by low-pay and low skill clerical workers and retail employees. Many work more than one service job. Their major expenditures on leisure, if any, are made before they are 50 years old. They seldom have significant vested pension resources, live in rental housing or work to pay a modest mortgage, and have limited health care. Their incomes are directed primarily toward "necessities" of maintenance. They are a sizable recreation market, but mostly for at-home and community programs and resources with low cost thresholds.

- The poverty class whose lack of economic security intensifies maintenance problems in health, housing, nutrition, and transportation. Their leisure tends to be close to home and relatively cost-free, such as television and informal interaction.

Changing Market Segments:

- The new class with university degrees and managerial or technical employment. They have considerable but not unlimited discretionary income and expect to spend a portion of it on leisure. They have had a range of recreation experiences and usually have plans for expansion in the future. Their residence-base activity is important to them, but they also expect to travel and be involved in sport, cultural, and other community-based engagements. They are urban or suburban in location, often related to life course period and the age of children. Their tastes are cosmopolitan, but they take the nurture of one or two children very seriously. Almost all who are married are dual-income households.

- The middle mass have experienced relatively stable but limited work histories. More than their predecessors they may have two incomes, experience marital instability, and have small families. Investment in a residence is central. Their tastes are not sophisticated, but they believe they have the right to some enjoyable activity. They travel on a budget and usually by car. They are a major market segment for goods and services that support their lifestyles, even though they tend to be very price conscious. They may, however, invest in major items such as boats or vehicles that facilitate major interests employing local and regional resources.

Each of these five categories can be subdivided according to other salient factors. There are important gender differences in experiences, tastes, and expectations. Those in childbearing and child-rearing periods of the life course tend to center much of their recreation around their children in all the five categories. Older persons with health problems have a constricted scale of recreation, with smaller circles of social interaction and activities located in or closer to home. Those in the midst of family transition or disruption tend to orient more of their leisure toward finding new social contexts for activity and relationships.

Therefore, age, family status, and gender are all significant variables that affect recreation choices for each of the socioeconomic groups and segment the recreation market. In the activity trend analysis in the next three chapters, we will refer to such segments and factors that cut across them to identify those market segments most likely to increase or decrease in participation.

Another important factor is that of education. For those above poverty levels and within age categories, there is nothing that indexes the likelihood of different kinds of recreation participation as clearly as the amount and quality of education. Education not only is an index of economic resources and cultural opportunities, but also of the probability of experience with a variety of leisure activities and opportunities. Fortunately, the market studies on which we will base our current trend analyses include age, income, education level, and gender breakdowns.

Leisure Styles and Resources

Leisure Resources

For each market segment, changes in access to resources are already affecting leisure styles and choices. A summary of some of those changes includes time and space as well as financial, social, and skill resources.

Time: The general leveling of average employment hours is different for different occupations. Retail and service occupations have schedules that are more diverse and irregular. Time for recreation often does not occur on weekends and evenings. Also, time is becoming a resource more scarce for single parents, dual-income households, commuters in crowded metropolitan areas, and salaried employees, especially those in research and development in businesses attempting to increase productivity. The alleged "growth in free time" is uneven at best and inaccurate for most adults in the 1980s. The "average work week" may be slightly decreased (Robinson and Godbey, 1997) or slightly increased (Schor, 1991), but there is clearly a time crunch for those under the pressure of multiple role responsibilities. For example, there may be the most acute work career pressures precisely on those with the greatest family role requirements.

Space: Housing and energy costs are reducing the proportion of the population who will live in detached homes with considerable recreation space. Multi-unit housing and space-efficient design will reduce the at-home leisure space. At the same time, metropolitan areas, especially suburbs, will continue to grow, even if at decreasing rates. The resulting high cost of indoor and outdoor space limits the expansion of public and business provisions for recreation. Activities that require costly space will be limited by the ability of tax-supported agencies and users to pay for it.

Money: The distribution of income already outlined may be changing somewhat. Reductions in the size of blue-collar and white-collar clerical groups will decrease that segment of the recreation markets. The possible growth in "new class" size with their discretionary incomes may be balanced by the simultaneous growth of the segment whose incomes are close to marginal and whose employment is insecure. The stable, if limited, middle mass category—consistent markets for many kinds of public recreation as well as goods and services—may be reduced in size. As a consequence, more marketing attention will be given to the "new class" with their greater resources and orientations that place major value on leisure.

Social resources: Smaller families, increased family dissolution, the separation of work and residential locales, geographical mobility increased by employment shifts, and increased at-home entertainment have all affected the development of skills for activities that require regular interaction with other people. It may be harder and harder to gather a group for such activities as team sports, classes in the arts, political action, or organization building.

Skills: Higher education levels will raise the depth and breadth of skill repertoires for a variety of recreation activities. More and more people have had opportunities to gain interest and experience with activities previously reserved for the affluent. This may be a snowballing trend as more such families introduce their children to leisure possibilities and skill acquisition. Resources for such experiences may, however, be reduced for some who fall back from previous levels of economic stability. There is also a growth in specialized programs for children in which they are introduced to sports and other skill-based activities at young ages and pressured to concentrate on one or two activities to the exclusion of others. Provisions are made for year-round instruction and participation rather than the previous seasonality of sports. This phenomenon, largely upscale due to costs, will raise skill levels, but at the cost of introduction to a variety of recreation possibilities.

Choices: A review of the development of recreation resources, activities, and market-sector enterprises makes it evident that those engaging in recreation have more choices than 20 years ago. Simmons now monitors more activities that are market-related. Some activities involve specialized skills and create small, but consistent, niche markets. There are, for example, multiple ways of "going bicycling" with different equipment and environments. At the same time, there are more opportunities for mass engagement at different price levels in such activities as cruise ships and air travel. The countless leisure-based periodicals and special sections in Sunday newspapers illustrate the growth in provisions offered through the variety of markets.

In general, except for space, trends seem to be toward greater resources for recreation, but they are neither universal nor consistent. Households with more financial resources may have less time. Economic shifts in employment patterns and stability will affect more households throughout the life course. Therefore, market-sector providers could focus increasingly on target markets with disproportionate resources of every kind.

Leisure Styles

A common formula in marketing is the "20-80 rule." The proposition is that in most markets 20 percent of the total make up 80 percent of the actual demand. Translated to recreation, the rule would suggest that the 20 to 25 percent of the most active participants in an activity do 80 percent of the total participation as measured by frequency and duration. It would also imply that the 20 percent who are most committed to an activity constitute 80 percent of the demand for resources, facilities, equipment, and instruction. For most activities, the dedicated percentage varies from

20 to 50 percent, usually related to the skill and conditioning requirements of the activity, and the proportion of the total market is somewhat less than 80 percent. However, in almost all cases, a minority of participants constitutes the bulk of participation days and the major market for resources.

This focus on the minority who are most committed to particular recreation activities is reinforced by marketing research that has found that between 20 and 30 percent of those who engage in an activity at all do so with regularity. Leisure participation choices are not separate from the overall patterns of resource allocation of any lifestyle. Rather, we allocate resources and respond to opportunities according to learned value systems. A study based on a national survey of markets and media used by Mediamark Research, Inc. found that American adults are divided almost evenly between those engaged in a variety of leisure investments ("Actives") and those who are only peripherally involved in active engagements ("Passives"). The Actives are younger, with 45 percent aged 18 to 34 versus 21 percent of the Passives; another 21 percent of the Passives are aged 65 and over compared with 10 percent of the Actives. Actives are twice as likely to have attended college and live in households headed by those in professional or managerial occupations. A majority of those in the lowest income categories are Passives, while Actives are most often found in the highest categories. Middle income adults are about evenly divided. In short, Actives are those with the most resources: social, economic, and age-indexed physical capabilities. Note, however, the ratios are about 2 to 1. Actives may also be older, of moderate incomes, less educated, and generally identifiable as members of the middle mass. (Mediamark Research, Inc., 1986).

The study found that about half of all adults are "Actives" who make up a disproportionate share of markets for leisure goods and services. The half who are "Passives" tend to watch television, engage in informal activity around the home, and take fairly traditional vacation trips by car. They are in many cases the "family-focused."

The Core plus Balance Model

The stylistic distinction that identifies market segments based on activity clusters is limited because it does not incorporate what most of them have in common. Reanalysis of a number of studies has revealed that most adults have a core of activities that remain central to their leisure patterns throughout the life course. This core includes watching television and reading, informal interaction with family and friends, walking, doing projects around the residence, shopping, and playing with children. These are low-cost and easy-access activities that do not require special plans, expenditures, resources, or skills. Beyond this core, most adults have a balance of activities that reflects developed interests and changes somewhat through the life course. Particular sports, outdoor activities, cultural engagement, travel environments, and skill-based activities reflect age, education level, community and regional resources, and family status. While some people concentrate on one kind of activity, more seek a balance of strenuous and relaxing, social and solitary, physical and intellectual, exploratory and familiar, and demanding and comfortable engagements. Although it is possible to identify leisure style differences, it is also important to note that the groups are not completely discrete. Overlaps and commonalities blur the differences.

Cohort Analysis and Lifestyles

A series of principles underlies the projections that will follow in the chapters analyzing markets by activity:

First, continuities and consistent behaviors are just as important as change.

Second, recreation participation will be affected by major population and economic shifts that include fertility and family size, marriage and divorce patterns, aging longevity, service-sector employment and schedules, women's employment, the distribution of income, and the overall strength of the economy.

Third, recreation choices and investments are made in the context of more general lifestyles that are related to age, gender, family status, education level, and income.

Fourth, recreation preferences and engagements change through the life course in relation to resources, role expectations, and abilities. Nevertheless, a core of accessible activities persists through the life course for most adults.

Fifth, age itself may be misleading in future projections because those who are now in their 30s may have different patterns in 20 years from those now in their 50s. There are shifts in health, expectations, past experience, and resources. Therefore, "cohort analysis" will be the model employed. Cohort differences such as consistently rising education levels will shape likely leisure styles in the future. While involving multiple factors, estimates can be reasonably reliable for a period as short as a decade or even two.

Sixth, recreation activities are seldom fixed for any individual moving through the life course. There are almost always alternative activities and environments, sometimes in direct competition for time and other resources. Recreation demand, therefore, cannot be estimated in quite the same way as the future demand for refrigerators or frozen vegetables. Recreation choices are subject to influence by companions, weather, crowded facilities, conflicting timetables, and countless other factors. The value placed on a particular activity, therefore, is related to consistency of participation. We will use frequency figures, then, to distinguish those who are committed to any activity from those who are occasional participants.

Seventh, relatively new activities with short histories are not included in this trend analysis. While there are principles for assessing the likelihood of an "activity life cycle," such analysis is too unstable for inclusion here. In the case of activities for which there are only two or three years of data, an analysis of the development of the activity and its participation base are offered without any projection of long-term trends. This is especially necessary for activities in the early years of rapid, technology-based growth.

Market Segmentation

It is, of course, impossible to include every possible factor in every analysis. Our aim is to identify general trends rather than to provide a complete analysis of participation in any one activity. Further, some kinds of information are consistent and available while others are incomparable and esoteric. Therefore, demand groups for particular activities will be identified using available trend data as indices for more complex factors. Although their significance varies from activity to activity, age, gender, education level, income, and family status are the factors that have been found most consistently reliable in distinguishing regular participants from occasional and non-participants.

Further, these variables can help identify the cohorts that will be in the various age categories in the 21st century. For example, the "Baby Boom" cohort has been identified as they moved out of school into early establishment periods and child rearing and in time entered post-parental and retirement periods of the life course.

These variables will be used to identify the market segments most significant for each kind of activity. In many cases we can identify the following:

> **Growth markets** that promise increased participation
> **Established markets** that promise consistency of demand
> **Low (or declining) markets** that offer only slight chances for growth

The projections, then, will be based on past participation, on consistencies as well as trend trajectories, and on identification of lifestyle groupings based on economic and social factors.

Continuities and Changes: A Summary

Before going on to the projections for particular activities, one further review will offer a more complete background on leisure in general: continuities and changes in leisure contexts, resources, styles, and meanings.

Continuities in Leisure and Recreation

(1) Although the 6.5 percent average household expenditure directly on leisure has now risen toward 8 percent, an infinite expansion of recreation spending cannot be anticipated. Even though the key concept is discretionary income—and those who have higher incomes tend to exceed the 8 percent average—expenditures have consistent limits, especially when the economy is not growing.

(2) The "core plus balance" model remains valid through the life course. Special recreation activities are part of more comprehensive leisure and lifestyles that include regular participation by most adults in accessible activity, especially at home.

(3) Leisure is embedded in the life course with its continuities and changes. As a consequence, both meanings and activities shift somewhat as individuals age, take up and drop various family and work roles, and change in interests and self-definitions.

(4) Time remains scarce for most adults. Whether or not there is an increased time crunch, the time costs of recreation participation may be a greater constraint than financial costs, especially for dual-income households with children.

(5) The one really profound social revolution of our era is in the sexual realm. Major behavioral changes since the 1950s permeate every aspect of the society, including leisure. Sexual expression is accepted, diversity is legitimized, and sexuality is presumed as a dimension of activity. Recreation meanings and choices have recognized sexual dimensions even when focused on a specific activity or environment. Intimate relationships will continue in diverse contexts other than those of marriage and the family.

(6) Considerable recreation involves self-display and style. How participants manage impressions to gain approval and acceptance involves styles of participation, clothing, equipment, and being with the "right" companions. Display also emphasizes the consumption element of leisure. Impression management may be more important than the game for some leisure events. Related to such image projection is the

increase in the purchases of recreation-related shoes, clothing, and even vehicles for everyday use. While comfort and convenience may be involved in the choices, there may also be some of the classic "Veblenesque" presentation of the self as one who can afford leisure.

(7) The distance costs of recreation continue to mount in growing urban areas. Distance is translated into time costs increased by crowding and "rush hour" time-tables that affect leisure as well as work. Private transportation may be a recreation necessity for time-efficiency.

(8) Race-intensified poverty, especially in urban ghettoes and rural fringes, is set against the affluent life and leisure styles portrayed on television. Anger and alienation may focus on leisure as much as on economic rewards and opportunity.

(9) Shopping continues as a central leisure activity for American adults, both in the home community and while traveling. Shopping malls and boutique boulevards are major leisure environments. Such recreational shopping and "malling" merit serious study as major leisure phenomena.

(10) Travel remains important for adults even when styles and costs vary widely. In 1991, 130 million Americans took trips, 75 percent by car. Styles, however, are very different for the rich in comparison to the middle mass, or for parents in comparison to the retired.

(11) Leisure and recreation investments are an important component of marriage and family life. For both intact and serial marriages, recreation choices can be conflict-ridden as well as contexts for expressing and developing relationships. Disappointment in leisure companionship and support can be a major factor in marriage dissolution.

(12) Developmental aims for families with children will be important in selecting recreation investments. Parents, perhaps especially those with only one or two children, will seek recreation that will improve their children's chances to compete in the worlds of school and work.

(13) Every younger cohort, up to the current student generation, has a higher level of education with consequent variety of leisure interests and experiences. Level and quality of education are significant predictors of recreational behavior, especially in the arts and developmental activity.

(14) The quality of relationships remains central to satisfaction with most recreation experiences.

(15) Concerns over the environment will continue to be in conflict with development for recreation and other uses.

(16) The trend toward securing blocks of time—long weekends as well as vacations—for leisure engagements will also continue. Travel-based activity will remain special, but somewhat more frequent, with the "mini-vacation" punctuating the time between major vacations.

(17) The trend toward more independence and self-reliance for women will also continue. This means that women's interests will become more and more important in determining patterns and resource allocation. With most adult women in the paid work force, their interests will be increasingly recognized in the leisure marketplace. Further, since the passage of Title IX requiring gender equality in educational opportunities including sports, each cohort of young women has been more likely to engage in a variety of recreational activities including ones previously dominated by

males. While school participation is only one factor in adult recreation, it is probable that the succeeding cohorts of females will continue to be more engaged in physically demanding activity as they age.

(18) There will continue to be an "other side" of leisure. Gambling is currently a growth industry despite the failure of many poorly-located casinos and riverboats. The sex industry exists almost everywhere. Entertainment of all kinds is available in cities and through electronic media. Too great a focus on traditional recreation obscures much of the larger and more inclusive markets. Such activities present measurement problems and have not been tracked in the same way as more conventional activities, but are a major segment of the leisure spectrum, both public and covert.

Changes in Leisure and Recreation

(1) The 50-plus age groups will be recognized as growing markets for recreation goods and services.

(2) Leisure opportunities for women, both married and single, will be more diverse and less tied to the family.

(3) The increasing size of the "new class" with discretionary income and more education will attract disproportionate attention from those planning for recreation programs and provisions, especially in the market sector.

(4) Major attention will have to be given to "off-hour employment" and the potential for recreation participation during weekdays and at odd times, especially by those employed in the service sector of the economy.

(5) Sunset or declining activities will balance sunrise recreation. For example, the basis of hunting seems to be shrinking at the same time that golf, a more urban activity, is growing. Education levels as well as urbanization are factors in such changing tastes.

(6) More and more adults at any one time are either single or in a period of transition. Leisure settings and opportunities will increase for those who do not come in couples or families. Singleness will be accepted as a more common and less extraordinary mode of life, whether temporary or relatively permanent. Different sexual orientations will also distinguish a variety of leisure styles, especially in metropolitan areas.

(7) The business sector will become more central to recreation provisions. Market-sector leisure is in an investment growth period. There are even stock mutual funds specializing in leisure-based industries that have outperformed the overall stock market averages. The complementary and conflicting relationship between market and public sector resources and programs will become increasingly significant, and public managers will be under increasing pressure to make public resources available to market-sector developments. Public-private partnerships will increase.

(8) The bias of market-sector leisure investment is toward the consumption of goods and services yielding the greatest return. Emphasis will be on entertainment rather than durable goods and challenging experiences (Kelly and Freysinger, 2000).

(9) Space scarcities will become more acute, especially in prime environments such as national parks, major museums, and urban facilities. The urban space crunch will be intensified by more multiple-unit housing and the shrinking of the private residential yard. Space-intensive activities such as golf will become more expensive and constrained at prime times.

(10) Home electronic entertainment will become more diverse and less costly. Those technologies that are compatible with current lifestyles will gain enormous markets and increase the attraction of at-home entertainment. Interactive formats and games will continue to be marginal to most leisure styles due to costs, skill requirements, and investment costs. The connectivity of a variety of networks will even offer activities such as fantasy games that make possible "electronic communities" of joint participants who never meet face-to-face.

(11) The changing diversity in life and leisure styles will continue despite the power of mass marketing. In fact, many "market segments" will be identified more by their leisure styles than by economic factors.

(12) Concentration on the "high end" for leisure businesses will saturate the market and cause business failures. Middle mass markets in time may become recognized by more kinds of businesses. In the meantime, however, the imbalance of opportunities for the affluent will intensify.

(13) Reduced public subsidies in areas such as the arts and outdoor resources will open many possible markets for businesses and diversify programs for the public resources. Reliance on cost recovery will tend to raise user fees for public provisions even further.

(14) The higher activity levels and greater financial resources of the retired will bring increased attention to the "active old" as recreation participants. Most retirement adults "age in place" in their home communities, but a significant number spend all or part of the year in environments that provide opportunities for more active engagement in walking, golf, fishing, and other activities.

(15) New technologies will impact on particular activities, much as fiberglass did on boating and skiing. Such technologies are extremely important when they lower the costs or reduce the pain of acquiring enough skill to gain satisfaction from the activity. New activities will also be developed around innovative recreation devices and products. Examples from the recent past include in-line skating, snowboarding, and mountain biking.

(16) Non-family leisure settings and organization will become more and more important due to demographic changes and the long post-parental period of the family. With most children experiencing some period of single parenting and schools reducing subsidized activity programs, there will continue to be a growth in community programs, public and market, that teach skills and provide venues for children and youth to engage in skill-based activities such as sports and the arts. Families may provide, at least for the affluent, more financial than personal support.

(17) Travel provisions will become more varied to accommodate various styles. Packages will be more diverse and almost any amenity will be available for rent.

(18) "Big toys" will be purchased by some. At the same time, however, some highly educated adults will avoid being tied down to particular locales or equipment. They will seek variety by refusing the big-ticket purchases. The "special use" car as a personal expression will become increasingly common with its allure of possession and symbol of individuality. The most rapidly growing markets in personal transportation have been sport utility vehicles (SUVs), fancy pickup trucks, mini-vans for vacation and family hauling, and new "concept cars" that are anything but conventional transportation. What were considered "niche" leisure-based markets have become mainstream, but may still make a leisure-related symbolic statement.

Chapter 2
A Framework for Projections

(19) The skills associated with recreation will become more important as more individuals define themselves and their competence in terms of what they can do and accomplish off the job. As a result, provisions for enhancing skills at levels above "beginner" will grow in public and market sector programs. At the same time, gains in skills will create new demand for programs and resources.

(20) Employed women will be recognized as a market opportunity almost equal to men. Over time the established bias toward male programs and provisions may almost disappear.

How will all these continuities and changes meld into a varied but integrated whole? There are too many dimensions of change to produce a neat picture of the future. Much more is possible than any set of scenarios can encompass. Nevertheless, it is important to try to keep such general continuities and changes in mind as we focus on particular activities and contexts.

References

Farley, Reynolds, ed. 1995. *State of the Union: America in the 1990s* (Vols. 1 and 2). New York: Russell Sage Foundation.

Fromm, Erich. 1955. *The Sane Society*. New York: Holt, Rinehart, and Winston.

Fuchs, Victor. 1983. *How We Live: An Economic Perspective on Americans from Birth to Death*. Cambridge: Harvard University Press.

Kelly, John R. 1987. *Peoria Winter: Later Life Styles and Resources*. Boston: Lexington Books, D. C. Heath.

Kelly, John R. 1996. *Leisure* (3rd ed.) Boston: Allyn and Bacon.

Kelly, John R., and Valeria Freysinger. 2000. *21st Century Leisure: Current Issues*. Boston: Allyn and Bacon.

Maslow, Abraham. 1954. Hierarchy of Human Needs, in *Motivation and Personality*. New York: Harper and Row.

Masnick, George, and Mary Jo Bane. 1980. *The Nation's Families: 1960–1990*. Cambridge: Harvard-MIT Joint Center for Urban Studies.

Mediamark Research, Inc. 1986. *Leisurestyles*. New York.

Mitchell, Arnold. 1983. The *Nine American Lifestyles*. New York: Warner Books.

Riesman, David, 1950. *The Lonely Crowd: A Study of the Changing American Character*. New Haven: Yale University.

Robinson, John, and Geoffrey Godbey. 1997. *Time for Life: The Surprising Ways Americans Use Their Time*. College Park, PA: The Pennsylvania State University Press.

Schor, Juliet. 1991. *The Overworked American*. New York: Basic Books.

Section II
RECREATION PROJECTIONS

Projections will be presented under seven general categories of activities:

Community Activities
Team Sports
Fitness Activities
Outdoor Resource Activities
Water-Based Activities
Winter Activities
Travel Activities
Home and Local Activities

In general, there will be two levels of analysis. Some activities will include relatively complete analyses of long-term and short-term trends, participation by age cohorts, and "target markets." Less trend data are available for other activities. Analysis for them will consist of a more concise review of current participation and particularly significant market segments. Some activities, especially home, and entertainment—based activities, lack total participation figures. Overall, the stress is on activities that require public or market sector provisions and have more identifiable markets.

The categorization of the activities is somewhat arbitrary. The primary factor is the most common location of participation. Most activities, in some form, can be engaged in at special travel-related locales as well as nearer home. The categories, then, are a combination of place and form.

Sources of Data

Limitations of the database were outlined in Chapter 1. Even the series of national outdoor recreation surveys is not comparable in sampling, instrumentation, or measurement. Further, the raw data are no longer available for some of the earlier surveys. The Nielsen survey lasted less than ten years and ended in 1983. Two market surveys, Mediamark and Simmons, moved slowly into recreation with a small number of activities in 1976 and gradual additions in the next decades. Most recently, National Family Opinion Research and the Standard Rate and Data Service have added recreational activities to their surveys. Further, data from proprietary surveys can only be released for general use a year after publication for clients who require confidentiality. Breakdowns by age, gender, and income level are now available only for the later national surveys. Moreover, the categories of activities have changed. For example, in some surveys, camping in developed areas is now distinguished from camping in dispersed sites, beach and lake swimming is distinguished from pool swimming, and distance running is distinguished from jogging. Earlier data aggregates such differences and requires judicious estimates of the types and styles of participation. Finally, there are "outlier" years for some activities in which participation data are inconsistent with the overall trends for the decade. Sometimes there are unusual years based on weather conditions for such activities as downhill skiing. In other cases, there is no clear explanation for the aberrations. The method used in our analysis has been to take a moving average of two years for the long-term trends to compensate for outlier and spike years.

Section II:
Recreation Projections

The data employed in the trend analysis and projections of this study are primarily from the Simmons Research Bureau's Study of Media and Markets from 1976 to 1996. The national sample of over 15,000 households in early years grew to samples of over 23,000 households. The data were weighted based on census projections for each year and extrapolated to the adult population, age 18 and over. This did not include children's participation, but gave overall patterns for families with children living at home. These data are used by permission after they are made available to universities for research and education. There will also be occasional references to other more specialized studies for particular activities. The most common reference will be to the public-access data of the surveys of the National Sporting Goods Association of Mt. Prospect, Illinois, and their annual surveys of a balanced sample of up to two adults and two children in 35,000 U.S. households and to the Sporting Goods Research Network of Princeton, New Jersey.

In the participation trend graphs, the percentages are rounded to the nearest percent or tenth of a percent, but should not be treated as precise and absolute. It is the overall trends that we are seeking here. Exact percentages are subject to enough error that small differences should not be given much weight. Year-to-year figures on gender and age differences and trends are, on the other hand, usually consistent and reliable.

Analysis Format

For each full analysis, the following format will be employed: (1) general trends when available, (2) market identification with growth, established, and low markets, and, (3) future projections.

To identify target markets, the market segments will be evaluated in three categories:

(1) "Growth market," for which there is evidence of continued increasing short and/or long-term participation.

(2) "Established market," which is currently significant but will likely remain relatively stable.

(3) "Low market," for which demand is expected to remain relatively low.

Life Course Periods

The life course does not always proceed without disruption. One study found that about 60 percent of adults over age 40 had experienced either a major turning point or a series of disruptions requiring significant change in order to cope (Kelly, 1987). Further, periods of the life course are not sharply disjunctive. Rather, the transitions are anticipated and tend to be relatively smooth for most making their life journeys. Nevertheless, life course period does identify common role expectations in work and family as well as shifts in access to resources and developmental aims. The following life course categories are useful in market analysis:

(1) "Preparation." The period of young adulthood in which school and work engagements are still geared toward later commitments and careers. It is a time of exploration in which many role expectations are still relatively open.

(2) "Free singles." The period in which work roles are being inaugurated, but marriage and family commitments are still in the future. It is a period for seeking

intimacy and relatedness in which leisure is oriented toward both personal development and exploring relationships. There is also an intermediate state for couples who have made a commitment to each other, but have not yet begun childbearing and child rearing.

(3) "Young parents." The transition to parenting has drastic impacts on time and money resources, aims for recreation, the use of space, and work career trajectories. Increasingly the marriage commitment is now tied to a decision to have children, usually no more than two and in a brief period. With most mothers now in the paid work force, this tends to be a period of time scarcity and high demands.

(4) "Establishment." The period of productivity in work, family, and community. Commitments to work, family, and other salient roles are at a peak. Resources are allocated in ways that enhance and express these commitments. It is, for most adults, generally coincident with the time children are in school.

(5) "Transitionals." For a high proportion of adults, the time of parenting and establishment is interrupted by change. Marriages dissolve, work careers are diverted or ended, and other traumas impact life. Therefore, more and more adults at any one time are in a period of transition rather than stability.

(6) "Late singles." Such transitions will be resolved for many by re-entry into established work and family roles. For others, however, singleness will become more permanent. They will be adult singles, with or without parenting responsibilities, who will not have the context of a stable marriage or other intimate relationship.

(7) "Pre-retirement adults." Their children are more or less out of the home and on their own. They may be at the peak of their earnings curve and have more freedom to allocate time than in any period of their lives. Further, they often are assessing their priorities and making changes based on what they want for the remainder of their lives. As a consequence, they are a prime market for many kinds of recreation provisions.

(8) "Active oldsters." They are in the earlier retirement period, yet retain reasonable health and competence for activity. Each cohort entering this period has been equipped with a more adequate income and higher education background than the one previous. They have expectations for a satisfying life period and usually believe that they have earned the right to enjoy themselves.

(9) "The frail." Those in the final period of life with limited abilities and resources. Their lives have often become constricted in social circles, geography, and range of activities. Their recreation is usually home-centered.

Life course analysis here is based on age and the composition of the household. Further, for key years market segments are tracked by age, gender, education, region, and income. This makes possible identification of growing and declining market segments. Some activities change their market patterns. A once-exclusive activity, such as golf, may become more diffuse. Costs for other activities may restrict their markets. Some niche activities become more inclusive as technologies lower costs and even skill requirements. These trends, while often difficult to discern, are examined when the data permit.

Resource-Based Categories

Recreation participation requires resources of time, skill, and usually financial cost. These resources vary through the life course, but even more according to one's place in the social system. Individuals may be categorized variously according to their general access to social and economic resources. Four categories are based primarily on amount and source of income. These economic factors are usually consistent with type and stability of employment and education preparation.

(1) "Low-end markets." The poor and those with marginal incomes and employment. They may move in and out of arbitrary "poverty" classifications but are never far from exhausting their very limited resources.

(2) "Middle-mass markets." With more stable employment that has very limited potential for advancement, the middle mass includes those working in factory, office, retailing, and other jobs where replacements are nearly always available. Nevertheless, many are buying homes, have adequate transportation, take a little vacation, engage in low-cost recreation, and often hope their children can go to college somewhere.

(3) "Discretionaries." The key to recreation spending is discretionary income, a level that permits the allocation of a consistent and substantial portion to leisure including travel, equipment, skill-acquisition, and special events. They may be in any life course period, but their aims change in relation to their social roles and expectations. They are most likely to be "active" in their leisure styles.

(4) "High-end market." The five percent or so who possess wealth comprise this market. They make major leisure purchases, rent or buy especially attractive environments including second homes, travel far and often, and are the target for many high-investment kinds of recreation provisions. Recreation for them is often tied to real estate investments and travel to destinations where numbers are limited by costs.

The sizes of these four socioeconomic segments can be calculated in several ways. In general, the "low-end market" comprises 15 to 20 percent of households in the United States, "middle mass" approximately 40 to 50 percent, "discretionaries" about 25 to 30 percent, and the "high end" 5 to 10 percent of the total. Of course, they are not discrete categories. Many households "fall into the cracks," with some characteristics of two classifications. Educated young parents, for example, have the social characteristics of "discretionaries" but often have some of the financial constraints of the "middle mass."

Gender: In what is still a profoundly gendered society, both resources and expectations for recreation vary by gender. Despite increased opportunities for women and girls and expanded sex-role definitions, gender is still a significant factor in recreation choices, motivations, contexts, and access to resources.

References

Kelly, John R. 1987. *Peoria Winter: Later Life Styles and Resources*. Boston: Lexington Books, D.C. Heath.

Kelly, John R., and Geofrey Godbey. 1992. *The Sociology of Leisure*. State College, PA: Venture Publishing.

Lipsey, Richard A. 1996–97. SGRnet. Princeton, NJ. (web site: www.sgrnet.com)
National Sporting Goods Association. *NSGA Research: Participation*. 1999. Mt. Prospect, IL: NSGA.(web site: www.nsga.org)

Simmons Market Research Bureau. 1976–96. *Sports and Leisure*. Study of Media and Markets. New York: Simmons Market Research Bureau.

Standard Rate and Data Service. 1993–96. *Lifestyle Market Analysis*. Wilmette, IL. SRDS Publications.

Chapter 3

Community Activities

Many activities take place primarily in the residential community. They may also be tied to vacation trips or even weekend outings to nearby locales. Some require special facilities provided by public recreation agencies or market-sector businesses. Some take place most often in the yard, neighborhood, or even the streets and sidewalks. Local rates of participation are affected by the quality and availability of resources, community histories of organization, ethnic background, and levels of income. The factors that are significant for national participation rates, however, may be factored into the analysis of a specific community. Another significant factor is space. Some residential communities have large private yards, numerous neighborhood and magnet parks, open school gyms and pools, and a rich array of private organizations offering recreation opportunities. Others are crowded, ill-planned, and even dangerous. No national trend analysis can take the place of local research and planning.

Not included in this section are such important leisure activities as shopping, mall walking, media use, and some activities related to the arts and culture. Nor is there analysis of such activities as gambling, drinking, or substance use. For individuals, activities such as car repair and restoration, growing plants, animal care and training, or a hundred other activities may be far more important than those for which we have trend statistics. The activities included in this volume are, for the most part, those that have resources provided by public or market-sector organizations and that require physically active participation. A later section includes cultural and other local activities. This chapter is designed to be a basic market identification analysis, not a complete picture of American community leisure.

Bicycling

Bicycling trends are confounded by the multiple uses of the vehicle. Some use bicycles entirely for recreation. Some commute to work on their bicycles. For those too young to drive a car, they may be a primary mode of transportation. Even for adults who do not commute by bicycle, the bike may be used for family outings on Sunday, to run errands on Saturday, and for exercise on weekday evenings in good weather. The trend data conflate all these uses. It is clear, however, that in this age of the automobile, adult use of bicycles is largely recreational. As such, bicycling has evolved into a new subset of activities that include road touring, mountain biking on and off trails, and other styles based on different types of bicycles.

General Trends

The overall trend since 1976 has been one of gradual decline. A slight increase in the early 1990s seems to have been temporary. In general, the trend follows that of the aging of the population. Further, despite the promotion of safety devices such as helmets, there has been concern over dangers associated with bicycling on roads shared by cars and the slow development of bike paths in most communities (see Table 3-1).

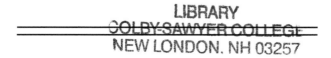

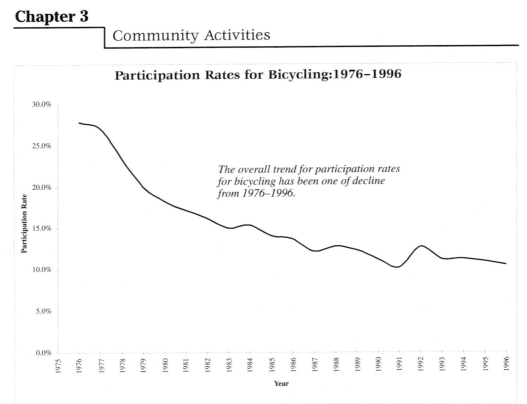

Participation Rates for Bicycling:1976–1996

The overall trend for participation rates for bicycling has been one of decline from 1976–1996.

Source: Simmons Market Research Bureau. *Study of Media and Markets.* New York, NY.

Table 3-1

There are, of course, committed cyclists who make major investments in equipment, ride regularly and rigorously, and provide a viable market for specialty businesses in some communities. The larger market, however, is for children whose equipment is most often purchased in discount retail establishments. There are also some communities such as Davis, California, with elaborate bike paths and trails that enable a high level of multiple-use riding. Regular users comprise about 46 percent of the total.

For adults, about 11 percent of the population rides bicycles with about one-third being very occasional (less than five times a year). This is a decline from 18 percent in 1980. The overall rate change of a minus 3 percent has yielded a total of 20 million cyclists with 489 million participation days.

Market Identification

Cyclists are evenly divided by gender. Rates are lowest in the South. High-income adults bike at almost twice the rates of those of middle-income. College graduates use bicycles at twice the rate of those with only high school education, 17.6 percent to 8.5 percent. The most significant factor is age, with rates of 8 to 9 percent for those 45 to 64 and 15 percent age 25 to 44. Thus, the aging of the population is the major factor in the consistent decline. Riding bicycles for recreation is specific to the resources available as well as the population composition. Protected and relatively safe paths and trails can alter local rates significantly (see Table 3-2).

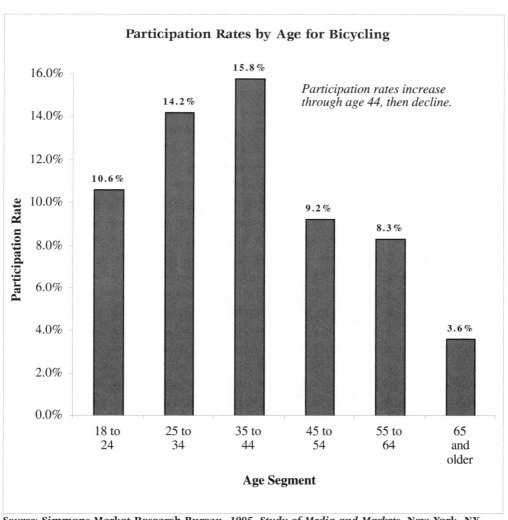

Participation Rates by Age for Bicycling

Participation rates increase through age 44, then decline.

Source: **Simmons Market Research Bureau. 1995. *Study of Media and Markets*. New York, NY.**

Table 3-2

Growth markets: Communities where there is a consistent program to provide safe venues are probably the main growth market. National funding of local trail efforts could enlarge this market. Younger singles and families with young children can be target markets in such areas.

Established markets: The largest market segment is children under age 16 who use bicycles for both transportation and recreation that include social interaction. A second market, although declining gradually, is those under the age of 45 who may also have multiple uses for their bikes with recreation, often with other family members, primary.

Low markets: Those in crowded cities, especially with low incomes in high theft areas, are a low market. Also, the drop with age suggests that safety and other considerations will continue to limit the number of older riders, especially age 65 and over.

Other Market Segmentation Factors

The overall trend suggests limits on market identification. Clearly, younger adults, with or without children, are one important segment. Communities willing to invest in paths are usually those with higher income and education levels. Males and females ride equally. There is no indication of any emerging age cohort that promises to reverse the overall trend.

Projection

As the population continues to age and the "Baby Boom" cohort moves toward retirement, adult bicycling is likely to continue to decline at a slow but consistent rate. Further, the tendency to transport children by car to recreational and educational activity sites suggests that the children's market will also decline gradually. There is, of course, a niche market for those who cycle regularly as a primary fitness and even sport activity. Overall, the future of bicycling is heavily dependent on the local development of protected paths and recreational trails. Also, further development of specialized types of bikes and related styles of cycling such as tour and mountain biking may create specialized markets.

Billiards and Pool

Billiards and pool are played both in residences and in "billiard parlors" (upscale) and "pool halls" (working class). A new kind of market-sector establishment combines regular and pocket billiards with a male-oriented night club decor targeted at younger "yuppie" males with or without dates. There are still the old country club billiard rooms. In "blue collar" and poorer neighborhoods pool attracts quite a different clientele, although still with a male core.

General Trends

Since 1990, the years for which trend data are available, billiards and pool have demonstrated consistent gradual growth with an annual change rate of over 15 percent. The rate has grown from 9 percent in 1991 to over 15 percent in 1996. The gender ratio is over 2 to 1 with a male rate of 21.6 percent. Despite the new emporiums, the market is primarily single young males with less than a college degree, including college students. There are about 30 million participants with under 500 million participation days.

Market Identification

One problem with market identification is that over half, about 56 percent, of those who played in the last year did so occasionally. About 29 percent were regular players, yet provide most of the market for businesses. As indicated, 65 percent of players are male, 65 percent under the age of 35, 90 percent with less than a college degree, and 60 percent with moderate incomes. It would appear that the market is a divided one: young males with access to facilities in colleges or upscale venues versus young males in neighborhood pool halls. About 60 percent are not married. Regionally distribution is about even except for a lower rate in the South.

Growth markets: Younger single males use billiards and pool establishments as a meeting place and social environment. Even so, the growth rate is modest although consistent. For establishments that market to women, there may be some potential growth as a place to meet or date (see Table 3-3).

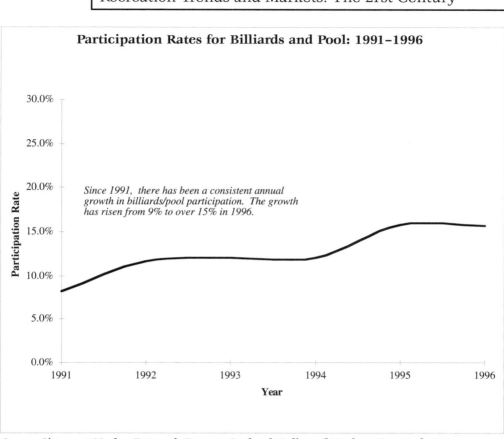

Participation Rates for Billiards and Pool: 1991–1996

Since 1991, there has been a consistent annual growth in billiards/pool participation. The growth has risen from 9% to over 15% in 1996.

Source: **Simmons Market Research Bureau.** *Study of Media and Markets.* **New York, NY.**

Table 3-3

Established markets: The traditional pool hall contrasting with the upscale country club are probably both established. Demographically, the first is decreasing in size and the second limited by the low rates of high education and income players in the current 45 to 64 age cohorts. Only 2 percent of those over age 54 played at all in 1996. **Low markets:** Older women, older men without a history of play, and young adults with families and college education are unlikely markets unless the current student cohort is caught up by a new set of opportunities combined with a revised social approval.

Projection

The question is whether the sport is undergoing a temporary growth fueled by opportunities and social acceptance that will carry over into later years. At present the market is so age-specific that the probability is that an aging population will take over and keep billiards/pool a special age-biased and gendered activity. The widespread cultural interest evidenced in Britain by snooker and televised matches seems unlikely. Businesses may develop markets if situated carefully and promoted to maximize clienteles expanding to attract young women. The breakdown of ethnic neighborhoods in most cities also suggests a limited future for the traditional pool hall (see Table 3-4).

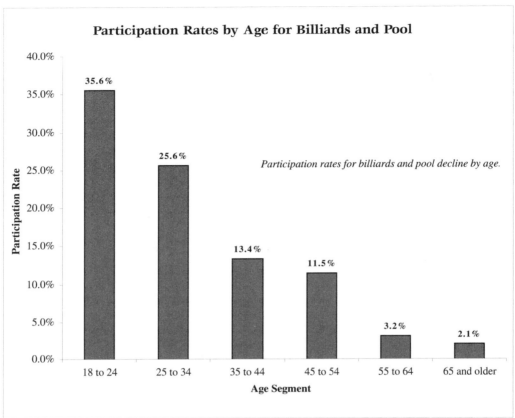

Participation Rates by Age for Billiards and Pool

Participation rates for billiards and pool decline by age.

Source: **Simmons Market Research Bureau.** *1995. Study of Media and Markets.* **New York, NY.**

Table 3-4

Bowling

Bowling is almost entirely located in commercial establishments despite a few facilities in private clubs and public venues. The traditional bowling alley relied heavily on organized leagues that filled prime after-work hours. Some leagues included representatives of industries and businesses with their insignia and long-term affiliations. This represented a time of relatively stable employment and fixed work schedules.

General Trends

Bowling was a markedly declining activity from 1979 to 1991, with an overall rate decline from 21.5 percent to 14.5 percent. Then, bowling had a recovery period with a gain back to 20 percent in 1996. The proportion of occasional bowlers, however, rose from 56 to 69 percent. Regular bowlers dropped from 31 to 21 percent indexing the decline of leagues and other weekly schedules. Bowling does not have dramatic biases; it is 55 percent male with markets spread over the age up to 45 and including those with and without college degrees and high and moderate incomes. Rates are lowest in the Northeast and South with about 25 percent in the Midwest and West. There are about 38 million bowlers and 500 million participation days (see Table 3-5).

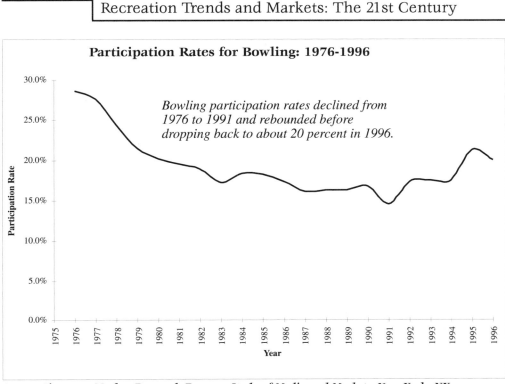

Participation Rates for Bowling: 1976-1996

Bowling participation rates declined from 1976 to 1991 and rebounded before dropping back to about 20 percent in 1996.

Source: **Simmons Market Research Bureau.** *Study of Media and Markets.* **New York, NY.**

Table 3-5

Market Identification

Bowling has traditionally been identified as a "blue collar" sport for young and midlife adults of both genders. That market remains primary, but there are some surprises. For example, the age factor is one of decline from 39 percent age 18 to 24 to 16 percent age 45 to 54. Education is not a major differentiating factor: 23 percent for college graduates, 28 percent for those who have attended college, and 20 percent for high school graduates. The high income rate is 27 percent and moderate income rate 19 percent. The national surveys suggest that bowling is an occasional activity for a wide range of adults with a decline in regular scheduled (and perhaps "blue collar") bowlers. In winter climates, it has also been a sport available in weather preventing outdoor activity.

Growth markets: If any, growth would have to come from those who now play occasionally and would increase their winter participation. In specific locales, such an increase might depend on upgraded facilities that offered a more gracious social environment. The problem is the aging of the traditional market with a greater likelihood of multiple service-sector jobs in a household with irregular employment schedules. The current rebound does not indicate any obvious growth market segments. The exception appears to be "couple bowling" and groups at special events in a semi-flexible and attractive format and environment. Such changes make bowling more a social than a sports activity.

Established markets: The core market remains adults in winter climates who bowl regularly for social as well as sport reasons. The key is to rebuild those markets in a community with more diverse employment patterns or a stable industrial base.

Low markets: As always the poor are a limited market, especially if facilities are upgraded and priced higher. Other than that factor, there does not seem to be any clearly-identified group that might not be a potential market in a situation where they feel socially comfortable. Issues of management have to be addressed in relation to decor, noise, smoking, food, scheduling, and identification of group affiliations (see Table 3-6).

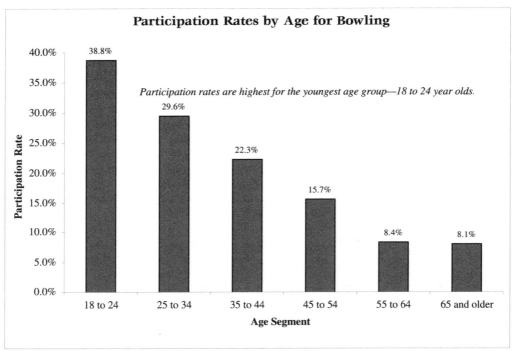

Participation Rates by Age for Bowling

Participation rates are highest for the youngest age group—18 to 24 year olds.

- 18 to 24: 38.8%
- 25 to 34: 29.6%
- 35 to 44: 22.3%
- 45 to 54: 15.7%
- 55 to 64: 8.4%
- 65 and older: 8.1%

Source: **Simmons Market Research Bureau.** *1995. Study of Media and Markets.* **New York, NY.**

Table 3-6

Projection

Can younger populations be attracted to bowling? Any answer has to be specific to a particular facility—its attractiveness and management. A population of 50,000 or more could support a business only if younger cohorts can be persuaded that bowling is a total social and sport environment that provides a viable winter opportunity. There is no demographic category that will provide a core except in areas that still have a substantial industrial employment base with stable schedules. It is likely that the rebound for bowling is self-limiting despite individual success stories.

Golf

The special feature of golf is the persistence of play into later life. Unlike every other outdoor and physical skill sport, it maintains a relatively high level of participation into the 60s, 70s, and even 80s for a few. As a consequence, it benefits from the graying of American rather than taking a loss. The critical factor is space. Most golfers are in urban areas where space is scarce and expensive. Lower-cost public links, then, tend to be crowded and often degraded in quality. Private courses tend to be costly. Therefore, there is a cost/space crunch affecting the growth of golf. A related issue is environmental. Golf courses not only replace natural areas and farmland, but in most climates require intensive watering and chemicals to maintain the fairways and greens. Water use in areas of scarcity and chemical runoff into streams and aquifers are coming under increasing criticism from environmental perspectives. High space and environmental costs are being weighed against the recreational and development benefits of a minority of the population. The National Golf Foundation reports that a high proportion of new courses are high-end public courses with upscale fees. As such, costs will continue to limit growth, especially if public agencies do not have the funds to subsidize construction and operation of courses with lower fee schedules.

General Trends

Golf participation indicates a steady, if gradual, pattern of growth since about 1980. Discounting dips related to weather, this growth runs across all demographic categories and is likely to be slowed or halted more by resource access than interest. The average change rate is plus 4.5 percent. This rate may have moderated somewhat from the growth rate in the 1980s. About one-third of golfers are regular and almost half occasional. The greatest growth has been among the core of regular golfers. Overall, the rate of adult golfers has risen from 8 percent in 1979 to 15 percent in 1996, an unparalleled growth in consistency. These rates yield about 30 million golfers and 550 million participation days.

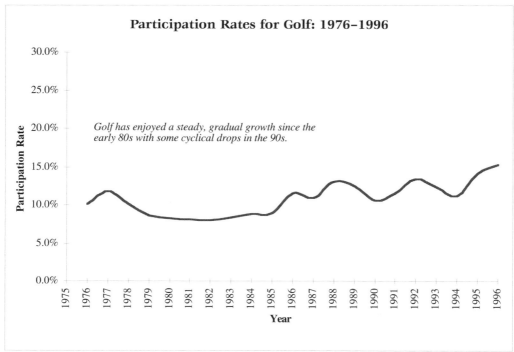

Participation Rates for Golf: 1976–1996

Golf has enjoyed a steady, gradual growth since the early 80s with some cyclical drops in the 90s.

Source: **Simmons Market Research Bureau.** *Study of Media and Markets.* **New York, NY.**

Table 3-7

Market Identification

As suggested, the remarkable element of golf is that older persons continue to play. In fact, golfers age 55 and over comprise almost 20 percent of the total market. Further, there is growth in all age segments (see Table 3-8).

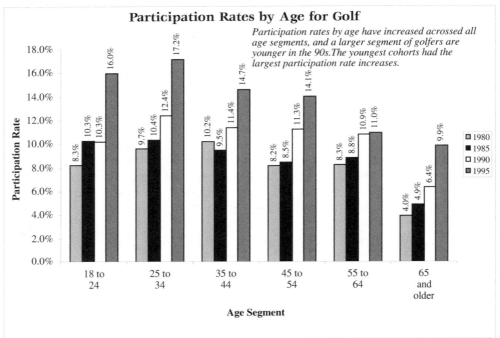

Participation Rates by Age for Golf

Participation rates by age have increased acrossed all age segments, and a larger segment of golfers are younger in the 90s. The youngest cohorts had the largest participation rate increases.

Source: **Simmons Market Research Bureau.** *1980, 1985, 1990, 1995. Study of Media and Markets.* **New York, NY.**

Table 3-8

Note that the 16 percent rate for the usual sports-prone age, 18 to 24, is not that much higher than the 11 percent for those 55 to 64 or even the 10 percent of those 65 and over.

Because of its cost and usual histories of participation, golf is related to education and income. Over 25 percent of adults with college degrees play versus 11.5 percent of those with just high school education. Exactly the same distribution is found for income: 25 percent for high income adults and 11 percent for moderate income and less than 5 percent for low income. Currently the gender ratio is over 2 to 1. 20. 5 percent of males and 8.3 percent of females golf, but the growth rate is slightly higher for females. The Midwest and West are the regions with the highest percentage of golfers, despite the Florida oldster market. There is some indication that golf, a time-intensive activity, is negatively impacted by parenting.

Growth markets: Since the growth pattern crosses most categories, the likelihood is that the limiting factors are primarily access to courses, especially in prime times, and cost. A second limiting factor may be skill, a limitation that now is somewhat mitigated by the proliferation of a variety of learning contexts. To be specific, however, the greatest growth may be expected among older men and women of all ages. Advances in orthopedics may also keep more older golfers in the game. The alleged time crunch for upper-income workers, however, may also be a limiting factor.

Established markets: Males of higher and upper-moderate incomes are the traditional market that continues to grow gradually. Some college students are now being introduced to golf at affiliated courses and often in coed social settings. The relationship between higher education and golf is likely to continue. There is also the upscale market of private clubs, often connected with housing developments, and retirement resorts built around golf courses.

Low markets: Cost and costly urban space limit participation by those of lower incomes. Also, adults working two service-sector jobs are unlikely to have either the time or income for the sport.

Projection

Continued moderate growth is probable if the supply can keep up with the demand. There are indications of a reduced rate of increase in the post-1995 period that should be watched carefully. Time along with cost remains a factor. How far are busy adults willing to drive to play, especially at inconvenient times? On the other hand, reduced household size and an increasing acceptance and even encouragement of women golfers suggests a growth potential. Nonetheless, those up to the age of 55 most likely to play are also those most likely to experience time scarcities.

Racquetball

Racquetball is a special indoor sport with introduction often related to opportunities in institutions of higher education. Once promoted as a winter alternative to tennis, it has become a niche of specialized activity. It simply never developed the level of participation predicted during the late 1970s and early 1980s. As a consequence, many market-sector and private racquetball facilities have been turned into general fitness centers.

General trends

Overall participation rates are low, dropping slightly from 6 percent in 1980 to about 5 percent in 1996. Half those who play are occasional and about 30 percent frequent. The nearly flat trend curve is partly one of disappointment, the failure of the sport to develop as predicted by its promoters. Despite the fact that racquetball is a relatively easy sport to learn, over two-thirds of the market are males under the age of 35. Overall, there are about 9 million players and 175 million participation days (see Table 3-9).

Market Identification

Racquetball is most common in the West with a rate of about 8 percent. The sport is gendered with males twice as likely to play as females. It is age-based—over 13 percent for those under 25 versus 7 percent for those 25 to 34 and less than 4 percent for those 35 to 44 (see Table 3-10).

Further, half the market is single and those with "some college" have a rate of 6.6 percent versus 1.8 percent of college graduates. All this indicates that this is basically a student sport, especially for males, that is continued after graduation by relatively few. Analysts have suggested that the cost/time scarcities have limited the markets to upper-income urban areas, preferably with locations near white-collar employment concentrations. It is, then, a niche sport with limited markets. It has almost no older players, either male or female.

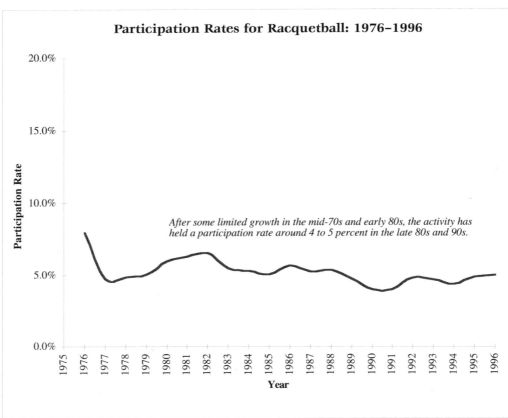

Participation Rates for Racquetball: 1976–1996

After some limited growth in the mid-70s and early 80s, the activity has held a participation rate around 4 to 5 percent in the late 80s and 90s.

Source: **Simmons Market Research Bureau.** *Study of Media and Markets.* **New York, NY.**

Table 3-9

Growth markets: Other than students, probably primarily locations where a concentration of college-graduate males can play before or after work or during lunch hours. **Established markets:** College students who have free and accessible facilities, usually built during the 1980s and expensive to alter for other sports. Even here, however, forms of volleyball, aerobics, and weight training have taken over some court space. **Low markets:** Any locations other than the above. In form, it could be a sport for older adults in a winter climate, but just hasn't attracted this market segment.

Projection

Probable continuation for the niche market and locations, but little likelihood of introduction or development elsewhere. Among investors, the word is out, especially among those burned during the "hype" period.

Roller Skating

Roller skating is confused by the two venues, indoor rinks and outdoor skating on sidewalks and where off-street paved pathways are available. The long-term trends for roller skating include both indoor and outdoor skating although adult skating is primarily in rinks. In-line skating data collection begin in 1992 and will be treated separately. The new sport of roller hockey is also a subset of in-line skating.

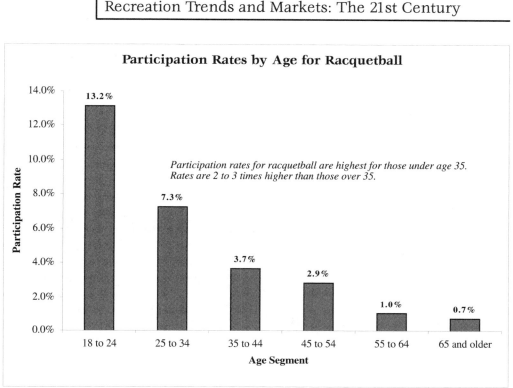

Participation Rates by Age for Racquetball

Participation rates for racquetball are highest for those under age 35. Rates are 2 to 3 times higher than those over 35.

Source: **Simmons Market Research Bureau.** *Study of Media and Markets.* **New York, NY.**

Table 3-10

General Trends

Overall, roller skating has been a declining activity since 1979 with a major drop from 9.2 percent to a plateau of about 3.5 percent in the early 1990s. The decline was most rapid during the early 1980s followed by relative stability. Any recent increase is probably from an inability to distinguish in-line skating. The rate of decline has been about 3 percent a year. NSG data for 2x2 skates indicates a 5 percent rate of loss. The impact of in-line skates has been a major factor in the traditional 2x2 reductions. There are about 7 million skaters age 18 and over with 60 million participation days (see Table 3-11).

Market Identification

Age has been the major distinguishing factor in skating with an 8.4 percent rate for ages 18 to 24 falling to about 7 percent for ages 25 to 44 and then 2 percent for 45 to 54 and less than 1 percent for those 55 and over. The activity is also gendered, with the female rate of 5.4 percent half again higher than the male rate of 3.8 percent. Income, education level, and region are not significant in market segmentation. However, both singles and households with children in school have higher rates (see Table 3-12).

Traditional skating has been a children's activity that has been a prelude to rink skating for older children and young adults. The overall decline is partly due to the substitution of other social activities and partly the incursion of in-line forms. Declines have been greatest among older skaters and those with higher incomes. About 80 percent of all skaters are occasional.

45

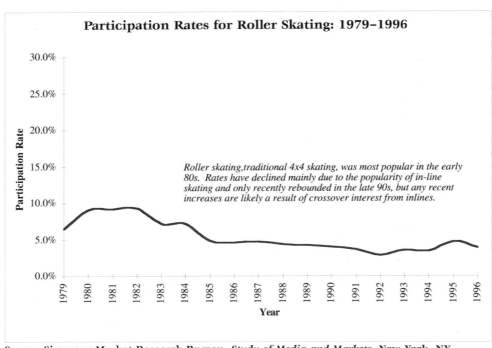

Participation Rates for Roller Skating: 1979–1996

Roller skating,traditional 4x4 skating, was most popular in the early 80s. Rates have declined mainly due to the popularity of in-line skating and only recently rebounded in the late 90s, but any recent increases are likely a result of crossover interest from inlines.

Source: Simmons Market Research Bureau. *Study of Media and Markets*. New York, NY.

Table 3-11

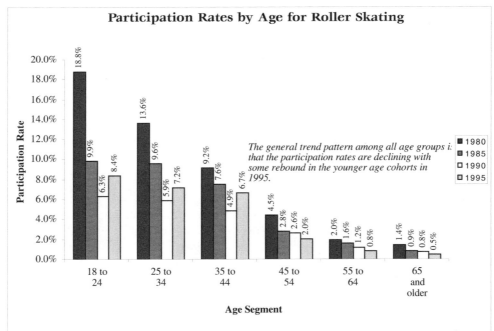

Participation Rates by Age for Roller Skating

The general trend pattern among all age groups is that the participation rates are declining with some rebound in the younger age cohorts in 1995.

Source: Simmons Market Research Bureau. *1980, 1985, 1990, 1995. Study of Media and Markets*. New York, NY.

Table 3-12

Growth markets: Probably none for 2x2 skating.

Established markets: School-age children and their families. There is some remaining interest among singles.

Low markets: The competition from other activities seems to have impacted almost all traditional skating markets. Especially older adults are reducing rates of rink skating.

Projection

The impact of in-line skating may continue to erode participation in 2x2 skating with declines similar to but not as rapid as that of the 1980s. Traditional 2x2 skating is probably an activity in peril.

In-Line Skating

In-line skating has several forms. There are those who skate outdoors on sidewalks and bike paths, even using the skates for transportation. There are those who play hockey and other games on in-line skates, often commandeering flat paved surfaces designed for other activities such as tennis. And now there is even an attempt to revive television "roller derby" with in-line skates that may stimulate further growth.

General Trends

The growth since 1993 has been one of rapid increase from about 12 percent to over 25 percent in 1996. NSG data indicates a doubling of in-line skaters in the 1990s. SMRB shows an increase of from 3.8 million to over 10 million skaters in 1996. The pattern is that of any new activity based on design or technology that takes off and creates a market. The question is at what level the activity will peak and what will be the subsequent plateau. Market segmentation gives some clues to this question (see Table 3-13).

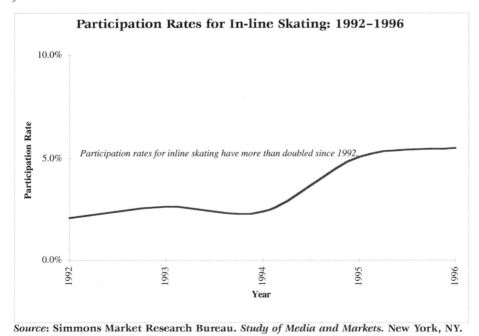

Participation Rates for In-line Skating: 1992–1996

Participation rates for inline skating have more than doubled since 1992.

Source: Simmons Market Research Bureau. *Study of Media and Markets.* New York, NY.

Table 3-13

Chapter 3
Community Activities

Market Identification

Some markets are similar to traditional skating. Males, however, slightly exceed females 5.3 percent to 4.9 percent. The 11 percent rate for ages 18 to 24 drops to 8 percent for 25 to 34, 6 percent for 35 to 44, 2 percent 45 to 54, and less than 1 percent for 55 and older. Singles have rates twice as high as those who are married. Rates are highest in the West and lowest in the South. The surprise may be the correlation with education and income. In-line skating rates are doubled for those with college education and almost doubled for those from households with high incomes. In-line skating, then, is more than a variant of traditional roller skating. It has tapped a different market, more upscale and less based on childhood participation. The use in games may partly explain the gender ratio (see Table 3-14).

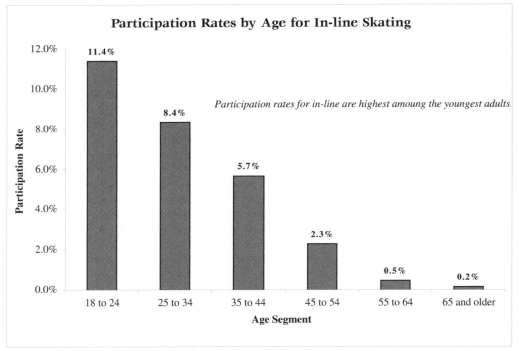

Participation Rates by Age for In-line Skating

Participation rates for in-line are highest among the youngest adults.

Source: **Simmons Market Research Bureau.** *1995. Study of Media and Markets.* **New York, NY.**

Table 3-14

Growth markets: Current growth is among college-educated single young adults and students. The second growth area is for those playing games on skates such as in-line hockey. In-line skating provides a second season for any ice skating activity and may add to interest in ice hockey.

Established markets: An activity so new is still in an overall growth mode. However, students seem to be the most stable market.

Low markets: Older adults are not viable markets, probably due to the accident and injury fear factor.

Projection

The growth will slow and level off as the primary markets become saturated. A second limiting factor is the injury issue that will likely have the same dampening consequences as with running and bicycling. This is especially related to age. The growth in in-line sports is still in question and may become the major area of growth. There are some indications that the growth curve is flattening, usually a sign of a developing plateau or market saturation.

In-Line Roller Hockey

NSG data on roller hockey are available only from 1993 to 1997. They indicate substantial growth for this niche sport from 1.5 percent to 3 percent. Of these, about a third are regular players. This sport is in its initial growth phase. Like ice hockey, it is likely to peak at a relatively low level of participation. Its market is primarily school-age males. While it can be played informally on any paved surface, its growth as an organized competition sport will require purpose-built outdoor facilities or competition with the relatively rare indoor soccer venues. In general, it will probably parallel indoor ice hockey as a special activity, primarily for school hockey players, unless it becomes a general playground activity that does not conflict with other surface uses. NSG data indicates there are about 3 million in-line hockey players with one-third playing regularly.

Jogging/Running

Included here is jogging and running as recreation and as fitness activities. Competition distance running is separated although some respondents may indicate participation in both. Such recreational/fitness jogging and running may take place outdoors on streets and pathways and on indoor tracks in some localities. Participation is seasonal for some in winter climates, but others run all year. Running is, like other recreational activities, subject to a high rate of discontinuance, starting and stopping in a few weeks or months. In this case, injuries are often a factor.

General trends

The long-term participation rates have been cyclical with periodic rebounds. Overall, the number of runners and joggers has gradually declined, but the number of days running has increased slightly. That is, more of those who jog or run at all do so regularly. There is a committed core of joggers and runners. The overall rate went from about 13 percent in 1980 down to 11 percent in 1984, up slightly and then down to a low of 7 percent in 1990 and 1991. In 1995–96, there has been a rebound back to 12 percent. Running may have a periodic "Olympic effect."

Total joggers/runners have increased from 20 million in 1980 to 23 million in 1995–96. In the last two years, the increase has been most pronounced among regular runners, and the total participation days increased to over 900,000. In general, then, the overall trend is one of decline, but the more recent trend is upward. NSG figures show a similar pattern with the 1996–97 increase most pronounced among those who run/jog at least 110 days a year. It should be noted, however, that the increase among regulars is from about 4.5 percent to 5 percent of the population. The cycles are not clearly explainable (see Table 3-15).

Community Activities

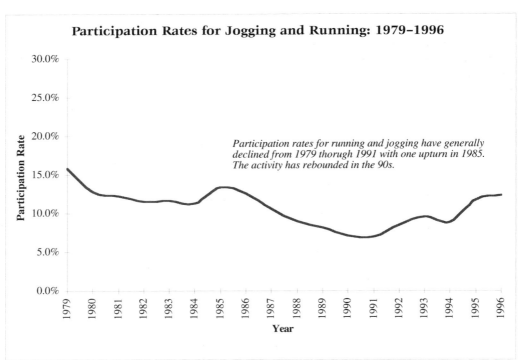

Participation Rates for Jogging and Running: 1979–1996

Participation rates for running and jogging have generally declined from 1979 thorugh 1991 with one upturn in 1985. The activity has rebounded in the 90s.

Source: **Simmons Market Research Bureau.** *Study of Media and Markets.* **New York, NY.**

Table 3-15

Market Identification

Rates vary by gender, almost 15 percent for males to 9 percent for females. There is also a strong inverse age correlation: 26 percent for those 18 to 24, 14 percent for 25 to 34, 12.6 percent 35 to 44, 9 percent 45 to 54, 4 percent 55 to 64, and 3 percent 65 and over.

Running/jogging is also biased toward those with college education, almost 3 times the high-school graduate rate for college grads and twice for those with some college. Those with high incomes run at twice the rate of others and singles over twice as much as those who are married. The highest regional rates are in the West followed by the South.

Growth markets: Regular runners with a fitness orientation, especially young singles with college education. Warm climates for year-round running are also a factor. There is also some growth among older runners, but from a low base. The on-demand nature of running makes it viable for employed parents and others with time scarcities. It is an easy access and low cost activity.

Established markets: Runners under age 45 who prefer this on-demand activity for fitness reasons. Singles with cosmetic aims are still a major market. Suburban space augments the fitness goals of those with higher education levels and younger males conditioning for sports.

Low markets: Almost anyone physically capable can jog or run, but it is uncommon in inner city neighborhoods where safety is a factor, especially in the Northeast and rural areas with older populations (see Table 3-16).

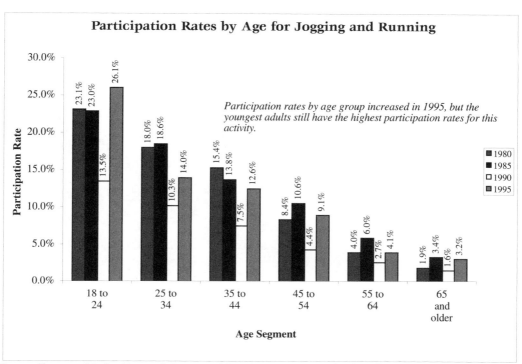

Participation Rates by Age for Jogging and Running

Participation rates by age group increased in 1995, but the youngest adults still have the highest participation rates for this activity.

Legend: ■ 1980 ■ 1985 □ 1990 ■ 1995

Values by age segment:
- 18 to 24: 23.1%, 23.0%, 13.5%, 26.1%
- 25 to 34: 18.0%, 18.6%, 10.3%, 14.0%
- 35 to 44: 15.4%, 13.8%, 7.5%, 12.6%
- 45 to 54: 8.4%, 10.6%, 4.4%, 9.1%
- 55 to 64: 4.0%, 6.0%, 2.7%, 4.1%
- 65 and older: 1.9%, 3.4%, 1.6%, 3.2%

Age Segment

Source: Simmons Market Research Bureau. *1980,1985,1990,1995. Study of Media and Markets.* **New York, NY.**

Table 3-16

Projection

The aging factor suggests an overall slow decline despite rebounds among the potential growth segments. Development of safe off-street paths in some communities and planned developments may have a small impact. Current segmented growth may continue, but is unlikely to fully counter the "aging of America." The critical issue is whether "Baby Boomers" will jog as they enter their 40s and 50s, turn to exercise walking and even treadmills, or become inactive. The low cost and easy access characteristics make it likely to retain a core of participants.

Distance Running

Distance running distinguishes those who run in competition and who keep records of times and distances. They strive to improve performance, not just meet a quota for fitness purposes or take a group "social jog." Most, but not all, enter competitions at least occasionally. As such, they are a dedicated niche market. There are some difficulties with distinguishing those who jog and run for exercise from those who are truly "distance runners." This problem may inflate the totals somewhat. The reported "highs" of dedicated runners may be countered in midlife by stress-related injuries.

General Trends

There has been a steady increase in distance running since 1980, both in numbers of runners and in participation days. Unlike activities that have 75 to 80 percent of occasional participants, distance running has 75 percent of participants running regularly. Further, the growth has been among the committed. The base, however, is

51

not large: the rate of participation has risen from 1.6 percent in 1980 to about 5.5 percent in 1995 and 1996. Participation days increased from 80,000 to 440,000. The number of runners increased from 2.5 million to 10.7 million. What has occurred is that the activity has changed to one of greater commitment and regularity with a supporting industry. It is an evolving niche activity (see Table 3-17).

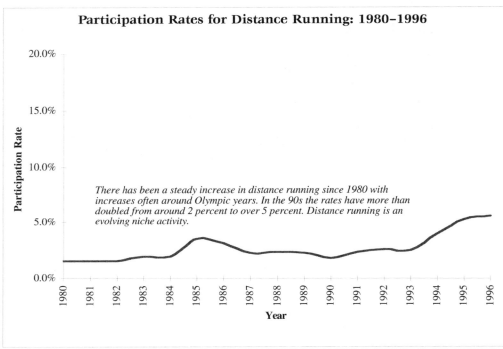

Participation Rates for Distance Running: 1980–1996

There has been a steady increase in distance running since 1980 with increases often around Olympic years. In the 90s the rates have more than doubled from around 2 percent to over 5 percent. Distance running is an evolving niche activity.

Source: **Simmons Market Research Bureau.** *Study of Media and Markets.* **New York, NY.**

Table 3-17

Market Identification

The modal distance runner is a single young male who is either a student or has some college education. Gender rates are 6.4 percent male to 4.2 percent female. The 13 percent rate for those 18 to 24 is double that for the next age category and falls to 3.4 percent for those 45 to 54 and less than 2 percent for those over 54. Rates are lowest in the Midwest and about the same for the rest of the country. The singles rate is over 10 percent and married under 4 percent. Student running makes high and low incomes most common. Although it is primarily a sport for young, athletically-inclined students and young adults, there is a smaller cadre of committed older adults who appear to be able to cope with the demands.

Growth markets: Primarily young adults with the women's rate growing faster than men's. The Northeast is the region of highest growth. The student market is the one growing most rapidly. Unusual is the increase among regular runners rather than those who are occasional. This core continues to run more (see Table 3-18).

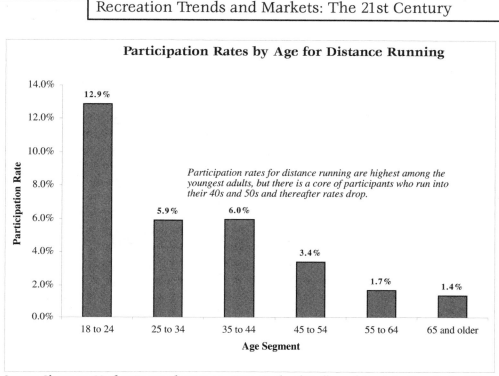

Participation Rates by Age for Distance Running

Participation rates for distance running are highest among the youngest adults, but there is a core of participants who run into their 40s and 50s and thereafter rates drop.

Source: **Simmons Market Research Bureau.** *1995. Study of Media and Markets.* **New York, NY.**

Table 3-18

Established markets: Young adults who combine the on-demand features of running with an orientation toward strenuous exercise. Distance runners form a community, almost a subculture, who practice together and meet at competitions. They are supported by an industry centered on shoes, sports medicine, and a health orientation.

Low markets: Older adults who lack a strong fitness and high-demand orientation. Distance running demands a high level of commitment as well as the physical ability to cope with high stress and related injuries, fatigue, and pain.

Projection

The aging of the population suggests that distance running numbers may have peaked despite the long-term growth trend. Nonetheless, continued increases among young women may counter the age factor. Further, running can be done on demand for younger educated workers with high work demands and a central orientation toward strenuous physical activity and competition. The growth segments are not the population growth segments. In their 50s and 60s, runners may become walkers or turn to various exercise equipment. Increasing provision of trails could increase safety and reduce injuries.

Tennis

Tennis is played outdoors, largely on public courts during warm weather. There is also a niche market of year-round players in the Southwest and South or who use relatively expensive indoor courts. The general market tends to be divided among regulars and the very occasional, most of whom will not become regular.

Chapter 3

Community Activities

General Trends

Tennis is a classic activity on the decline with a possible leveling in the mid-1990s. The overall decline has been from a high of over 12 percent in 1979 to about 7 percent in 1990–91 and just under 8 percent in 1995–96. About 25 percent are regular players and half occasional. Participation days have sunk from over 300 million in 1979 to 268 million in 1996, falling far behind the population increase. The number of participants has fallen from almost 20 million in 1979 to 15 million in 1996. NSG trends indicate consistent decline through the 1980s and early 90s and possible leveling or slight increase after 1995. The popularity of tennis in the 70s may have been linked to media attention to popular stars and rivalries (see Table 3-19).

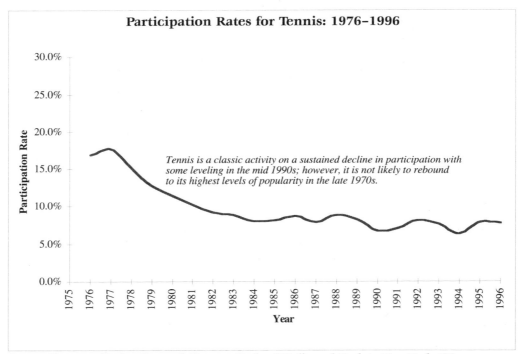

Tennis is a classic activity on a sustained decline in participation with some leveling in the mid 1990s; however, it is not likely to rebound to its highest levels of popularity in the late 1970s.

Source: Simmons Market Research Bureau. *Study of Media and Markets*. New York, NY.

Table 3-19

Market Identification

Tennis is not highly gendered, 9 percent male to almost 7 percent female. It is age-graded with the largest decrease at age 25, 17 percent for 18 to 24 to 9.5 percent for 25 to 34. There is a significant older cohort with rates of almost 3 percent for age 55 to 64 and 2 percent for 65 and older. Tennis is strongly related to education with college graduates playing at over three times the rate of those without any college education. Tennis is strongest in the West and lowest in the Midwest. Rates for those with high incomes are over twice as high as moderate and low levels despite public facilities. The modal player is under 25, single, and has a college education and a substantial income (see Table 3-20).

54

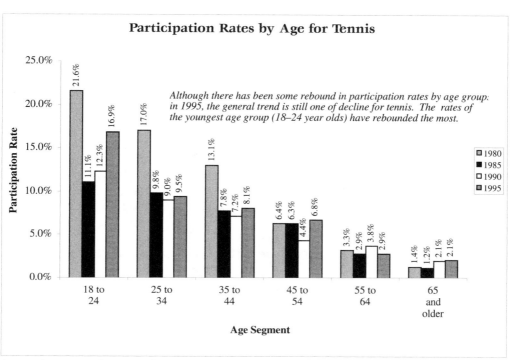

Participation Rates by Age for Tennis

Although there has been some rebound in participation rates by age group in 1995, the general trend is still one of decline for tennis. The rates of the youngest age group (18–24 year olds) have rebounded the most.

Source: **Simmons Market Research Bureau.** *1980,1985,1990,1995. Study of Media and Markets.* **New York, NY.**

Table 3-20

Growth markets: Regular players in the "Baby Boom" age cohorts, perhaps more women than men. Age 65 plus players are increasing slightly already. There is some growth among low income players, but from a low base. Larger households may also find tennis a family activity, but usually not regularly.

Established markets: Students and other young adults, both single and married. Tennis can be a "couple sport." Declines have been lowest in the South and West, suggesting a climate factor. Overall, declines have been general rather than for market segments.

Low markets: Generally the poor in winter climates.

Tennis is a general rather than niche sport with the segmentation factors that are common for most physical activity except for the lack of a gender bias.

Projection

Probable stable trends with the possibilities of some small growth as indicated above. The keys are the "Boomers" who enter the usual dropout age periods and give some indication of higher retention and the developmental programs, usually for children from affluent households and less commonly in urban low-income areas. Despite promotion, a return to the levels of the 70s is unlikely.

Walking for Exercise

Some exercise walking takes place on indoor tracks. Some takes advantage of walkways especially provided for walkers and runners or shared with bicycles and in-line skaters. There are also planned communities with special provisions for walking.

For the most part, however, exercise walking begins at the front door and take place on sidewalks and streets. It is an on-demand activity requiring no advance scheduling or costly equipment although some walking is a group activity and walking shoes are now a marketed product.

General Trends

It is no accident that the two large-participation activities with the clearest growth trends are golf and exercise walking, both engaged in by that growing population segment of older adults. As a designated activity, the trend data begin in 1988 and demonstrate a clear pattern of growth. The annual change rate is plus 10 percent. Further, almost 80 percent of exercise walkers do so regularly. The overall rate has risen from 19 percent in 1988 to 35 percent in 1995 and 1996. This means that there are over 66 million walkers with 2,800 million participation days. This is despite the fact that most communities are slow to make special provisions for safe walkways with even surfaces (see Table 3-21).

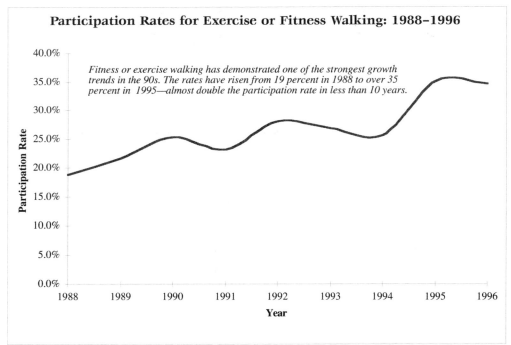

Participation Rates for Exercise or Fitness Walking: 1988–1996

Fitness or exercise walking has demonstrated one of the strongest growth trends in the 90s. The rates have risen from 19 percent in 1988 to over 35 percent in 1995—almost double the participation rate in less than 10 years.

Source: Simmons Market Research Bureau. *Study of Media and Markets*. New York, NY.

Table 3-21

Market Identification

There is no gender bias with 12 percent male and 11 percent female rates. Nor is there any significant market differentiation by education level, moderate or high income, or marital status. Walking is least common in the South and Northeast at about 8 percent and higher with 13 percent in the Midwest and 20 percent in the West. The most remarkable factor is age. As indicated in the bar graph, the age-related decline, while significant, retains a relatively high rate of walking for older adults: 7 percent for 55 to 64 and 9.5 percent for 45 to 54 ages. Even 65 and over retains about 3 percent. The adult rate below age 45 is about 15 percent (see Table 3-22).

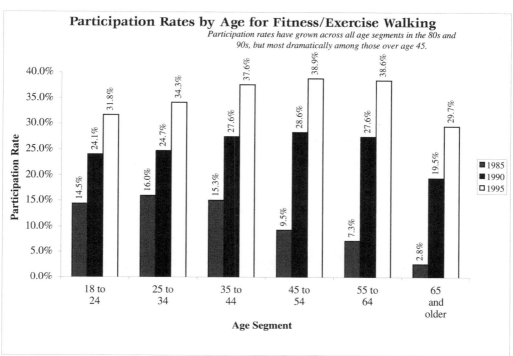

Participation Rates by Age for Fitness/Exercise Walking

Participation rates have grown across all age segments in the 80s and 90s, but most dramatically among those over age 45.

Source: Simmons Market Research Bureau. 1985, 1990, 1995. *Study of Media and Markets*. New York, NY.

Table 3-22

Growth markets: The "Boomers" are the major growth market as they age. The current growth trend includes all except low income and the frail elderly. It is an activity for those with moderate incomes and fitness aims, especially for women whose rates are increasing twice as fast as men's. Specifically, the target growth market is middle-aged women of moderate incomes. There are also indications of growth in the Northeast and South where rates are currently the lowest.

Established markets: Quite general. Exercise walking is a general, not niche, activity. No market segment is excluded except for the urban poor in crowded cities and dangerous neighborhoods. Further, the 80-20 rule is reversed, with almost 80 percent of exercise walkers engaging in the activity regularly.

Low markets: The urban poor.

Projections

Some data suggest a slowing of the growth rate in the late 1990s. The aging of the population and continuation of midlife patterns suggest a growth rate commensurate with the population trends. That is, the large aging cohort will probably walk at slightly higher rates than those now in their 60s and 70s. The increase in this population group should support continued, if gradual, growth in total participation. The smaller cohorts of young adults will, however, counter that trend. The focus will be on older adults, especially in communities that provide safe and attractive venues for walking. The sizable core of walkers is likely to remain strong in the next decade with possible spillover to indoor venues and treadmills.

Chapter 4

Team Sports

The analysis of team sports trends requires some compilation of data from the Simmons national survey (SMRB) and the National Sporting Goods (NSG) survey of 35,000 households that includes children age 7 to 11 and youth 12 to 17. Team sports are played on several distinct levels. The first is, of course, the school. Schools have organized sports programs for children. Secondary schools have both interscholastic sports that include a few elite athletes and intramural sports with wider inclusion. Also for children and youth, there are community programs, many of which are highly organized with uniforms, leagues, coaching standards, and even post-season tournaments. There are also both private and public developmental programs in sports that include children as young as five or six.

Participation rates in team sports drop precipitously on leaving the set of opportunities and rewards of the school. For many, sport ends with leaving high school and for others on leaving college. There is a succeeding level, however. Many communities have organized sports programs for adults. Most are primarily for younger males and fewer are for females. Complicating the picture, however, is the growth of leagues for older adults with minimum age requirements. There are also organized programs in private venues such as Ys and clubs.

The third level is informal. There is always the opportunity for self-organized sports, especially in sports such as basketball that can be played 2 on 2 or 3 on 3. Self-reports from surveys do not, for the most part, differentiate these venues and types of programs. Parents may also play team sports informally with their children.

There are sports surveys that do not differentiate school-age players from older ones. This radically distorts the overall picture. Surveys of high school sports participation are not fully comparable with household surveys. In the analysis that follows, age will be used as a proxy for educational attachment. For all team sports, age is the most powerful index of participation. It is combined, however, with student status to make the transition from student status and school opportunities the watershed of diminished team sports engagement.

Basketball

Basketball may be played indoors or outdoors, on full courts or half, in formal competition or self-organized games. Where space and "hoops" are available, it is low cost and often the sport of choice in urban settings. Its popularity is linked to the sports industry and its highly-promoted star system.

General Trends

The SMRB data show a cyclical but increasing rate of adult basketball in the 1990s. Just over 7 percent of those 18 and over played basketball in 1996. Of those, about half played frequently. NSG data for the same period also indicates growth at a modest 3.5 percent per year rate. Overall participation increased from 26 million to 31 million including children and youth. Participation for frequent players who played 50 or more times a year was 26 percent of the total. The increase for children 7 to 11 from 1990 to 1996 was 26 percent and for youth 12 to 17, 10.5 percent Basketball, then, is a growth sport, partly because of its overall popularity and partly due to its low cost and relative flexibility in numbers and space requirements (see Table 4-23).

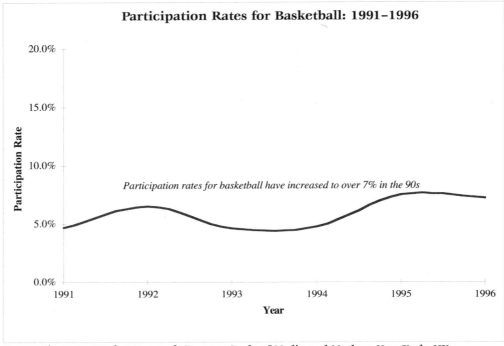

Participation Rates for Basketball: 1991–1996

Participation rates for basketball have increased to over 7% in the 90s

Source: Simmons Market Research Bureau. *Study of Media and Markets*. New York, NY.

Table 4-23

Market Identification

Basketball, like most team sports with a long history of male support, is strongly gendered: 12 percent male participation for adults 18 and just over 3 percent for females. It is also age-based with a 22 percent rate for those 18 to 24 dropping to 11 percent age 25 to 34, 7 percent age 35 to 44, and 3 percent age 45 to 54. Basketball players are most likely to be single males in school including college. There is no strong regional bias. Unlike most sports, there is also no income factor. Basketball is played by those with low as well as moderate and high incomes. It is urban and rural and crosses racial lines. One reason is that it is the most common indoor school sport for males. Support for female basketball in schools may alter the gender bias in time, but in the 1990s the growth rate was about the same for males and females 18 and over.

Growth markets: Basketball is a mainstream sport that remains school-related. The general gradual growth pattern for males and females under 25 may shift somewhat as females now in elementary and secondary schools play more basketball. The highest growth rate is for low-income players. Increased levels of participation and quality of play are likely to continue unless adequately-equipped court space is saturated.

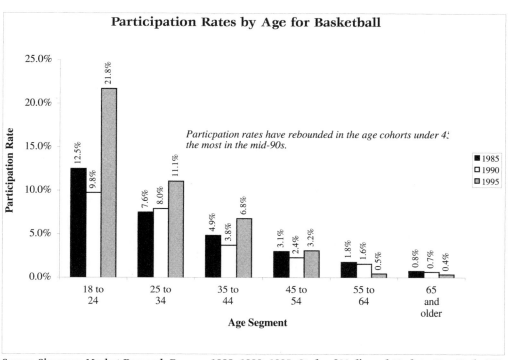

Participation Rates by Age for Basketball

Particpation rates have rebounded in the age cohorts under 4: the most in the mid-90s.

Source: **Simmons Market Research Bureau. 1985, 1990, 1995.** *Study of Media and Markets.* **New York, NY.**

Table 4-24

Established markets: The central market remains that of students. A critical factor is the availability of courts and programs for those who have left school. However, basketball is a self-organized activity at many gyms and playgrounds. As such, it is less subject to scheduling than most sports.

Low markets: Both men and women age 45 and over. Despite a few programs for older players, the physical demands of the sport preclude heavy later-life participation. Upper income and educated adults have alternative physical activities while downscale markets are limited by health factors.

Projections

Basketball participation will likely grow somewhat among younger females due to greater opportunity in school programs. Otherwise, participation rates may have slight growth by age category due to low cost and cross-racial inclusiveness, but the aging of the society makes dramatic growth in total participation unlikely. Injury rates are relatively high. It is both a strenuous and accessible sport so that age remains the primary factor in participation.

Football

Football is the classic school sport for young males despite some public programs for children and youth. It is primarily a spectator rather than recreational sport due to the complications of arranging for full teams, equipment required for safety, and physical requirements. Despite occasional informal "touch" football games for young

61

adults and intramural games in schools, it is a niche sport with overall low rates of participation. Concerns for injuries also are a limiting factor in parental support for children and youth.

General Trends

Football is growing slightly but consistently since 1990 at about a 3 percent annual rate. The 18 and over rate of just under 4 percent reflects informal games for the 70 percent of the total who are occasional. About 7.4 million adults report playing in some venue with 147 million participation days. NSG data are helpful. They report almost 12 million players of whom 1.9 million played 40 or more times a year. Tackle football has 8 million players of whom 3 million played frequently. Tackle, then, tends to be an organized sport for younger players, mostly students. Touch is most often an occasional informal game and attracts some older players. NSG is no longer tracking touch football. Overall, then, football is a divided sport with low rates of participation in organized programs, interscholastic (tackle) and intramural (touch or flag). There is also some rugby football among students. This low rate of participation runs counter to the importance of football as a spectator sport, media attraction, and business enterprise (including university programs) (see Table 4-25).

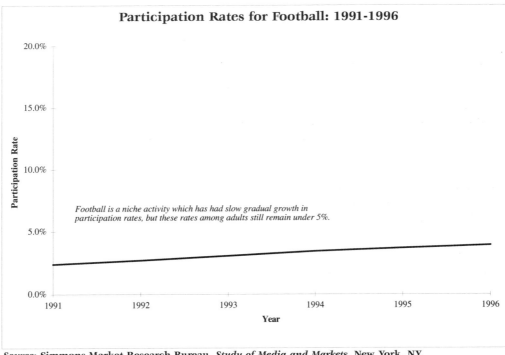

Source: Simmons Market Research Bureau. *Study of Media and Markets*. New York, NY.

Table 4-25

Market Identification

Football is, of course, highly gendered with 6.4 percent male to 1.2 percent female participation. It is also primarily a sport for the young, the 15 percent rate for those 18 to 24 falling drastically to 3 percent for age 25 to 34. It is primarily a student sport with the highest rates in the West and lowest in the Northeast. The rate for singles is seven times higher than for the married (see Table 4-26).

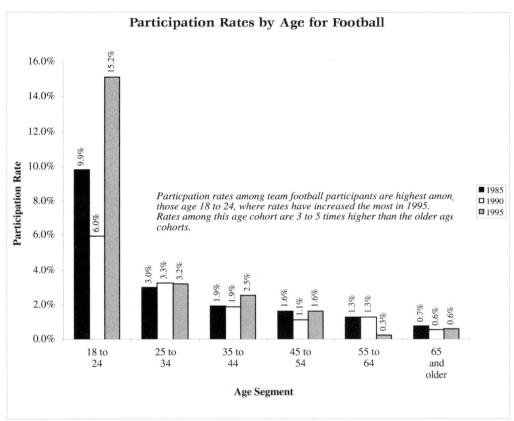

Participation Rates by Age for Football

Particpation rates among team football participants are highest among those age 18 to 24, where rates have increased the most in 1995. Rates among this age cohort are 3 to 5 times higher than the older age cohorts.

Source: **Simmons Market Research Bureau. 1985, 1990, 1995.** *Study of Media and Markets.* **New York, NY.**

Table 4-26

Growth markets: There is little likelihood of growth in recreational football.
Established markets: Schools with interscholastic and intramural programs at high school and college levels.
Low markets: Females and males out of school.

Projections

Football will probably continue to flourish as a spectator sport and attract players with its particular physical requirements. As a recreational sport, it is primarily an informal and intramural activity for those who played in younger years and have been winnowed out by the special requirements of the sport at higher levels. It is, then, a niche sport with a "young male" image and aura. The growth of other sports, such as soccer, places another limit on football participation. Tackle football is an expensive sport requiring expensive school or community sponsorship.

Ice Hockey

Ice hockey is a sport with a strong tradition in Canada and concentrated cores in the Northern tier of states with natural ice in the winter. It can also be played informally where ice is available, but has increasingly become an organized sport played in indoor arenas. The sponsors are both schools and public or private organized programs for youth. It is relatively costly for equipment and indoor ice time rental.

General Trends

Ice hockey had a period of growth in the early 1990s that appears to be leveling off. Cost and climate as well as injury risk limit its markets. The SMRB data for adults shows a 32 percent growth rate in the 1990s. This is from a low level, however, 0.4 percent in 1991 to 1.4 percent in 1994–96. That yields 2.6 million hockey players of all types and 68 million participation days. The NSG data including children shows no increase from the 1.9 million level in 1990, of whom about 25 percent play regularly. There was an 11 percent increase among children at 7 to 11, but a 3 percent loss for youth 12 to 17. Overall, ice hockey appears to be a niche sport with a growth curve that has leveled due to costs and rink limitations. Growth in specific areas will be due to improved facilities and organized programs (see Table 4-27).

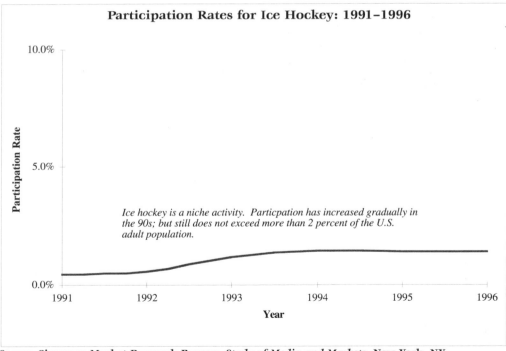

Participation Rates for Ice Hockey: 1991–1996

Ice hockey is a niche activity. Participation has increased gradually in the 90s; but still does not exceed more than 2 percent of the U.S. adult population.

Source: **Simmons Market Research Bureau.** *Study of Media and Markets.* **New York, NY.**

Table 4-27

Market Identification

Ice hockey is 75 percent male and almost entirely a youth sport. The 5 percent rate for those 18 to 24 drops to 1.4 percent for age 25 to 34 and 0.7 percent for those

35 to 44. It is a student sport with a high proportion of players in college. Singles play at four times the rate of those who are married. It is, of course strongest in the Northeast and upper Midwest and weakest in the South. Players are predominantly from higher income households due to costs. The largest cohort of ice hockey players come from schools with hockey programs or communities with youth hockey and/or outdoor ice in the winter. New in-line hockey programs may provide some crossover growth (see Table 4-28).

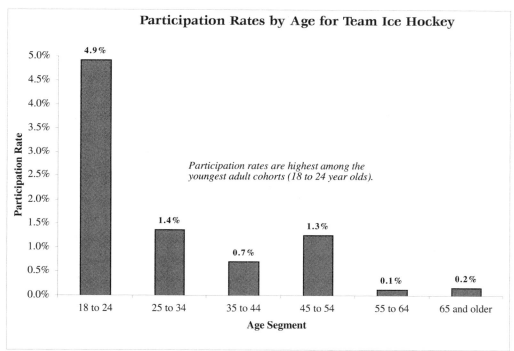

Participation Rates by Age for Team Ice Hockey

Participation rates are highest among the youngest adult cohorts (18 to 24 year olds).

Source: **Simmons Market Research Bureau. 1995.** *Study of Media and Markets.* **New York, NY.**

Table 4-28

Growth markets: Any further growth will be located in communities that enlarge and develop programs for youth. It is a site-specific niche activity concentrated in locales with facilities and an adequate supply of children and youth from households that can afford the activity.

Established markets: Youth, primarily males from households with adequate discretionary income, in communities with facilities and programs.

Low markets: Most of the country, especially communities with lower income levels, are limited markets, even for the young. For the most part, despite a few exceptions in traditional hockey areas, ice hockey is not an adult sport.

Projections

Limited community-specific growth. The economic and logistical limitations make this a niche sport with little likelihood of general growth. In communities and areas with a skating history and adequate economic resources, however, there may be strong programs that grow and saturate the resources.

Soccer

Soccer (football) is the major sport in Europe and Latin America. As such, its growth is partly related to immigration. Nevertheless, expanded opportunities and interest have produced growth across all ethnic lines. While World Cup hype exaggerated probable growth, it has become a major team sport in the 1980s and early 1990s. Youth soccer programs in schools and communities have supported participation in an increasing number of locales.

General Trends

The growth of soccer in the 1990s has been significant, with an overall rate of plus 20 percent. Like any activity cycle, the period of greatest growth may have been reached. It is an activity that is growing from the ground up, with participation growth strongest among children. Therefore, the adult rate of participation obscures much of that growth. Adult soccer playing has increased from 1 percent in 1991 to about 2.5 percent in 1994, 1995, and 1996. That produces 4.5 million players and 124 million participation days. NSG data including children shows a 4 percent overall yearly increase with 11 million players in 1990 and 13.7 million in 1997. Of these, about one third play regularly. The greatest growth has been among children age 7 to 11, a 27 percent increase between 1990 and 1996. However, the 12 to 17 age youth demonstrated a 5 percent loss in the same period. This may be explained by the increase in children's programs and the greater selectivity of those for youth age 12 and over. The growth, then, especially among regular participants, is largely among preteen children (see Table 4-29).

Market Identification

Over twice as many adult males play soccer as females, 3.7 percent to 1.4 percent Those 18 to 24 play at four times the rate of those 25 to 34, 8.5 percent to 2.1 percent The 2 to 3 percent rate falls rapidly after age 45. For adults, soccer is biased toward those with college education, including students. The model adult player is a single young male, suggesting school program facilitation. The West is the strongest area. Adult soccer players tend to have high incomes, suggesting a basis in upper-level school programs (see Table 4-30).

Growth market: Current growth is among children in organized programs that are increasing in many communities. A special growth opportunity is for girls in gender segregated and integrated programs. The long-term growth depends on these children continuing the sport. The second growth area is in communities where immigration is increasing the population who are from soccer football playing cultures. For example, there is a market among young Latin males in Los Angeles County, Dade County, and in Texas. Carryover to indoor soccer programs in the North is more income-based.

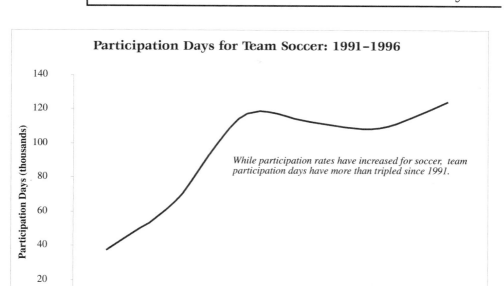

Source: Simmons Market Research Bureau. *Study of Media and Markets*. New York, NY.

Table 4-29

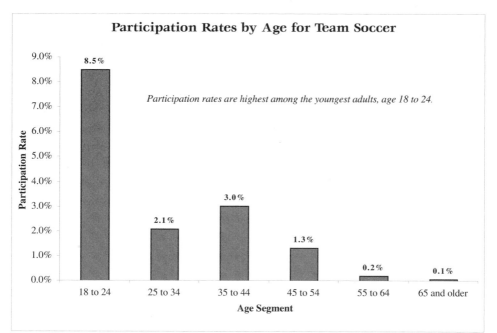

Source: Simmons Market Research Bureau. 1995. *Study of Media and Markets*. New York, NY.

Table 4-30

67

Established markets: The major market depends on organized programs in urban communities where soccer has become established as a children's and youth sport. Much will depend on fields being available to accommodate this sport in urban areas where space is scarce. As a relatively low-cost sport for equipment, public space is the key factor. Indoor arenas for year-round play may enhance the sport for the committed, but change the low-cost nature of the sport.

Low markets: All the adults who were raised prior to the introduction of soccer in school and public programs, including the "Boomer" cohort, are unlikely to take up the sport in midlife. The appeal is to the children of the "Boomers" rather than adults.

Projections

The growth of soccer is likely to continue, if at a somewhat slower or reduced rate. The two areas of growth are children in communities with organized programs and adequate space, especially among the less-developed female market, and areas with large European and Latin populations, especially first and second generation immigrants who bring both interest and skills with them. This suggests that growth may be most pronounced in the Southwest and South. The most significant growth, then, will be among frequent players as families and communities develop a soccer tradition.

Softball and Baseball

Softball is played in both school and league formats that include both males and females. It can also be an informal activity for children and youth in warm weather where space is available. Baseball, on the other hand, with its greater space requirements tends to be more limited to organized formats including school teams and the Little League and Babe Ruth Leagues for children and youth. The data for adults are combined, but those for children and youth separate the two related sports.

General Trends

Adult participation in softball and baseball shows little growth or loss. Combining softball and baseball confounds differences between the two. Baseball, despite being labeled the "National Pastime," has lost its centrality in American communities. It is a declining sport for adults, while softball has some small increases partly related to female and older male participation. The adult rate for the combined sports was just over 6 percent in 1991 and was about 7 percent from 1993 through 1996. The 13 million players produced just under 300 million participation days. About 40 percent play regularly. NSG data including children and youth show a steady rate of participation for softball since 1990 with between 17 and 20 million players of whom about 30 percent played 30 days or more. Gender equality programs have been a factor in the last two decades. Children age 7 to 11 showed a 1 percent decrease in softball from 1990 through 1996 and youth age 11 to 17 a 10 percent gain. Baseball has fewer players, about 14 million, of whom 30 percent are frequent. The trend indicates a very slight loss. For children 7 to 11, however, the decline from 1990 through 1996 was 5 percent and for youth 12 to 17 almost 10 percent (see Table 4-31).

Market Identification

For adults age 18 and above softball/baseball is gendered, 10.5 percent male to 4.8 percent female. This difference may be less pronounced, however, for children's softball. The sports are age-related with a 15 percent rate for those 18 to 24 falling to 13

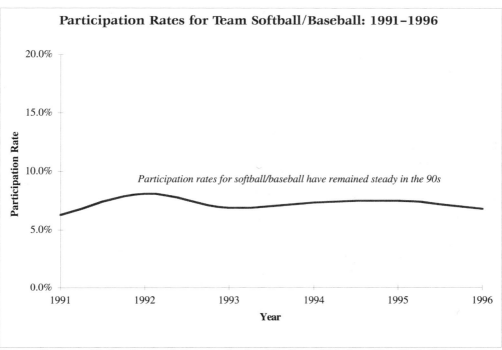

Participation Rates for Team Softball/Baseball: 1991–1996

Participation rates for softball/baseball have remained steady in the 90s

Source: **Simmons Market Research Bureau.** *Study of Media and Markets.* **New York, NY.**

Table 4-31

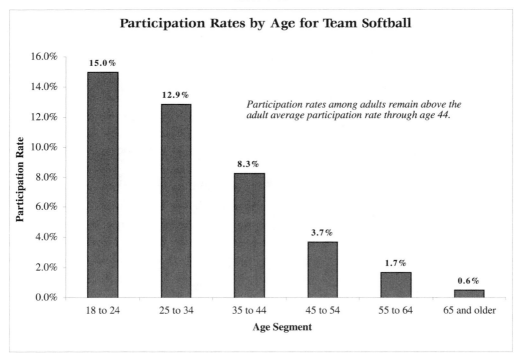

Participation Rates by Age for Team Softball

Participation rates among adults remain above the adult average participation rate through age 44.

Source: **Simmons Market Research Bureau. 1995.** *Study of Media and Markets.* **New York, NY.**

Table 4-32

69

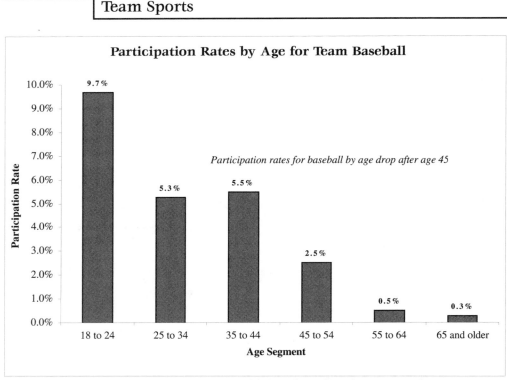

Participation Rates by Age for Team Baseball

Participation rates for baseball by age drop after age 45

Source: Simmons Market Research Bureau. *Study of Media and Markets.* New York, NY.

Table 4-33

percent age 25 to 34, 8 percent 35 to 44, 3.7 percent 45 to 54, 1.7 percent 55 to 64, and 0.6 percent 65 and older. There is little education or income bias above the poverty line. Rates are lowest in the Northeast and South and highest in the Midwest and West. Softball/baseball still demonstrates a level of inclusion that is higher than most sports (see Table 4-32).

Growth markets: There may be some growth in percentages among younger women and possibly older males where there are special programs. In general, softball and baseball are stable rather than growth sports. Gender equity can be expected to have some impact.

Established markets: Children, youth, and young adult males in communities with adequate fields and developed programs are the central market. There is, of course, some informal softball played by children and at gatherings such as picnics.

Low markets: Older females and those in urban areas too crowded or poor to provide fields are of low market potential.

Projections

The general projection is for little change. There is both developed interest and an investment in programs and facilities in communities with age-graded softball programs and Little League baseball. Schools continue to support baseball, but opportunities for those who are not "stars" are limited after leaving school. Females who have gained skills as children may expand that market somewhat. The negative side is the competition from growing sports such as soccer, especially in urban areas with high ethnic growth from European and Latin regions. Softball especially is a general, not niche, sport, but with major growth unlikely. It exemplifies "middle America," with 70 percent of players from households of moderate income and a strong base in the Midwest.

Volleyball

Volleyball is played in a variety of formats and venues. There is informal picnic play. There is interscholastic and league 6-per-side competition. There is beach and sand volleyball played 2 on 2. Volleyball can be single sex or mixed, informal or formal, indoors and outdoors. It is different from many sports in that it has a relatively small children's component, partly due to net height, player height, and related skills. In many schools, its main or primary competition format is for females.

General Trends

Volleyball has had fluctuating growth since 1990 among adult players. The adult rate has risen from 5.5 percent to an average 7 percent level in 1994–96 yielding about 14 million players and 215 million participation days. Of these, about 30 percent play regularly. NSG surveys including children indicate a negative 2 percent change rate since 1990 with total players falling from 20.5 to 18 million. The loss in frequent volleyball players has been somewhat less, from 7.3 to 5.7 million. The loss seems to be among children and youth, with a total 20 percent loss for children age 7 to 11 and 17

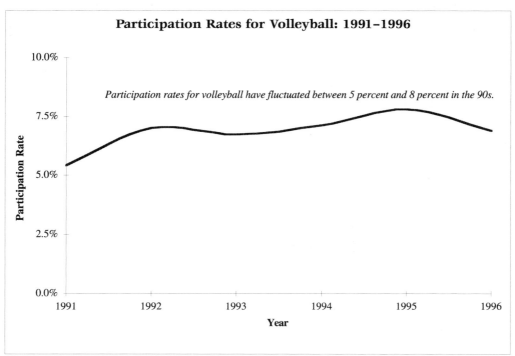

Source: **Simmons Market Research Bureau.** *Study of Media and Markets.* **New York, NY.**

Table 4-34

percent loss for youth 12 to 17 from 1990 through 1996. One factor may be the new pressures for year-round commitment to one or two sports. Although from different surveys, the trends suggest overall stability or slight growth with the gains coming from young adults, especially those with lower incomes, and the losses occurring among children and youth (see Table 4-34).

Market Identification

Volleyball players are about evenly divided by gender, 6.7 percent male to 5.7 percent female. There is the usual sport decline by age from 13 percent for young adults age 18 to 24 to 8.6 percent age 25 to 34, 6.5 percent age 35 to 44, 3.5 percent 45 to 54, and about 1 percent for those over 54. Rates are similar for education levels from high school graduates up. Volleyball is least common in the South and highest in the West and Midwest. Singles play two times as often as those who are married, reflecting the student cohort. While low income adults play at half the rate of those with moderate or high household incomes, the rate of increase is three times higher. Volleyball is more a general than a niche sport, partly due to the variety of venues in which it is played. It is playground, beach, yard, and gym based. The markets are somewhat different for each venue (see Table 4-35).

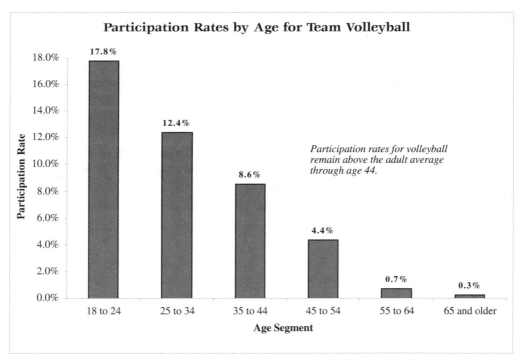

Source: Simmons Market Research Bureau. *Study of Media and Markets.* New York, NY.

Table 4-35

Growth markets: The largest growth market is young adult women where opportunities are available and school opportunities were increased by Title IX. A second, partly hidden, growth market may be in low-income areas where nets and courts are available in public neighborhood locations. Beach and sand volleyball are being promoted, but separate data are not available for analysis. The transformation of racquetball courts for "wallyball" may be growing in some indoor recreational centers, but no data are available on this change.

Established markets: The central markets remain that of male and female students where there are programs and facilities. Volleyball is also an occasional park recreational activity related to social gatherings. It is a standard sport with both competition and recreational/social formats and traditions.

Low markets: Older adults are not major markets except in locations such as some Ys where there is a tradition of organized adult play.

Projections

There may be minor growth among young adults, especially females, and in park courts in low-income areas. However, the reductions among children and youth will not support long-term growth. The overall projection, however, is for stability. The unknown factor would seem to be new forms of the sport which are likely to have fluctuating cycles of participation.

Chapter 5

Fitness Activities

All sorts of activities are engaged in with physical fitness and health as a significant motivating factor. Exercise for fitness may prompt a commuter to walk from the train to the office, a home- owner to mow her own lawn, or a midlife adult to continue a sport. There are, however, a number of activities, some with special devices, that are clearly for physical enhancement purposes. Sometimes there are specific health aims related to cardiovascular conditions or problems. Sometimes exercise is related to weight, which may be a matter of health or appearance. The large proportion of young adults engaged in fitness activity indicates that the aims are frequently more cosmetic than health-related. In fact, the high dropout rates for fitness activities may be partly due to the fact that exercise does not change basic body type or overcome poor nutrition habits. This section focuses on activities that are primarily for physical exercise, whatever the aims.

There is also a problem with the type of programs. Much of the growth in fitness activity has not been at locations away from home. There has been a large market for devices that can be used on demand in the home. At-home on-demand exercise is responsive to the time pressures of young adults with upper-level jobs that are a major segment of the fitness market. In some cases, participation data distinguishes residential from external venues. Most do not. Further, most devices purchased in the last five years lie in a corner or a closet, broken or unbroken, gathering dust. Therefore, sales figures do not represent use. What the trend data do provide is an overall view of the development of the various kinds of exercise activities and equipment.

A final factor is that of marketing. New devices and refinements of older ones are highly promoted with great promises as to their effectiveness. Advertising attempts to bypass qualified evaluation and any testing to appeal directly to the consumer dissatisfied with his or her appearance. The consistency and discipline in use required to gain substantial results leads to discontinuance rates for at-home equipment and fitness center programs estimated at 75 to 80 percent in periods of months or even weeks. Research indicating that a strong motivation combined with positive feedback and social support are required for an effective program are seldom included in promotional material.

Aerobics—General

Aerobic exercise in general includes any sustained exercise activity with a fitness aim. However, most references are to group exercise programs, sometimes combined with dance and music, individual routines, and use of equipment but excluding walking, jogging, and sports. Some participants combine organized programs at special locations with at-home exercise. The data, however, give a picture of overall aerobic activity separated from the promotional cycles of any specific equipment or fad.

General Trends

There have been fluctuations since the mid-1980s, but overall participation has been declining. What is clear is that the journalistically ballyhooed "fitness craze" never existed. The proportion of the adult population consistently engaged in physical exercise for fitness and cosmetic purposes has remained at modest levels. The adult participation rate in general aerobics was about 8 percent in 1986, declined to 6.5 percent in 1991, and then rose slightly to between 7 and 7.5 percent in 1995 and 96. This yields about 14 million exercisers and 500 million participation days. NSG data including children and youth demonstrates a similar pattern. Total aerobics participants numbered 23 million in 1990 and fluctuated through the decade to a level of 26 million in 1997. Frequent exercisers, just over 25 percent of the total, also increased to 7 million. Different samples account for the differences. In general, however, aerobic exercise is at most growing slightly and possibly at a steady state after a decade of slight decline. Clearly, there is no "boom" (see Table 5-36).

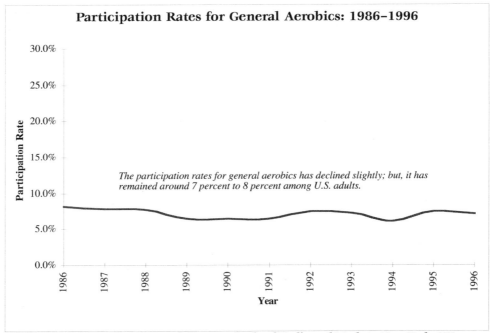

Participation Rates for General Aerobics: 1986–1996

The participation rates for general aerobics has declined slightly; but, it has remained around 7 percent to 8 percent among U.S. adults.

Source: **Simmons Market Research Bureau.** *Study of Media and Markets.* **New York, NY.**

Table 5-36

Market Identification

Aerobic exercise is gendered, but in the opposite way from most sports. Females outnumber males almost 3 to 1 or 11 percent to 3.6 percent. Aerobics is age-graded, but not as dramatically as many physical activities. The 12 percent rate for those 18 to 24 shrinks to 10 percent for 25 to 34, 8.6 percent for 35 to 44, 5.7 percent for 45 to 54, 4.3 percent for 55 to 64, and just under 3 percent for those 65 and over. Aerobic rates for those with some college education are twice those with just high school diplomas. Singles engaged in aerobics only slightly more than married, but those with high incomes double the rates for moderate income levels. The West and Midwest rates are highest. Unlike most activities, aerobics is either a regular or not at all activity with 72 percent being frequent participants. A possible explanation of the lack of "Boomer" growth in general aerobics is the development of a variety of exercise programs and equipment (see Table 5-37).

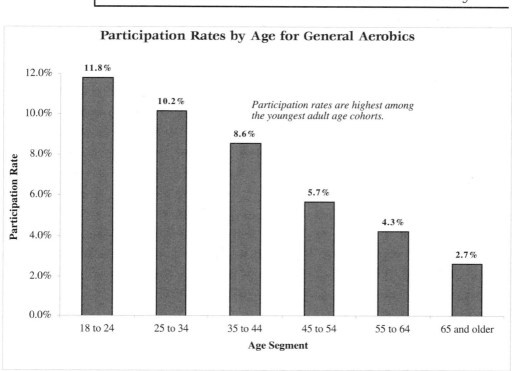

Participation Rates by Age for General Aerobics

Participation rates are highest among the youngest adult age cohorts.

18 to 24: 11.8%
25 to 34: 10.2%
35 to 44: 8.6%
45 to 54: 5.7%
55 to 64: 4.3%
65 and older: 2.7%

Y-axis: Participation Rate

X-axis: Age Segment

Source: **Simmons Market Research Bureau. 1995.** *Study of Media and Markets.* **New York, NY.**

Table 5-37

Growth markets: Despite lower rates, the highest growth rates have been among those age 45 and over. This growing population segment is the most significant market opportunity. However, there are indications of growth among those with low incomes and education levels as well. Continuation among "Baby Boomers" may produce some growth. There is also some indication of an increase in male participation.

Established markets: Young adult women with cosmetic aims remain the central, if stable, market. Marketing has to take into account that these women are in the work force so that time and schedule are major factors.

Low markets: Older males, especially with lower incomes and education levels, are not a major market segment.

Projections

No dramatic growth is likely. The long-term trends are clear. However, the indications of some modest growth among older adults and the significance of the "Boomer" cohort suggests that their participation may at least offset the smaller numbers of young adult women. The problematic factor is the incursion of variations of activities such as step and water aerobics and the marketing of at-home exercise equipment, especially for those with time scarcities. On-demand exercise has a convenience appeal over any scheduled activity.

Exercise With Equipment

The NSG survey has tracked a general category of activity that does not specify the kind of exercise equipment since 1993. The equipment can include portable and stationary types of machines, some of which are specific to one part of the body. Surveys demonstrate some increase in such activity, especially for frequent users. The 1993 total including children and youth is 35 million participants of whom 10 million engaged in the activity 110 or more time a year. This total rises to 44 million in 1995 and 48 million in 1997 for an 8.6 percent rate of gain. The increase of frequent users, about 30 percent of the total, is to 11 million in 1995 and 14 million in 1997. The value of this analysis is that it bypasses the rise and fall of particular kinds of equipment to give an overall view of the market that includes treadmills, step machines, rowers, stationary bicycles, weight devices, and other variations of stationary equipment As a comparison, this indicates that the total equipment exercise market is somewhat less than twice that for aerobics or four times that for step exercise alone. Convenience and the on-demand nature of such exercise appeals to those who feel a time scarcity.

Aerobics—Step

Step aerobics, in various forms, has become popular at many fitness centers and with in-home devices. In general, the markets are similar as for other aerobic formats except that it exemplifies self-scheduled activity. There is a problem distinguishing step aerobics from exercise employing a stair-walking or climbing machine (see below). Step aerobics is a variation of general aerobics with an adjustable step built into the routines. The machine may be at a market, public, or private location or in the home. Technically, an exerciser could also use real steps, but there is no research on this variant.

General Trends

Data are not long-term. SMRB shows sustained growth since 1994, rising from a rate of 4.7 percent to 5.6 percent in 1996 with a total of about 11 million adult users and 400 million participation days. NSG data begin with 1991 and indicate a marked increase in participants from 6.8 million to just under 10 million in 1997 with a rate of increase of almost 10 percent. Of these, about 20 percent are frequent exercisers, a very different pattern from that of general aerobics programs. This is typical of on-demand exercise as distinguished from commitment to a regular group program which one tends to do or not.

Market Identification

Step aerobic exercisers are predominantly female, 8.8 percent female to 3.6 percent male. They are most often young adults, the highest rate being for age 25 to 34, 10.2 percent, with 8 percent for those age 18 to 24, 6.7 percent of 35 to 44, 6 percent for 45 to 54, 2.6 percent for 55 to 64, and 1.5 percent for 65 and older. Singles do step aerobics at a 50 percent higher rate than the married, and those with high incomes at almost twice the rate of those with moderate or low incomes. There is no significant regional bias. Those with college education use the step at twice the rate of others. The modal step exerciser is a young adult woman who values the convenience of the device.

Growth markets: The time-scarcity young adult is the continued growth market, perhaps especially the "second shift" employed mothers. Convenience is a major factor so that those desiring exercise but finding a scheduled group difficult are a target market. The in-home step program adds to the convenience, but lacks the reinforcement of meeting others at a facility.

Established markets: Essentially the same young adult female market along with students who have access to school facilities.

Low markets: Adults over 55 and those who cannot afford the device.

Projections

Probably there will continue to be short-term growth followed by a market saturation. One major question will be the continued use by women as their children age. Another factor is the competition of exercise devices such as treadmills and stationary cycles that may lessen the demand for step aerobics. Competition among such machines along with the many variations for standing and sitting exercisers may erode markets for each specific style. Further, the discontinuation rate for on-demand exercise is so high that individuals come in and out of the market at a high rate. It is a highly competitive and promoted market.

Aerobics—Water

Water aerobics is most often an organized activity in larger pools, but can be individual and in private pools. One problem is that the activity interferes with swimming, especially lap swimming that may be a demand with similar time preferences. Water aerobics has also been promoted for older adults and those with physical limitations or health problems. As such, it is more health oriented and rehabilitative and less cosmetic than other aerobics.

General Trends

In the brief period tracked, water aerobics seems to have increased at a 7 percent rate with a leveling since 1995. The rate of participation is low, 2 percent of adults, making short-term trends unreliable. About 60 percent of these exercisers are frequent. This rate yields about 4 million participants and participation days fluctuating between 115 million and 150 million during the period examined. The 1996 reduction may be unreliable, especially since the central market is increasing in size and older segments are less reliable in trend analysis (see Table 5-38).

Market Identification

The market is skewed toward females, 4.3 percent to 1.8 percent. There is essentially no age-related reduction with a rate of just over 3 percent from ages 25 to 65 and 2.9 percent for 65 and over. There is also no market differentiation by education level, marital status, or income. The rate is somewhat lower in the Northeast. In overall size, this is a niche activity, but in distribution it is broad-based. What is suggested is that it is need and opportunity-based. Those who have a health factor in choosing this kind of exercise and access to a pool and program engage in it frequently if at all. It is probably more health-based than most exercise, accounting for the remarkable lack of age bias (see Table 5-39).

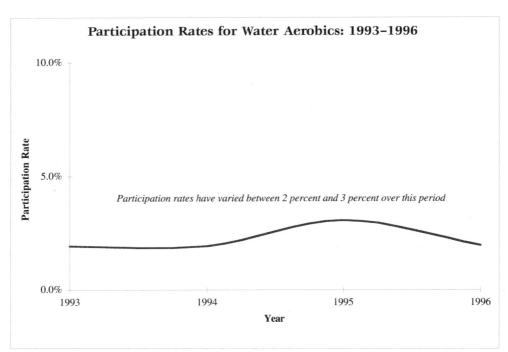

Participation Rates for Water Aerobics: 1993–1996

Participation rates have varied between 2 percent and 3 percent over this period

Source: Simmons Market Research Bureau. *Study of Media and Markets*. New York, NY.

Table 5-38

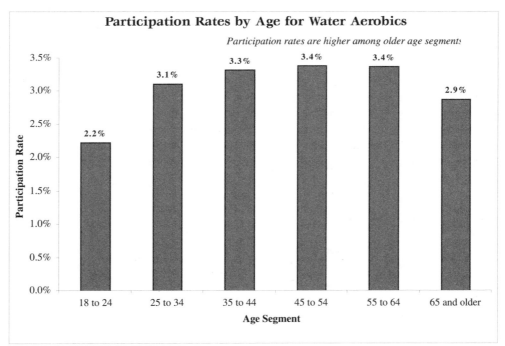

Participation Rates by Age for Water Aerobics

Participation rates are higher among older age segments

3.5%

3.4%   3.4%

3.3%

3.1%

2.9%

2.2%

18 to 24   25 to 34   35 to 44   45 to 54   55 to 64   65 and older

Age Segment

Source: Simmons Market Research Bureau. 1995. *Study of Media and Markets*. New York, NY.

Table 5-39

Growth market: "Boomer" cohort women are the likely area of growth, especially those with health conditions that call for exercise that makes minimal impact on feet and legs. In this sense, then, it is a niche market.

Established market: A broad base of those seeking a more gentle cardiovascular or rehabilitative exercise. Very general in composition. Individuals can need this type of exercise at almost any age due to injuries, pregnancy, or conditions such as arthritis or heart disease.

Low markets: Those engaged in physically demanding activity and those who are fully sedentary are unlikely markets at any age.

Projections

The development of programs has led to an increase. It will continue as opportunities expand and will be augmented by the increase in the older population. Water aerobics is a special activity that really is exercise for health and fitness benefits.

Exercise—Stationary Bicycles

A high proportion of stationary bike riding is a residential on-demand activity. However, such equipment is also provided at fitness centers as part of a more varied workout. This is one of the older equipment-based exercise activities, so trend data begin in 1986.

General Trends

This is a growth activity with signs of leveling since 1995. Competition with other types of exercise equipment may account for the end of market growth. The adult rate grew from about 7.5 percent in 1986 to 105 percent in 1990, 8.5 percent in 1993 and 1994, and back to 10.5 percent in 1995 and 1996. This yields 20 million users and 700 million participation days. Over 60 percent of users are frequent participants and comprise a committed core of exercise cyclists (see Table 5-40).

Market Identification

There is a small bias toward females, 12 percent to 9.4 percent for males. The age-related decline is smaller than for most physical activities: 13 percent age 18 to 24, 10.7 percent 25 to 34, 12 percent 35 to 44, 11 percent 54 to 54, 9.4 percent 55 to 64, and 8 percent 65 and older. The rate for those with college education is 60 percent higher than for high school graduates. Except for lower rates in the South, there is no regional bias. Singles and married have equal rates. In general, stationary bike exercise has an inclusive market distribution based on its convenience, relatively low cost, and longer period of availability. It is the "traditional" piece of exercise equipment (see Table 5-41).

Growth markets: Due to the competition and promotion from other exercise devices, bikes probably have a consistent and somewhat stable, but not growing, market. Like others, they appeal to those who want uncomplicated exercise on demand and most often at home A special niche may be the retirement generation for whom the bike is a familiar machine. The growth potential is with the aging "Boomer" cohort and those in winter climates who ride conventional bicycles in the summer.

Established markets: The very general exercise market is based on the stationary bike's early introduction, longer history, and relative simplicity (once it is assembled). Further, it can be used at a self-determined pace that crosses ages and fitness conditions. The technologies have added to feedback and monitoring in using exercise bikes.

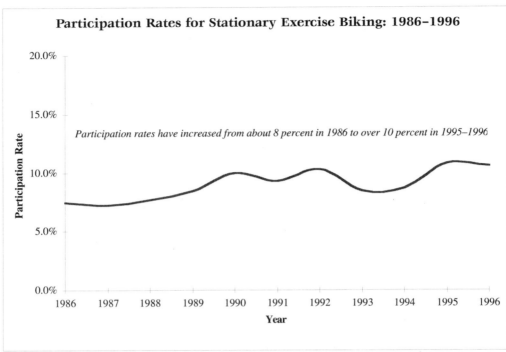

Participation Rates for Stationary Exercise Biking: 1986–1996

Participation rates have increased from about 8 percent in 1986 to over 10 percent in 1995–1996

Source: Simmons Market Research Bureau. *Study of Media and Markets*. New York, NY.

Table 5-40

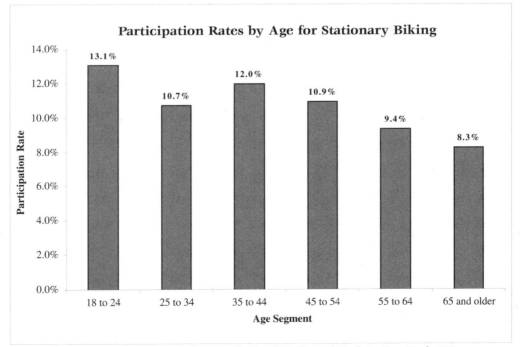

Participation Rates by Age for Stationary Biking

Source: Simmons Market Research Bureau. *Study of Media and Markets*. New York, NY.

Table 5-41

Low markets: Almost anyone wanting a machine for on-demand exercise is a potential market. The market is probably smallest for older people in warm climates.

Projections

There are no indications that the bike is being completely replaced by the competition, but any growth is likely to be gradual when other types of machines are getting most of the promotional budget. Current growth is highest among the young under 25 and those 65 and over.

Working Out at a Club

NSG has tracked exercise at fitness clubs that does not specify the type of exercise or machine. This generic category has grown slightly from 20.3 million participants in 1990 to 22 million in 1995 and 21 million in 1997. Of these, 25 to 30 percent are regular. In general, these data support the analysis that there is no strong increase in exercise activity, but that the forms fluctuate as new machines and programs are promoted and participants become bored and want to try something different. Time-diary data, while sparse and dated, also indicate no increase in exercise activity overall.

Exercise—Rowing Machines

The rowing machine is another of the traditional exercise devices. It exercises somewhat different parts of the body than those involving walking, running, or cycling. This is its appeal to some, but also a limitation due to stress on the back. It is also found both in the residence and in fitness centers. It has crossover appeal to outdoor rowers including the growing number of females in school programs.

General Trends

Adult data run from 1990. There was gradual growth in overall use through 1995, but not in regular use. The rate increased from 2 percent in 1990 and 1991 to 2.8 percent in 1995, but fell back to 2 percent in 1996. Frequent users, however, who are close to half the total, did not increase, suggesting purchases followed by occasional use. The total participants number about 4 million with just over 100 million participation days. As with other exercise machines, competition in the marketplace has restricted growth (see Table 5-42).

Market Identification

There is little gender difference for adults, 2.6 percent male to 3 percent female. There is remarkably little decline with age up to 55. Singles are 3.6 percent to 3 percent married. Rates are lowest in the Midwest and South. There is some upward income and education bias, but the low-income rate is almost 3 percent and those without college have 60 percent as high a rate as college graduates. Stationary rowing is, like bikes, a rather undifferentiated market (see Table 5-43).

Growth markets: Growth has been somewhat higher for those age 25 to 55. The fluctuating trends make it difficult to specify target markets. Rowing is one of the more strenuous exercise activities with particular stress on the back. Any measurable growth is unlikely regardless of market segment.

Established markets: Again the market is not clearly segmented by demographics. Competition from more heavily promoted machines and types of exercise suggests little change in the market composition.

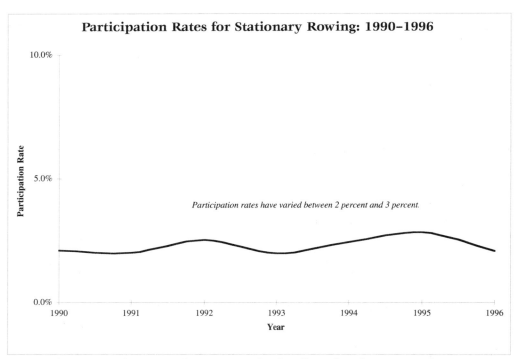

Participation Rates for Stationary Rowing: 1990–1996

Participation rates have varied between 2 percent and 3 percent.

Source: Simmons Market Research Bureau. *Study of Media and Markets*. New York, NY.

Table 5-42

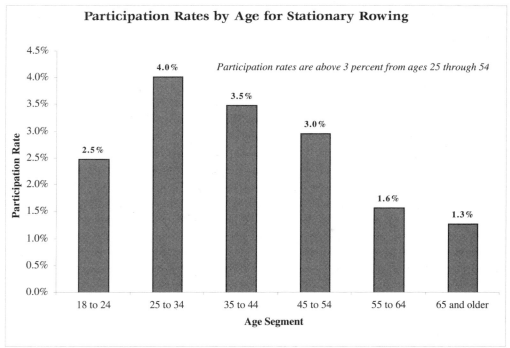

Participation Rates by Age for Stationary Rowing

Participation rates are above 3 percent from ages 25 through 54

Source: Simmons Market Research Bureau. 1995. *Study of Media and Markets*. New York, NY.

Table 5-43

Low markets: Adults 55 and over are not major markets due to the strenuous nature of the exercise and its stress on joints. Use by those of low incomes is increasing, but they remain only 7 percent of the total market.

Projections

There is no sign of continued growth. Product competition may send rowing machine use into a long-term decline. There will remain a market, however, for those who prefer this particular kind of conditioning and exercise. The niche market of female rowers may increase slightly.

Stair Walking and Climbing Machine

Again, in the survey data there is the problem of specifying the various similar kinds of exercise devices. One assumption would be that this category includes more than one kind of device and venue. Adult data are available only since 1991. There may be some crossover participation by those engaged in step aerobics.

General Trends

There is a reported increase in this activity since 1991 with a 3 percent adult rate doubling to 6.3 percent in 1996. The growth has been steady and now yields a total of 12 million participants and 400 million participation days. About 60 percent are frequent exercisers (see Table 5-44).

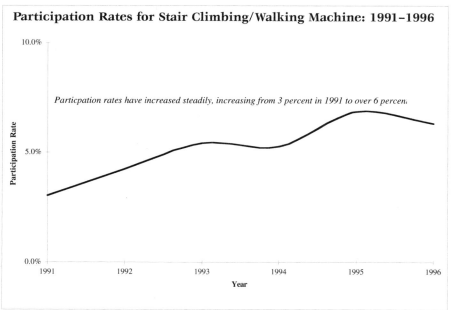

Participation Rates for Stair Climbing/Walking Machine: 1991–1996

Particpation rates have increased steadily, increasing from 3 percent in 1991 to over 6 percen.

Source: **Simmons Market Research Bureau.** *Study of Media and Markets.* **New York, NY.**

Table 5-44

Market Identification

This activity slightly favors females, 7.6 percent to 6.1 percent Again, there is little decrease with age up to age 55. The 8.5 percent rate for young adults age 18 to 24 increases to almost 10 percent for 25 to 34, drops back to 8.7 percent for 35 to 44, 6 percent for 45 to 54, and then halves. Singles are 50 percent more likely to use such devices than those with high incomes. Rates are lowest in the South and Midwest. The modal participant is a woman age 25 to 34, single, and living in the West or Northeast (see Table 5-45).

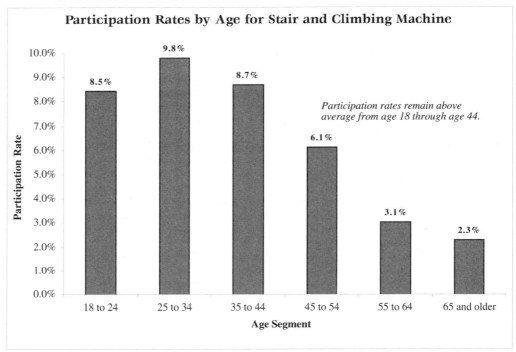

Participation Rates by Age for Stair and Climbing Machine

Participation rates remain above average from age 18 through age 44.

Source: **Simmons Market Research Bureau. 1995.** *Study of Media and Markets.* **New York, NY.**

Table 5-45

Growth markets: The greatest likelihood of growth would be midlife women as they age and retain a favored exercise mode. The highest growth rate, however, has been among the younger adults age 25 to 34. This is a post-school activity for many. A problematic factor in growth is the marketing of other forms of exercise machines.

Established markets: Young adults are the strongest market Stair walking, however, retains its appeal up to age 55.

Low markets: Low income adults and those who have not finished high school are low-demand market segments. The current low demand among those 55 and over may change as "Boomers" age.

Projections

Growth is likely to taper off to a longer-term trend of slow growth or niche stability. Again, competition among forms of exercise and devices is from a total market that is not growing. The possible exception would appear to be the retention of earlier habits and interests among the aging "Boomers."

Weight Training—Dumbbells

Dumbbells are used in facilities with a central weight training component, but may also be used at home. They are portable. However, the use of dumbbells is commonly combined with other weight training activity. Therefore, the category may serve as a proxy for a fuller program of weight training. The aims of this activity are multiple: some are involved in body building, some use weights for general fitness purposes, and others employ weights for the enhancement of strength and flexibility to be used in other sports. Another value of this category is the availability of participation data since 1982.

General Trends

There is overall growth in weight training at a participation rate of about 4.5 percent a year. The trend pattern, however, is more complex. The 7.5 percent adult rate in 1982 fell to about 5 percent in 1990 and 1991. Then it began to rise in 1992 to almost 12 percent in 1995 and 1996. There has clearly been a resurgence in weight training in the mid-1990s that now yields over 22 million participants and over 900 million participation days. Of these, 75 percent of weight training participants are frequent. There is a sizable committed core of participants (see Table 5-46).

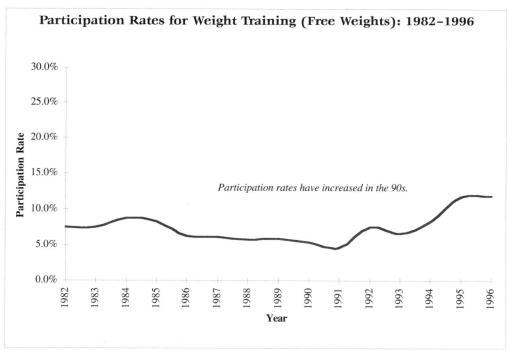

Participation Rates for Weight Training (Free Weights): 1982–1996

Participation rates have increased in the 90s.

Source: **Simmons Market Research Bureau. 1995.** *Study of Media and Markets.* **New York, NY.**

Table 5-46

Market Identification

As expected, weight training is gendered with about twice as many male as female participants, 16 percent to 8 percent. It is also age-graded: the 24.5 percent rate for those 18 to 24 falls to 16 percent for age 25 to 34, 13 percent for 35 to 44, 8 percent for 45 to 54, 3.7 percent for 55 to 64, and 3 percent for 65 and older. Those with college education train at over twice the rate of those with only high school education. Singles have a 23 percent rate to 9 percent for those who are married. High-income rates are almost 18 percent compared with 10 percent for moderate income and 7 percent for low income. As with many activities, the student market segment muddies these figures somewhat. Weight training is highest in the West and lowest in the South (see Table 5-47).

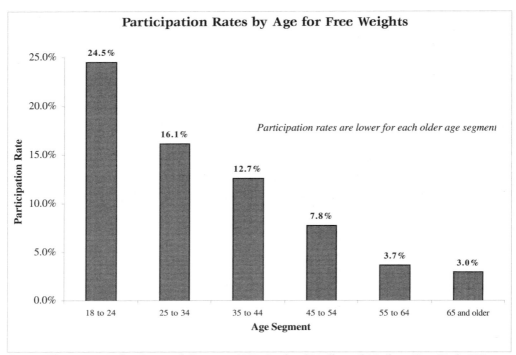

Participation Rates by Age for Free Weights

Participation rates are lower for each older age segment

Age Segment	Participation Rate
18 to 24	24.5%
25 to 34	16.1%
35 to 44	12.7%
45 to 54	7.8%
55 to 64	3.7%
65 and older	3.0%

Source: **Simmons Market Research Bureau.** *1995. Study of Media and Markets.* **New York, NY.**

Table 5-47

Growth markets: Growth among female weight trainers exceeds male increases. There is also marked growth among older trainers 65 and older, but from a very small base. Growth is somewhat general, but target markets may be older participants and students along with some attention to females. There is also some growth among lower income athletes building strength for other sports.

Established markets: Younger males are the central market, especially those with college education. A niche market is those engaged in weight training to enhance performance in sports.

Low markets: Traditionally, older adults, especially women, have been low markets. This may be changing somewhat as weight training is adapted to the retention of muscle mass and skeletal strength.

Projections

Continued growth is likely up to 8 to 10 percent per year before the market saturates. Weight training is changing from the traditional body building, a niche activity, to one that, when combined with other exercise, attracts a wider range of participants. Use of weights now overlaps with more general "working out at a club" activity. Some equipment such as dumbbells can also be used in the residence.

Weight Training—Machines

This activity is largely confined to weight training and fitness centers due to the size and costs of the equipment. However, there are now more portable machines in homes. Trend data for adults are available only since 1991 so that trends do not show the cycles of the previous category. Again, the aims include body building, fitness in conjunction with other exercise, and strength building for other sports.

General Trends

The trend since 1991 has been one of strong growth at a 22 percent per year rate. The adult rate in 1991 was 3.6 percent and has risen to almost 10 percent by 1995 and 96. This rate yields 18 million participants and 735 million participation days. Of such weight trainers, 75 percent are frequent. As with some, not all, other exercise activities, the tendency is to do it regularly or not at all. Exercise that is most demanding creates such a committed core of participants (see Table 5-48).

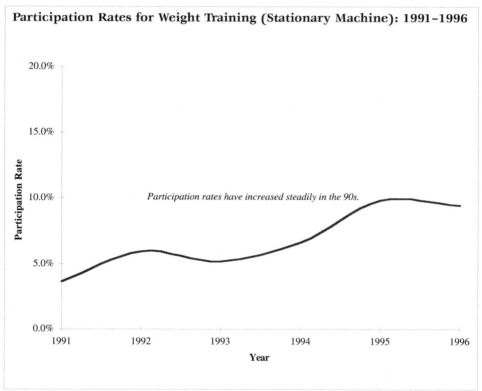

Participation Rates for Weight Training (Stationary Machine): 1991–1996

Participation rates have increased steadily in the 90s.

Source: **Simmons Market Research Bureau.** *Study of Media and Markets.* **New York, NY.**

Table 5-48

Market Identification

Market segmentation is similar to the previous category. Gender is somewhat less pronounced, 11.6 percent male to 8.2 percent female. The age curve is significant: 19 percent for 18 to 24, 14.5 percent 25 to 34, 10 percent 35 to 44, 7 percent 45 to 54, 4.5

percent 55 to 64, and 1.5 percent 65 and older. Those with college education, high incomes, and who are single have double the rates of others. Again, the activity is strongest in the West, perhaps related to the beach culture (see Table 5-49).

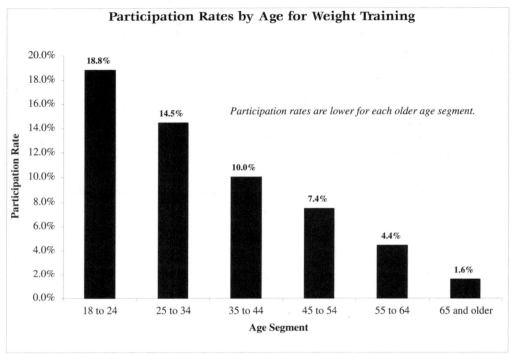

Participation Rates by Age for Weight Training

Participation rates are lower for each older age segment.

Source: **Simmons Market Research Bureau. 1995.** *Study of Media and Markets.* **New York, NY.**

Table 5-49

Growth markets: Again, the growth has reflected the general market segments. The greatest growth has been among those under age 35 and with moderate incomes. There appears to be an overall increase in the use of weight training machines suggesting a widening of the market from body building to incorporation into organized fitness programs. The tie to other sports would seem to be a growth market.

Established markets: Young males and body building are the traditional market. Certain kinds of equipment are now established and accepted in the field with many experienced users and trainers.

Low markets: The strenuous nature of the machine workout and their cost suggests that older persons and those with low incomes will remain small markets.

Projections

The issue after any period of strong growth in an activity is always market saturation. This is especially the case for an activity with markets focused by age and other factors. Most likely the rapid growth of the mid-1990s will slow, but that real long-term growth will continue limited chiefly by the aging of the population. Incorporating the machines into exercise programs with more general appeal is the key to long-term growth. Development of home equipment may sustain the market in the short term.

Martial Arts

Martial arts with its many forms, including the traditional karate, is engaged in for fitness purposes, but also has elements of self-defense and even spiritual growth. Programs are available for all ages and with a variety of venues, formats, and orientations. Some practice may take place in the residence, but training is given in group settings. Trend data for adults are available since 1988.

General Trends

The growth trend for adults since 1988 has been consistent despite some fluctuations. The tiny 1.2 percent rate in 1988 has increased to about 2 percent in 1994 and 96 with an unexplained spike to 3 percent in 1995. For 1996 this yields about 4 million participants and 140 million participation days. The annual growth rate of 12 percent is from a small base. Of the total, about 70 percent are frequent although the data are inconsistent varying from 60 to 80 percent. Martial arts remains a niche activity despite the growth (see Table 5-50).

Table 5-50

Source: Simmons Market Research Bureau. *Study of Media and Markets.* New York, NY.

Market Identification

The gender ratio is not marked, with participation rates of 3.8 percent male to 2.7 percent female. Other market segmentation factors do not tend to be strong. The age curve begins at just over 4 percent for young adults age 18 to 34, 3 to 3.5 percent for those 35 to 54, and then just over 2 percent for 55 to 64 and 1.4 percent for 65 and older. Those with college education and high incomes participate at twice the rate of those without, and singles double the married rate. The South and West are about 1 percent higher in participation rates than the Northeast and Midwest. The modal participant is a young adult male with a good income and some college education. Again, the student cohort somewhat confounds these figures. Programs in school and college settings are a significant market (see Table 5-51).

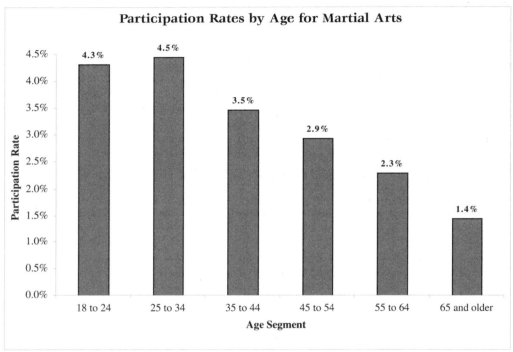

Participation Rates by Age for Martial Arts

Source: **Simmons Market Research Bureau. 1995.** *Study of Media and Markets*. **New York, NY.**

Table 5-51

Growth markets: Growth has been strongest among those under age 45 with at least a high school education. The region of fastest growth has been the South. Within these parameters, growth seems somewhat diffuse. The varying orientations of different forms of martial arts make market specification difficult.

Established markets: The traditional market of self-defense oriented toward young males has been increased by greater participation of females and young adults with some fitness aims.

Low markets: Despite some special programs, older adults and those with low incomes remain low growth market segments.

Projections

Interest in Asian culture may support some continued growth of this niche activity. The growth is more likely among forms that enhance health and fitness than actual fighting formats. The pattern of fluctuating growth with a possible gradual overall increase related to the variety of programs, especially for children, would seem likely.

Chapter 6

Outdoor Resource Activities

The category of "outdoor recreation" has always been somewhat ambiguous. Many kinds of activities take place in back yards, neighborhood parks, and even the streets. Some national surveys even include outdoor concerts and summer "theater in the park" as activities for Americans outdoors. Here we take the narrower definition of outdoor resource-based activities that specifically employ a natural resource environment for the activity. We also place water and winter activities in separate sections. What remains, however, includes four activities that may also be indoors: archery, horseback riding, wall and rock climbing, and target shooting. We also separate extractive activities because fishing is water-based and hunting land-based.

Archery

Archery is for the most part shooting at targets, commonly at outdoor sites but occasionally indoors. Archery is an ancient traditional activity. There are trend data beginning in 1979. A few schools have competition archery programs, and there are other competitive venues and occasions. Bow and arrow hunting is also the basis of some off-season practice. Archery is a niche sport, but with a long and consistent history.

General Trends

Archery has grown recently after almost twenty years of stability. The adult participation rate remained at about 2 percent from 1979 to 1992, then jumped to 2.6 percent until 1995 at 3.6 percent and a surprising 4.7 percent in 1997. There are between 7 and 9 million archers producing 115 to 175 participation days. The data on frequent participation are inconsistent, fluctuating between 20 percent and 60 percent depending on the measures used. About 30 percent would be an average for the proportion of frequent archers. The NSG surveys since 1990 do not indicate any measurable growth and show only about 5 million archers of whom about 25 percent are regular participants. The pattern, then, is of stability followed by some recent growth, but from a small base. The inconsistencies of the data are a problem in assessment (see Table 6-52).

Market Identification

Males engage in archery at over twice the rate of females, 5.4 percent to 2 percent in 1995. Young adults 25 to 44 are the highest age category with a rate of just over 5 percent in 1995. This builds from 2.8 percent for 18 to 24 and falls to 3 percent for 46 to 64 and 1 percent for 65 and older. There is little market segmentation by education level, but those with moderate incomes have higher rates than high and low levels. Singles do archery at 50 percent higher level than the married. The Midwest is the region of highest participation. Overall, archery is a niche sport in magnitude, but without strong or distinct market characteristics (see Table 6-53).

Growth markets: Growth has been greatest among older adult archers and in low-income groups in the Northeast and South. "Boomer" women and men are probably the main growth market. There may also be some increase in bow and arrow hunting.

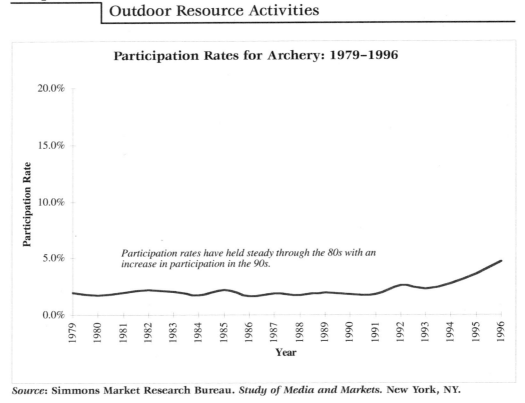

Participation Rates for Archery: 1979–1996

Participation rates have held steady through the 80s with an increase in participation in the 90s.

Source: **Simmons Market Research Bureau.** *Study of Media and Markets.* **New York, NY.**

Table 6-52

Established markets: Those in school programs and who continue participation are the traditional market. The hunting market is also relatively consistent.

Low markets: There is relatively little opportunity to learn and practice the activity in some urban areas. Beginning and practicing archery requires access to a program and facility. Such opportunities are unevenly distributed.

Projections

There is clearly no decline over a 20 year period and there may be recent increases in participation. Where there is growth, it appears to be among young adults and those in early midlife and focused among those who do the activity regularly. There is possible continued growth among the "Boomer" generation women and men, but from a small base. Archery remains a special niche activity.

Backpacking

This is most fully a natural resource-based activity. It requires access to back country and preferably a relatively low density of backpackers and other trail users. As a consequence there are management conflicts between backpackers and those who use back country trails with horses, bikes, and other apparatus. Most backpacking is in small groups who are specially outfitted for lightweight and compact camping and eating. Specialized equipment, including food, has become a niche business. Trend data are available from 1979. Backpacking is, of course, most often an occasional and even once-a-year activity.

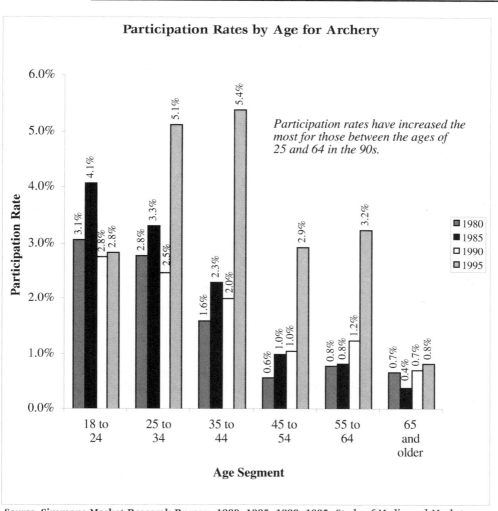

Participation Rates by Age for Archery

Participation rates have increased the most for those between the ages of 25 and 64 in the 90s.

Legend:
- 1980
- 1985
- 1990
- 1995

Values by age segment:

18 to 24: 3.1%, 4.1%, 2.8%, 2.8%
25 to 34: 2.8%, 3.3%, 2.5%, 5.1%
35 to 44: 1.6%, 2.3%, 2.0%, 5.4%
45 to 54: 0.6%, 1.0%, 1.0%, 2.9%
55 to 64: 0.8%, 0.8%, 1.2%, 3.2%
65 and older: 0.7%, 0.4%, 0.7%, 0.8%

Y-axis: Participation Rate (0.0% to 6.0%)
X-axis: Age Segment

Source: Simmons Market Research Bureau. 1980, 1985, 1990, 1995. *Study of Media and Markets.* New York, NY

Table 6-53

General Trends

The SMRB adult surveys show a decline in backpacking from a high rate of about 5 percent in 1979 and 1980, a 2 percent level from 1982 through 1986, a further decline to below 1.5 percent, and then more recent increase to 2.7 percent in 1993 and 1994, about 4 percent in 1995, and almost 5 percent in 1996. This trend yields 5 to 9 million backpackers and 95 to 143 million participation days in recent years. The NSG data from 1990 including children and youth begin at a 10.8 million participant level, decrease slightly in the mid-90s and rise to 12 million in 1997. The overall growth rate is just over 1 percent a year. Of these, less than 20 percent backpack over 20 days a year. There seems to be a problem of different definitions of the activity in the SMRB data that may partly be implied by the fluctuations in participation rates. Discounting the 1979 and 1980 aberrations, backpacking is a niche activity with possible recent growth since 1995 from its low base. In the 1970s and early 1980s, SMRD grouped backpacking with hiking so that trend comparisons are blurred (see Table 6-54).

95

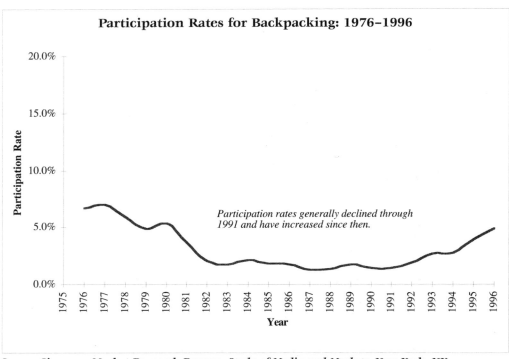

Participation Rates for Backpacking: 1976–1996

Participation rates generally declined through 1991 and have increased since then.

Source: **Simmons Market Research Bureau.** *Study of Media and Markets.* **New York, NY.**

Table 6-54

Market Identification

Participation rates are somewhat higher for males, in 1995 4.8 percent to 3.1 percent female. The age-related decrease is consistent from 7 percent age 18 to 24 to about 4.8 percent age 25 to 44, 2.4 percent age 45 to 54, 2 percent 55 to 64, and 1.3 percent 65 and older. Those with college education backpack at double the rate of high school or less. Singles triple the married rate, and low income rates are low. Not surprisingly, the rate in the West is over three times that in the rest of the country with the Northeast especially low. Those who backpack at all tend to do so at least once a year. There is also a market for families with school-age children, although at lower rates than for other young adults (see Table 6-55).

Growth markets: Growth patterns for this niche market are somewhat surprising. Growth is greatest for females, those over the age of 55, and those with low incomes. The growth rate is also highest in the Northeast. It must be noted, however, that except for women, these growth segments are from the lowest levels. There is also some growth in the "married with children" market. What is suggested is that the appeal of backpacking may be broadening from its traditional market concentrations as "Boomers" introduce backpacking to their families.

Established markets: The core market remains young adults in the West, especially those with some college education and viable incomes. Growth outside this core may be broad, but of limited size.

Low markets: As with all such activities, low income households in urban areas produce few backpackers. Age intensifies this limited segment.

96

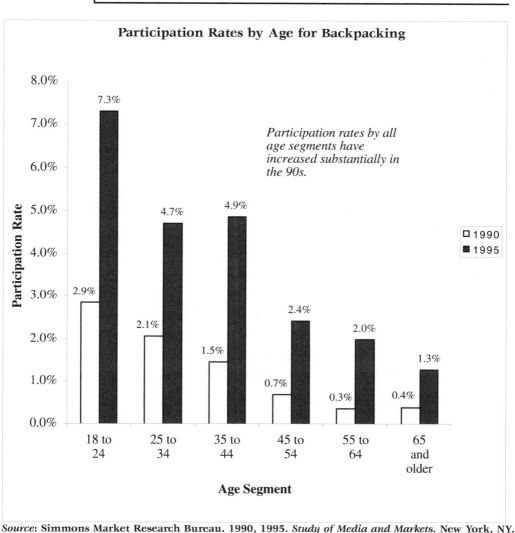

Participation Rates by Age for Backpacking

Participation rates by all age segments have increased substantially in the 90s.

Source: Simmons Market Research Bureau. 1990, 1995. *Study of Media and Markets.* **New York, NY.**

Table 6-55

Projections

The gradual widening of participation suggests a pattern of possible moderate but consistent growth. Backpacking remains a special activity requiring particular interests, resources, and access to environments. It can, however, appeal to a wider market seeking fuller contact with natural environments that are less crowded and impacted by use.

Camping—Overnight

Overnight camping may take place in public and market-sector campgrounds or, more occasionally, in undeveloped back-country sites. Equipment may be minimal or quite elaborate. Some camp in tents and cook over the fire. At the other end there is "V camping" with Recreation Vehicles (RVs), TVs, videos, and other portable comforts.

97

Chapter 6

Outdoor Resource Activities

Some camp occasionally and on vacations. Others live in campsites, evade the Northern winter in the South, and otherwise make camping a second-home lifestyle. Even labeling camping as a vacation activity does not narrow the category precisely. Adult data are available since 1979 for trend analysis. Camping should be divided among styles, but are not at this point.

General Trends

Camping overnight has not been a growth activity for adults. The SMS data indicate a gradual decline with a rate of just under 15 percent in 1979 falling to 11 percent through the 1980s and then to 9.6 percent in 1994. There are indications of a rebound to 12.6 percent in 1995 and almost 14 percent in 1996. This yields 26 million campers and over 300 million participation days. For most years, 12 to 15 percent are frequent campers. NSG data show an overall loss since 1990 from 46 million campers down to 43 million and then a small rebound to about 45 million in 1996 and over 46 million in 1997. Of these, about 15 percent camp 20 or more days a year. The overall trend, then, is one of gradual decrease with a significant rebound in the last two years of data collection (see Table 6-56).

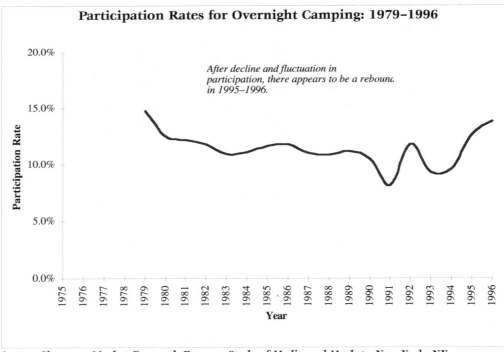

Participation Rates for Overnight Camping: 1979–1996

After decline and fluctuation in participation, there appears to be a rebound in 1995–1996.

Source: **Simmons Market Research Bureau.** *Study of Media and Markets.* **New York, NY.**

Table 6-56

Market Identification

Camping is a broad-based activity without clearly segmented markets. The gender ratio is about even, 13 percent males to 12 percent females. But by age a 17 percent adult rate for ages 18 to 44 declines to 9 to 10 percent age 45 to 54, 6.6 percent for 55 to 64, and 7 percent for 65 and older. High school graduates camp at almost the rate of those with college education, and those with moderate incomes are only 20 percent lower than high income campers. Singles exceed married adults by a 1.5 percent rate. Regional differences, however, are pronounced: 21 percent in the West, 13 percent in the Midwest, and about 9 percent in the Northeast and South. Camping rates are higher for those with school-age children rather than pre-school, but by less than 20 percent. Camping is a very inclusive activity with a solid and broad base of participation despite regional differences (see Table 6-57).

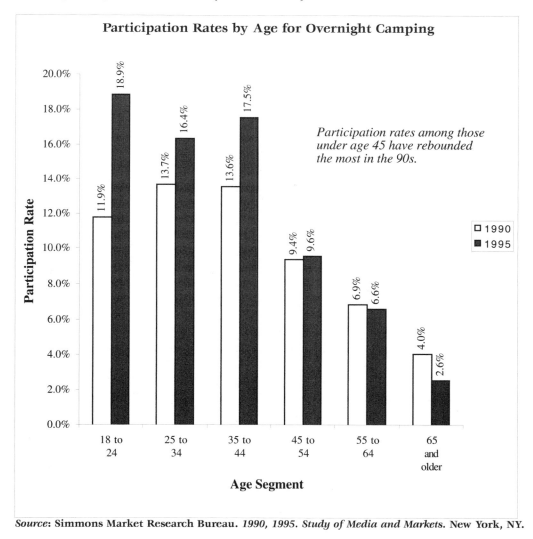

Participation Rates by Age for Overnight Camping

Participation rates among those under age 45 have rebounded the most in the 90s.

□ 1990
■ 1995

Source: **Simmons Market Research Bureau.** *1990, 1995. Study of Media and Markets.* **New York, NY.**

Table 6-57

Growth markets: The slight growth or stability rates have not been distinguished by demographics or region. Any segmented growth would appear to be among families with school-age children. The recent upward trend is, for the most part, general without clear segments. There are suggestions of an increase among single parents in safe and accessible environments.

99

Established markets: Again, camping is a broad-based activity so that the established market is simply those who have a history in this activity. One question might be about the "Boomer" generation who give some indications of wanting to travel more comfortably, even luxuriously, than camping affords. This may, however, be countered by interests in bringing children into contact with natural environments.

Low markets: Low income households in Eastern cities remain a low market. Camping does require reliable transportation and some equipment as well as access to camping sites.

Projections

The recent increase may indicate a small but significant increase in camping in natural environments. This would be limited, however, by current restrictions in federal and state funding for outdoor recreation sites. Households with children will not be a growing population segment in the next decade, so any marked increase in camping would seem unlikely. Camping remains an important activity, however, in its total participation and wide appeal.

Target Shooting

Target shooting can take place at indoor ranges, especially with handguns. The most common venue, however, is the outdoor shooting range, often sponsored by private clubs. Many target shooters are also hunters. Adult data are available beginning in 1978.

General Trends

Like the related hunting, the overall trend is downward. The average rate of 4.7 percent from 1979 to 1982 fell to about 4 percent from 1983 to 1993. There was, however, a rebound to about 7 percent in 1995 and 1996. The 1995 rate yielded, 13 million shooters and 200 million participation days. Overall, about 20 percent of target shooters are frequent. The NSG data including children and youth shows a stable level of 12 to 13 million shooters from 1990 to 1996 with a jump to over 15 million that year and then back to 13.7 million in 1997. Of these, somewhat less than 30 percent shot 20 or more days a year. The overall trend of stability from 1983 may have been broken by some recent growth (see Table 6-58).

Market Identification

The modal shooter is a male under the age of 45 with a moderate income and living in the West. He is probably a hunter. The gender ratio is 3 to 1 male. There is a decline from an average rate in 1995 of over 8 percent for those under 45 to an average of 5 to 6 percent for those 45 to 64. The rate for those 65 and over is about one-third. Education and income are not clear segmenting factors. Singles shoot at a 30 percent higher rate than the married. Regional differences are more significant, in 1995 9.6 percent participation in the West, 6.3 percent in the Midwest and South, and 5.2 percent in the Northeast (see Table 6-59).

Growth markets: Recent growth has broadened the market somewhat with increases among the 55 to 64 ages, college-educated, the married, and in the West. The differences, however, are not dramatic. Target shooting would seem to be just a little less blue collar and age-related. There is, however, no major growth segment.

Established markets: The male hunter in the West, Midwest, and South remains the core market. He is generally of moderate income. Competition target shooting would

Participation Rates for Target Shooting: 1976–1996

Participation rates have declined from the 70s through 1991, but rebounded through the 1995-1996 period.

Source: Simmons Market Research Bureau. *Study of Media and Markets*. New York, NY.

Table 6-58

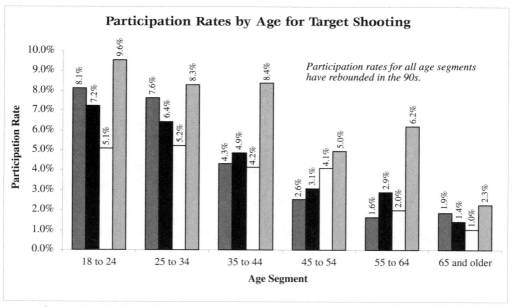

Participation Rates by Age for Target Shooting

Participation rates for all age segments have rebounded in the 90s.

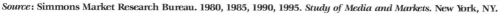

Source: Simmons Market Research Bureau. 1980, 1985, 1990, 1995. *Study of Media and Markets*. New York, NY.

Table 6-59

seem to be a niche. There are also regional niches such as "turkey shoots" in the South. Other niches of undetermined size would be those who shoot in conjunction with paramilitary programs and organizations and skeet shooting at private clubs.

Low markets: Excluding handguns, the urban Northern tier of states provides less opportunity and motivation for regular shooting. Women are also a relatively low market segment.

Projections

Despite the niches, in an urbanized and aging society, there seems little basis to project significant growth in target shooting. The recent upsurge, however, should be watched and may signify some broadening in the overall market. Note that this increase still does not produce a rate as high as the 1970s.

Hiking

Hiking is somewhat difficult to distinguish from backpacking on one side and extended walking on the other. The term connotes a special environment rather than the neighborhood streets, but may take place on community "hiking" paths, area trails, or in back-country natural areas. Adult trend data begin in 1979.

General Trends

The fluctuating trend in adult hiking may be partly an artifact of how the activity is defined in surveys. Nevertheless, both data sources indicate that the levels of 1981 through 1986 began to decline until an increase in the mid-1990s. The overall trend, then, seems to be one of growth, a trough, and then some rebound. In the SMRB adult surveys an overall rate of about 5 percent in 1979 and 1980 grew to almost 9 percent from 1982 to 1985, fell into the 6 percent level until 1992, and then began to rise to over 12 percent in 1996. Of these, 30 percent were frequent hikers. The total of hiking participants was almost 24 million in 1996 with over 350 million participation days. The NSG surveys show a similar trend with a level of 20 to 22 million hikers increasing to 25 million in 1994 and 95, 26.5 million in 1996, and 28 million in 1997. Of these, 10 to 13 percent hiked 30 or more days a year. The totals, then, include a large proportion of occasional hikers (see Table 6-60).

Market Identification

There is no gender difference. Rates by age fall about 50 percent after age 45 and halve again for those 65 and older. College graduates and those with some college education hiked at about twice the rate of high school graduates. Those with high income had a 16 percent rate in 1995 versus a 10 percent rate for moderate income adults. Hiking is most common in the West followed by the Midwest and Northeast and twice the rate of those in the South. Families with children hike at higher rates than those without, but singles hike more than the married. Hiking is a fairly general activity, then, but biased somewhat toward upper income and higher education levels and those age 45 and younger. There may still be some overlap between backpacking and day hiking in the survey data that dampens indices of backpacking growth (see Table 6-61).

Growth markets: Growth is at a somewhat higher rate for older adults including those 65 and over. This suggests that the "Boomers" of both genders may be the likely growth market. More accessible hiking trails and paths in or near urban areas would also increase participation, especially among older adults.

Established markets: Hiking is a general activity, but remains most common among young adults including those with children living at home. It can be a social or family activity. It is not an exclusive costly activity, but attracts more hikers with higher incomes and education levels.

Low markets: Low hiking rates may be more a matter of opportunity than interest. Rates are lowest in the urban Northeast and in the South. Access to trails is often a localized problem. There also may be cultural factors at work in some lower rates.

Projections

The current growth is in the older and growing age segments and among those who hike more frequently. This trend similar to fitness walking suggests long-term, if gradual, growth. Both data sources support this recent upward trend which would be accelerated by expanding safe and accessible hiking venues, especially local trail systems.

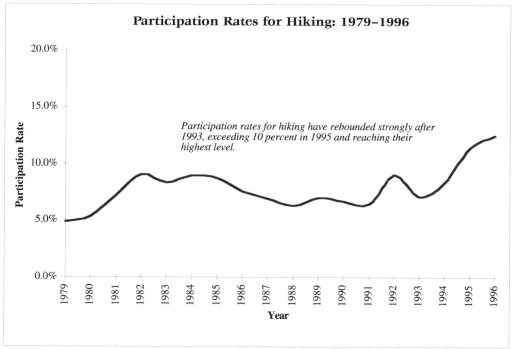

Participation Rates for Hiking: 1979–1996

Participation rates for hiking have rebounded strongly after 1993, exceeding 10 percent in 1995 and reaching their highest level.

Source: **Simmons Market Research Bureau.** *Study of Media and Markets.* **New York, NY.**

Table 6-60

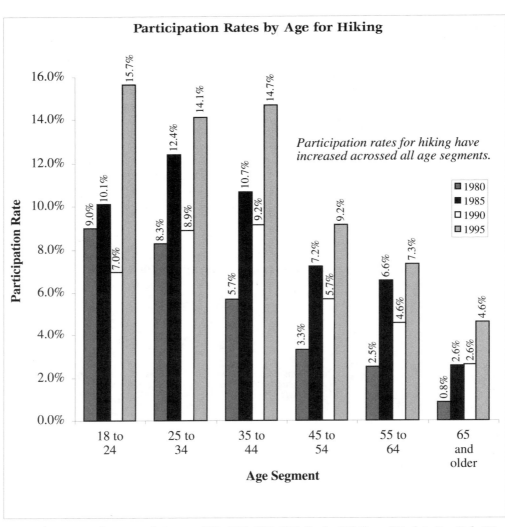

Participation Rates by Age for Hiking

Participation rates for hiking have increased acrossed all age segments.

Source: Simmons Market Research Bureau. 1980, 1985, 1990, 1995. *Study of Media and Markets.* New York, NY.

Table 6-61

Horseback Riding

Riding horses is also a varied activity. There is informal trail riding, competitive showing indoors and out such as dressage and jumping, Western forms of showing and racing, urban and rural rental stables, and a variety of learning programs for children and youth. In all cases, however, owning horses is a relatively expensive activity. Costs for a children's "pony club," however, are quite different from upper level dressage and jumping with top horses priced as high as six figures. Again, the overall numbers include those who train hours a day to those who rent a ride once a year. Horseback riding includes several niches. The adult trend data begins in 1979.

General Trends

The overall adult trend is one of stability since 1979 at a rate fluctuating between 4 percent and 5 percent. Three of the years between 1988 and 1991 dipped to just below 4 percent. Most recently, however, there has been a rise to 5.6 percent in 1995 and 6.1 percent in 1996. This yields about 11 million adult riders and over 200 million participation days. About one-third of the riders are frequent and most of the rest occasional. NSG data indicate a decline to just under 10 million riders in 1994 including children and youth and 8.7 million in 1996. Again, about a third rode more than six days a year. Horseback riding in all its forms, then, is a niche activity with about one-third of participants committed riders. Trend data are conflicting, with SMRB showing a recent increase, especially among regular riders, and NSG indicating a slight downward trend (see Table 6-62).

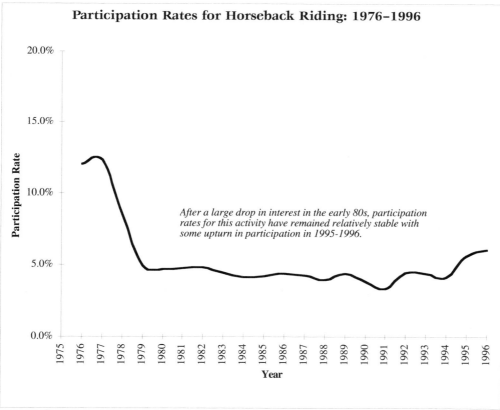

Participation Rates for Horseback Riding: 1976–1996

After a large drop in interest in the early 80s, participation rates for this activity have remained relatively stable with some upturn in participation in 1995-1996.

Source: Simmons Market Research Bureau. *Study of Media and Markets.* New York, NY.

Table 6-62

Market Identification

The various niches in horseback riding confound any market segmentation. There is the significant market for school-age children, especially females, that declines in the mid-teens. There is the adult "serious" competition horse showing and riding of adults, in "English" forms with a majority women and in "Western" forms more male. There are many more casual riders, usually renters. And there are still cowboys riding in the West. Overall, there is little gender difference: in 1990 it was 3.5 percent male to 4.1 percent female and reversed for 1995 to 5.9 percent male and 5.4 percent female. Rates stay above 7 percent from age 18 to 45 and then drop to 4.6 percent to age 55, 3.2 percent to age 65, and 2 percent for 65 and older. Costs make income a factor with the rate 60 percent higher for those with high versus moderate incomes. Those with college education ride at only a 20 percent higher rate than those without, reflecting the participation of those still in school. Rates are highest in the West followed in order by the Midwest, Northeast, and South. There are more riders in households with school-age rather than younger children. Again, these inclusive rates obscure the variety of markets in the category of horseback riding (see Table 6-63).

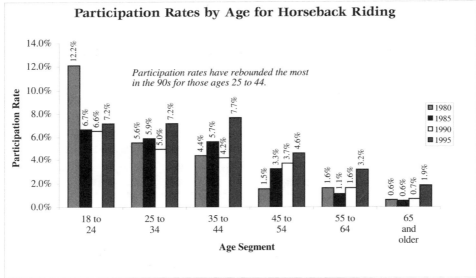

Participation Rates by Age for Horseback Riding

Participation rates have rebounded the most in the 90s for those ages 25 to 44.

Source: **Simmons Market Research Bureau.** *Study of Media and Markets.* **New York, NY.**

Table 6-63

Growth markets: Growth rates are highest among male riders and, from a low base, riders 65 and over and those of low incomes. The most significant growth market is among those committed to some form of riding and who ride regularly. They comprise at least 80 percent of the total market spending on horses, equipment, and services.

Established markets: School-age children and youth are the long-term established market along with those in particular forms of competition. There has been little study of entry and dropout patterns except for age. Styles of riding are largely regional despite New Jersey rodeos and Bay Area hunts.

Low markets: Those with low incomes and distant from opportunities are low markets.

Projections

Relative affluence may allow some who have been constrained by costs to engage in some form of horseback riding. There are indications of a recent upturn among frequent riders. Riding, however, remains a niche activity with overall stability or only slight increases probable.

Hunting

Along with fishing (see water-based activities), hunting is a resource-based extractive activity with a history as long as humankind. Now, however, in this time of urbanization and decreases of rural populations, it is becoming more of a niche activity, even connected with family histories of male hunting participation. Opportunities are also a factor, as the loss of environments to agriculture is now accompanied by residential sprawl. For more and more hunters, the activity requires travel to a special environment.

General Trends

It comes as no surprise, then, that hunting is an activity in decline, although gradually. Adults trends since 1979 show a decline from 8.4 percent to just under 7 percent in 1987–88, to around 6 percent in 1991–1994. Upturns in 1995 are back to 7 percent and in 1996 to 8.4 percent. In 1995 this rate yields over 13 million hunters and between 250 and 300 million participation days. Hunting is seasonal and limited so the proportion of regular hunters varies from 25 percent to 40 percent depending on the measure with 30 percent a fair average. NSG data including youth since 1990 have the total of hunters falling slightly from 18.5 million in 1990 to 17 million in 1997 (see Table 6-64).

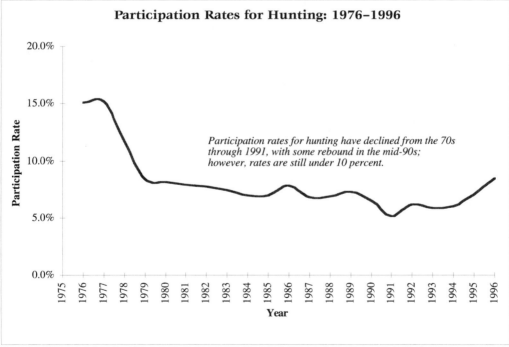

Participation Rates for Hunting: 1976–1996

Participation rates for hunting have declined from the 70s through 1991, with some rebound in the mid-90s; however, rates are still under 10 percent.

Source: **Simmons Market Research Bureau.** *Study of Media and Markets.* **New York, NY.**

Table 6-64

Market Identification

Hunting is quite gendered: in 1995 almost 12 percent male to 2.7 percent female participation. Age is less of a factor, with rates for 1995 holding at about 8 percent through age 64 and then declining to less than 3 percent. Education levels, household composition, and income do not differentiate markets except for low incomes. Hunting is most common in the Midwest with a rate over 9 percent followed by 6 percent in the South, 5 percent in the West, and 4 percent in the Northeast. Hunting, then, remains a male activity related to access to hunting locales. It also tends to have a father-to-son history of introduction. The hunting decline reflects geographical, demographic, and family style changes (see Table 6-65).

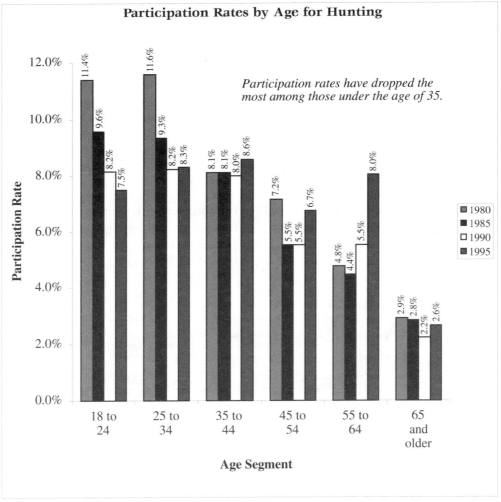

Participation Rates by Age for Hunting

Participation rates have dropped the most among those under the age of 35.

Legend: 1980, 1985, 1990, 1995

Source: Simmons Market Research Bureau. 1980, 1985, 1990, 1995. *Study of Media and Markets.* New York, NY.

Table 6-65

Growth markets: There are no real growth market segments except for those with very small totals.

Established markets: Those who are now hunting, males with a history of hunting, are a dedicated core market. They hunt regularly and may hunt more frequently in areas in which bag limits and the number of licenses are increased. The problem is that they are aging and not being fully replaced by succeeding generations. Declines have been greatest among occasional and younger hunters.

Low markets: Those without access to game environments and without a history of participation and, for the most part, females despite efforts to recruit them.

Projections

A sustained gradual decline is probable despite the recent upturns. Demographics of aging along with reduced access to resources in many areas indicate a continuation of the long-term trend. The main counter factor would be the attempts in some states to support and even introduce hunting as a seasonal activity to thin growing stocks of game.

Mountain Biking

Trend data for this activity are quite short-term. The activity is dependent on the development and marketing of this special form of bicycle designed for off-pavement riding. There are also limitations being placed on bike riding in some back-country areas due to trail damage and conflict with other uses. Recently mountain biking has been divided into off-road and on-road (trail) biking.

General Trends

Mountain biking is a growth niche activity in the initial stages of its "activity life cycle." It is based on an adapted technology and combines a high level of exercise with outdoor environments. The SMS data for only two years show a decline from 5 percent to 4.7 percent from 1995 to 1996 suggesting that the growth may have peaked. This yields 9 million adult riders and 225 million participation days. About 40 percent of the riders are frequent. NSG data from 1993 show total mountain bikers as 10.5 million followed by 9, 10.5, and then 11.3 million in 1996. The 1997 total jumps to 16 million. In general, such short-term trend data are not reliable. Overall, likelihood is that the growth may be peaking. The plateau level, however, remains to be determined.

Market Identification

In gender, the market is about 60-40 male. It is an activity for the relatively young. The rate is over 9 percent for those 18 to 24, 7.6 percent age 25 to 34, 5.8 percent 35 to 44, 3.2 percent 45 to 54, and about 1 percent for those 55 and older. Rates for those with college education double those for high school only. High income riders ride at 40 percent higher rates than moderate. Singles double the rate for the married and households without children are higher than those with. The 6 percent rate for those with school-age children, however, suggests some family riding.

The West is far and away the highest region at 8.5 percent participation followed by the Northeast at 4.9 percent, Midwest at 4.4 percent, and South at 3.3 percent. The modal rider is a college-educated young adult male who can afford to travel to the outdoor environments.

Growth markets: The growth market may be households with children old enough to participate, especially with parents who did such biking earlier. However, it remains a strenuous resource-based niche activity with built-in limitations in environments and requirements. Mountain bike sales continue strong suggesting some possible expansion or more general use and lowered costs. The popularity of this type of bikes may encourage their use on roads and trails (see Tables 6-66, 6-67, and 6-68).

109

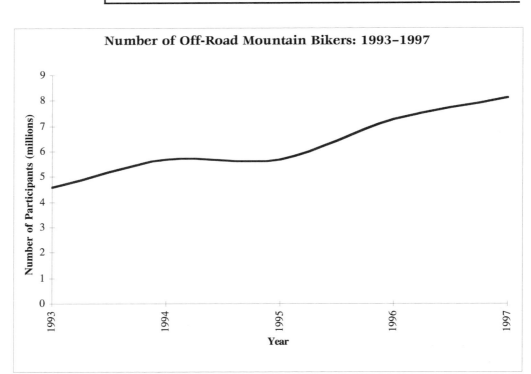

Source: SGRnet. National Sporting Goods Association. Princeton, NJ. (www.sgrnet.com).

Table 6-66

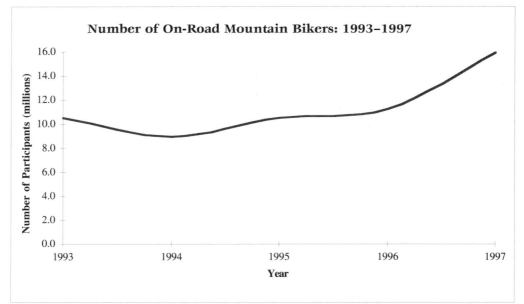

Source: SGRnet. National Sporting Goods Association. Princeton, NJ. (www.sgrnet.com).

Table 6-67

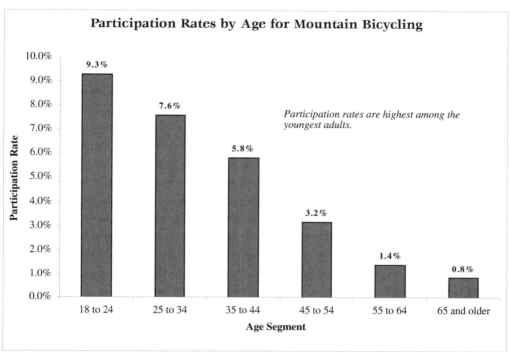

Source: **Simmons Market Research Bureau. 1995.** *Study of Media and Markets.* **New York, NY.**

Table 6-68

Established markets: There is a core of dedicated riders, especially among young adults in the West.

Low markets: Older adults and the urban poor, especially in the flatlands, are not major markets.

Projections

Growth may be approaching a peak, but trend data are not sufficient to be certain. The nature of the activity and its requirements indicate a peak at a niche level and a continuing plateau of riders who are committed to mountain biking's particular exercise and environmental combination. One critical factor will be access to back-country trails versus limits placed by those who are concerned with resource degradation.

Mountain and Rock Climbing

There is some off-season indoor wall climbing, but this is for the most part a resource-based activity. Trend data for adults is available from 1993 and for households including children and adults from 1990. Styles include high-tech climbing of rock faces, mountain expeditions, and relatively simple climbing of more accessible faces.

General Trends

For adults, this is an evolving niche activity. SMRB data indicates about 7 to 8 million climbers and up to 200 million participation days. The rates increased from 2.9 percent in 1993 to 4.4 percent in 1996 with 30 to 55 percent rates of frequent climbing. NSG surveys show a total of 4.7 million climbers in 1990 falling to 4.3 million in 1992,

3.4 in 1994, 4 in 1995, and 3.4 in 1996. Of these, about 30% climb more than 6 days a year. The decline may be a result of separating indoor wall climbing. This fluctuating total does not really produce a consistent trend (see Table 6-69).

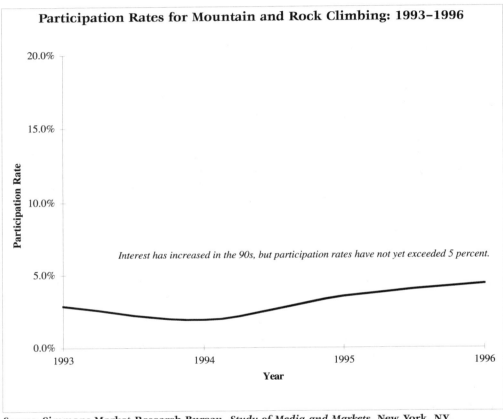

Participation Rates for Mountain and Rock Climbing: 1993–1996

Interest has increased in the 90s, but participation rates have not yet exceeded 5 percent.

Source: Simmons Market Research Bureau. *Study of Media and Markets*. New York, NY.

Table 6-69

Market Identification

Gender rates are about 55 percent male. This is an age-graded activity with the 8 percent rate for those 18 to 24 falling to 4 percent for age 25 to 44, 3 percent for 45 to 54, and 1 percent for those 55 and older. The rate for singles is double that for the married. Student participation has the "some college" rate higher than for graduates. High income climbers have a 5.3 percent rate compared with 2.9 percent for moderate incomes. For dedicated climbers, the age of children does not seem to be a factor. Climbing in the West is double the rest of the country with the Midwest the lowest, reflecting access to resources (see Table 6-70).

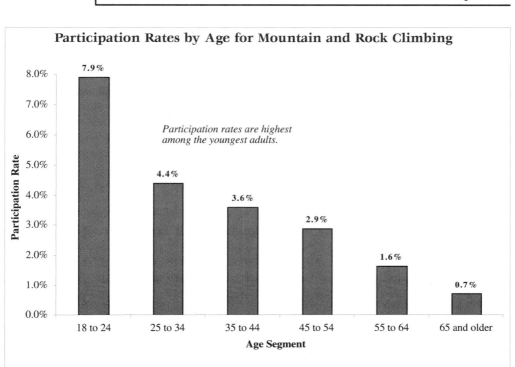

Participation Rates by Age for Mountain and Rock Climbing

Participation rates are highest among the youngest adults.

Source: Simmons Market Research Bureau. *Study of Media and Markets*. New York, NY.

Table 6-70

Growth markets: The growth markets are also the established markets for this demanding and resource-specific activity. The core growth market is young with adequate incomes and primarily in the West. There is also growth in the South. This core seems strong among frequent climbers and may be strengthened by those with fitness aims.

Established markets: Largely the same, active and fit young adults with access to rock faces and mountains. The regional bias is not likely to change. This is a niche market due to the demands of the activity and probably the perceived risks.

Low markets: Everyone else, especially older adults.

Projections

This activity may not have peaked, but any growth will be limited by its character. The core market is not growing in size. Climbing requires an orientation to high-demand activity, some risk, and access to rock faces. This is a self-limiting set of factors. Climbing, then, is likely to remain a niche activity with a core of dedicated participants.

Chapter 7

Water-Based Activities

The kinds of activities that require water environments include various kinds of boating, fishing, swimming, and skiing. There are limited data on beach behaviors in which swimming is secondary, on viewing and appreciation, or socializing and drinking on boats designed for groups rather than movement. A variety of forms are combined into a "swimming" category. In the "local activity" section there are data on visiting lakes and beaches, but public and private pools in clubs or in residential yards are not separated. The different kinds of water—lakes, streams, rivers, and oceans—are not differentiated except for fishing. As a consequence, the trend figures may obscure growth or loss in particular forms of activity, types of equipment, and orientations. SMRB categorizes "skin" diving and NSG "scuba." Further, a category such as power boating can include anything from a skiff with an outboard to the 60-foot luxury yacht. Those seeking to assess more specific markets will need to add to participation trends specific data in equipment sales, resales, and rentals.

Fishing—Freshwater

Freshwater fishing includes plug casting from a dock or bank, high-tech competition bass fishing, Great Lakes charter boats, and (despite a separate category) some fly fishing. It can be quite low cost or a high end market. Market segmentation for a particular form or locale requires site-specific analysis. An especially attractive and/or accessible resource can attract fishers and run against national trends.

General Trends

Adult fishing participation since 1979 declined from a 17 percent rate to about 12 percent in the late 1980s and then rebounded to 15 percent in 1995 and 1996. This rate yields 29 million participants and over 450 million participation days. Over half of those who fish are infrequent and about 25 percent frequent. The NSG data including children and youth shows a decline from 41.5 million in 1990 to 39 million in 1997, a gradual but consistent loss. About one-third fish over 20 days a year. Overall, freshwater fishing is a broad-based activity that has undergone a long-term and very gradual decline. Dramatic changes are dampened by the inclusive categorization (see Table 7-71).

Market Identification

Again, the markets for specific kinds of fishing vary from the generic composition. Overall, fishing is gendered with males fishing at over twice the rate of females, in 1995 21 percent to 10 percent. The age gradation is gradual: 17 percent age 18 to 24, 20.7 percent 25 to 34, 17.8 percent 35 to 44, 14 percent 45 to 54, 13 percent 55 to 64, and 9 percent 65 and over. Again, due to the inclusive category, education, income, marital status, and household composition do not identify markets significantly. Cost and fishing style, however, are correlated to income. Fishing is most common in the Midwest, 19 percent, followed by the West at 13 percent, South at 12 percent and Northeast far lower at 7 percent (see Table 7-72).

About the only modal profile is that of a male with access to fishing resources.
Growth markets: There are no strong growth segments. There is some increase for those age 35 and above, suggesting that the "boomers" are the most likely target for potential growth, especially if they introduce their children to the activity. Frequent fishers are more likely to grow as a market segment than those who are occasional.
Established markets: The core market is males who fish regularly in nearby water resources. Styles are to a large extent an adaptation to the resource.
Low markets: Again, any declines are very gradual, but they are most common among those under age 35. The market for fishing in general, however, is quite inclusive.

Projections

The styles of fishing may be becoming more segmented and distinct. For example, bass fisher(men) in the Midwest tend to have considerable investment in equipment specific to the style and resource. There seems to be a slight rebound since 1994, but any long-term growth is more likely to be gradual and based on the participation of the larger cohort of older males with higher retention rates than in the past. The stylistic markets need to be analyzed separately in order to target markets for investment.

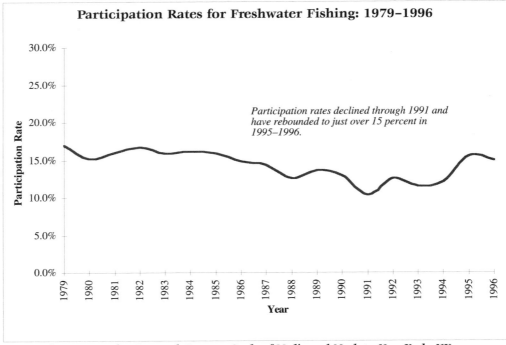

Source: **Simmons Market Research Bureau.** *Study of Media and Markets.* **New York, NY.**

Table 7-71

116

Participation Rates by Age for Freshwater Fishing

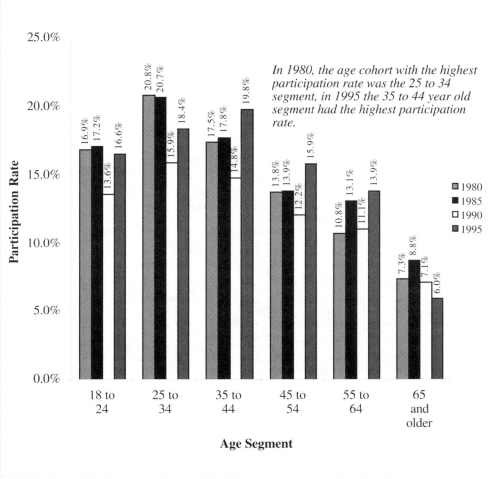

In 1980, the age cohort with the highest participation rate was the 25 to 34 segment, in 1995 the 35 to 44 year old segment had the highest participation rate.

Source: Simmons Market Research Bureau. 1980, 1985, 1990, 1995. *Study of Media and Markets*. New York, NY.

Table 7-72

Fishing—Saltwater

Distinct from the inclusive freshwater category, saltwater fishing is a more segmented niche activity. Some takes place on seashores and piers at relatively low cost. Other saltwater fishing requires boat ownership or charter and can be quite costly. Again, it would be most useful to be able to distinguish styles of saltwater fishing that are blurred by the category. Access to coastal waters limits the activity.

General Trends

Adult saltwater fishing had a long-term decline since 1979 with a more recent rebound beginning in 1994. The earlier rates of about 6 percent fell to levels below 4 percent in 1988 and 1989, gradually recovered to 4.5 percent, and then jumped to 5.6 percent in 1995 and 6.2 percent in 1996. In 1995 there were 10.5 million saltwater fishers and 120 million participation days. About 25 percent of participants were

117

frequent and 60 percent infrequent. The NSG data also show a long-term decline from over 12 million participants in 1990 down to 11 million and then increasing somewhat in 1995–1996 to 11 million and in 1997 to 11.6 million. Again, about 25 percent fished 20 days or more a year (see Table 7-73).

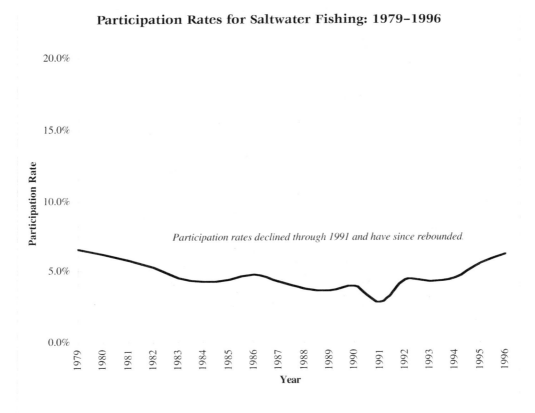

Participation Rates for Saltwater Fishing: 1979–1996

Participation rates declined through 1991 and have since rebounded.

Source: **Simmons Market Research Bureau.** *Study of Media and Markets.* **New York, NY.**

Table 7-73

Market Identification

Saltwater fishing is gendered, in most years at least 2 to 1 male. By age participation rates in 1995 average 6-7 percent up to age 45, drop to 5 percent age 45 to 54, and 3.5 percent for those 55 and older. The market is not highly age-graded. High-income adults fish in saltwater at almost twice the rate of those with moderate incomes, reflecting access to water and charter boats. Children in the household and education level do not discriminate. Other than gender, the main segmenting factor is region: rates are highest on the coasts at 8.7 percent in the South, 5.2 percent in the Northeast, 4.5 percent in the West, and 2 percent in the Midwest. Of course, snowbirds and others may engage in saltwater fishing on trips of various duration. However, no strong growth was indicated among retirement age adults. The modal saltwater fisher(man) lives near salt water for at least part of the year and can afford access, usually to a boat (see Table 7-74).

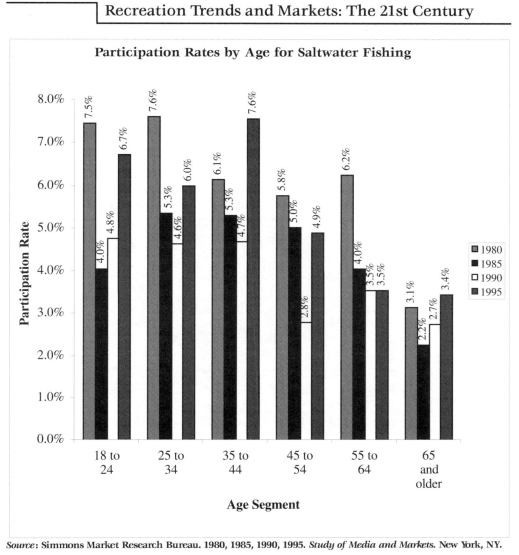

Participation Rates by Age for Saltwater Fishing

Source: Simmons Market Research Bureau. 1980, 1985, 1990, 1995. *Study of Media and Markets*. New York, NY.

Table 7-74

Growth markets: Growth is highest among frequent fishers, usually married, age 35 to 44. A niche market may be adult males vacationing or snowbirding in the South. Female rates are also increasing.

Established markets: Relatively well-to-do males, especially in the South and Northeast, are the core market. There are also, however, a core of lower-income males who fish off piers and in tidal waters whose increase reflects the aging of the population.

Low markets: Obviously those without access to salt water due to location or costs are low markets. There may be some shift in this previously male-dominated market.

Projections

The age group of frequent saltwater fishers is growing and more affluent retirements also would provide a wider market. The recent rebound in participation may level or become gradual, but some measured growth in saltwater fishing is quite possible. It remains, however, an activity limited by resource access and costs.

Fishing—Fly

Fly fishing is a niche activity. Some research suggests that it is a "specialized" activity with a high stress on the skills and special environments rather than high-yield harvesting. It is largely limited to streams and to species of game fish that take flies and offer a skill-based experience. Equipment is light and refined, but not high-tech. Segmented trend data are not available over a long term.

General Trends

There are no long-term trend data available. Such a specialized niche activity does not tend to have dramatic changes in either direction. An overall 3.2 percent rate produces 6 million fly fishers and over 100 million participation days in 1995. Twenty to 35 percent tend to be frequent and up to 60 percent infrequent. Access to streams and seasonality may make some dedicated fly fishers infrequent in participation.

Market Identification

The core market is composed of those who have developed the skills and give a high priority to the activity. The gender ratio is over 2 to 1 male with rate of 4.7 percent to 2 percent. Age rates do not decline significantly until age 55 when they halve to about 2 percent. The 65 and older rate is about 1 percent. This is not an elite activity as measured by education level, income, or family composition. Surprisingly, regional differences are not marked: 3.3 percent to 3.6 percent in the West, South, and Midwest and 3 percent in the Northeast. Rather, it is a niche activity with a special appeal that crosses demographic lines (see Table 7-75).

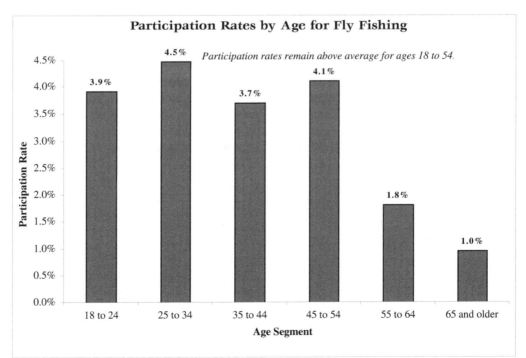

Source: **Simmons Market Research Bureau.** *Study of Media and Markets.* **New York, NY.**

Table 7-75

Growth markets: Growth comes from the introduction into the special skills by those who are already adept. Some research suggests that those taking up fly fishing are already engaged in other freshwater fishing. Introduction, often within families, tends to be person-to-person.

Established markets: Males with access to fishable streams and a history of such fishing are the core market.

Low markets: The skill and access requirements make fly fishing a limited casual activity. Urban low-income residents are a very low market.

Projections

Stream quality makes environmental conservation a major issue, as streams become degraded by extractive activity. Any growth of such a niche activity will be quite gradual. The decline at age 55 may suggest that the physical requirements are a problem for that growing older adult market segment. If so, then the probability of any marked growth is low. The combination of skill and environmental immersion, however, may prompt gradual growth where "a river runs through it."

Canoeing

NSG data on canoeing indicate stability with some fluctuation. Total participants went from about 9 million in 1990 as low as 7.2 million in 1992 and 1995 and as high as 9.7 in 1996 followed by a fall to 7.1 in 1997. There is no clear explanation for this fluctuation that produces no clear trend. It is an occasional activity for 80 percent of those who do it at all. The likelihood is that it will continue to be an occasional activity for a modest market. One countertendency is the possibility that the promotion of kayaking will lessen the demand for canoeing (see Table 7-76).

Rafting and Kayaking

Only NSG has recently tracked this water-based activity. Growth has been at about a 6 percent rate, but not among frequent users. The total participants increased significantly from 2.5 million in 1995 to 3.9 million in 1996. This activity appears to be in the growth phase of the activity life cycle accompanied by the more intensive marketing of the craft. Participants may come from canoe users and other boaters. Ease of transport for kayaks with cartop racks may create a somewhat different market with a continued growth curve and a viable plateau following the peak. Rafting is an activity with particular locations and includes both social rafting on more gentle rivers and "whitewater" rafting as a risk sport. Both are in a growth phase, but from a limited base. Future trend information will be available in the next edition of this book and reveal the outcome of these trends (see Table 77).

Outdoor Rowing

This is a niche activity that calls for specialized equipment and access to a relatively lengthy body of water. Trend data for adults are available since 1990.

General Trends

Outdoor rowing is a niche activity with some indications of growth with a spike year in 1995. The rate fluctuating around 1 percent until the 1.8 percent spike in 1995 and then a fall back to 1.3 percent in 1996. Ignoring 1995, the trend is of very gradual growth from a small base. The 1995 spike suggests a possible increase. The 1996 rate yields 2.4 million rowers and 40 million participation days. About 60 percent are

Water-Based Activities

infrequent and about 30% frequent. This may be a divided market with regular high-demand exercise and competition rowers making up one segment and occasional casual rowers another. If so, the market identification factors may be somewhat confounded (see Table 7-78).

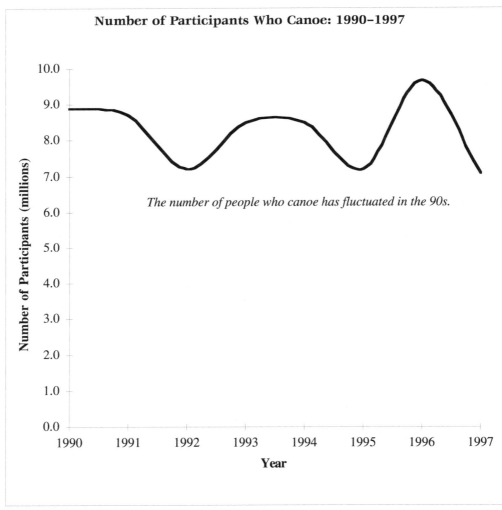

Number of Participants Who Canoe: 1990–1997

The number of people who canoe has fluctuated in the 90s.

Source: SGRnet. National Sporting Goods Association. Princeton, NJ. (www.sgrnet.com).

Table 7-76

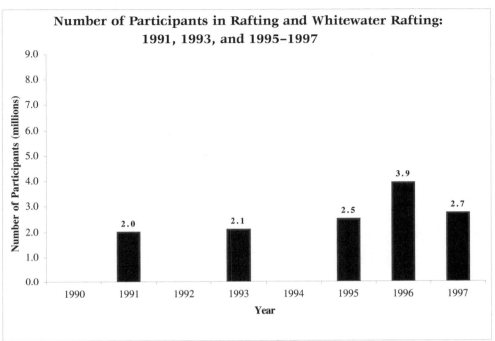

Source: SGRnet. National Sporting Goods Association. Princeton, NJ. (www.sgrnet.com)

Table 7-77

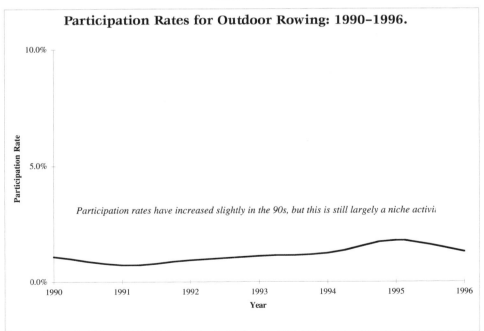

Source: Simmons Market Research Bureau. *Study of Media and Markets*. New York, NY.

Table 7-78

| Water-Based Activities

Market Identification

"Serious" rowers with their special shells and regular engagement tend to be young men and women, often single, with high education and income levels. The gender ratio is essentially 1 to 1 with females having a slightly higher rate, 1.9 percent to 1.7 percent in the peak year of 1995. Singles are almost twice as likely to row as the married and those with high incomes exceed moderate 2.5 percent to 1.5 percent. Again, the confounding of types of rowing makes the segmentation between shells and the high-end young singles different from the family-based rowboat users. Shell rowing alone is a very selective activity. Such rowing is highest in the Northeast, reflecting college and school programs. For all outdoor rowing, however, regional differences are not marked. Shells on the Potomac and rowboats on "golden pond" are quite different activities. Overall, there is a decline with age from over 2 percent to age 45, a decline to 1.4 percent age 45 to 54, and about 1 percent age 55 and over (see Table 7-79).

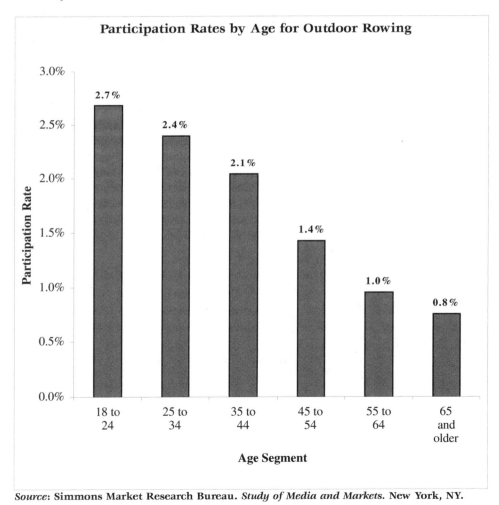

Participation Rates by Age for Outdoor Rowing

Source: **Simmons Market Research Bureau.** *Study of Media and Markets.* **New York, NY.**

Table 7-79

Growth markets: There may be slight gradual growth among the "serious" shell rowers, but from a very small base and quite localized.

Established markets: Casual rowboating, often related to fishing, is a more general activity. Most fishing boats, however, have motors.

Low markets: For specialized rowing, almost any segment outside the narrow elite young adult market. For generic rowing, the limitation is that most boats now have motors.

Projection

The spike 1995 year is problematic. There may even be an "Olympics effect." Rafting and kayaking are growing according to the NSG surveys, but mostly among occasional participants. With the aging of the society, there is little likelihood of significant growth in the number of shell rowers. Using rowboats for rowing is likely to decline in the face of more specialized craft and their marketing.

Power Boating

Like other forms of boating, there is a wide latitude in styles and costs. The increase in yachts of over 60 feet despite luxury taxes in a time of economic affluence is the upscale high end market. At the other end are a variety of smaller craft with outboard motors. There are specialty power boats such as high-powered "cigarette" boats and comfortable flat-bottom party boats. Again, the niche markets may vary from the overall market in significant ways and in particular places. Trend data are available since 1979.

General Trends

The overall trend for power boating is stable through 1990 at about a 6 percent level followed by a decline to 4.5 to 5 percent from 1991 to 1995. 1995 and 1996 return to a level just over 6 percent. This level has about 12 million boaters and 180 million participation days. Of these, 20 to 25 percent boat frequently and over half infrequently. NSG surveys from 1990 have fluctuating levels with 28 million boaters in 1990 falling to about 22 million for the next three years and then rebounding to 26 million in 1994 and 27 million in 1997. Of these, about 25 percent boated 20 or more days a year. The general trend, then, is one of stability with indications of an upturn beginning in 1994 or 1995 (see Table 7-80).

Market Identification

There is considerable market segmentation within the category. Overall, the activity is somewhat gendered, in 1995 rates were 7.5 percent male to 5.3 percent female. The age decline is minor up to age 55, with the highest rates between the ages of 25 and 45. A 6 to 8 percent rate falls to 4 percent for those 55 to 64 and just over 2 percent for those 65 and over. Power boating, however, is skewed toward higher incomes, 11 percent for high incomes and 5 percent for moderate income boaters. Those with college education have an 8 to 9 percent rate compared with 6 percent for high school graduates. Boating is highest in the Midwest, 35 percent higher than the rest of the country. Boaters come in a variety of demographic profiles, depending partly on the type of boat and water resources (see Table 7-81).

Growth markets: Midlife adults, younger "Boomers," are a growth segment, especially college graduates who are mostly likely to have adequate discretionary income. Boating is frequently a family activity with a sizable market among those with school-age children at home. Conversely, there may be some loss of the speedboating market to jet skiing, especially among those 18 to 25. Data are now beginning to be collected on jet skiing.

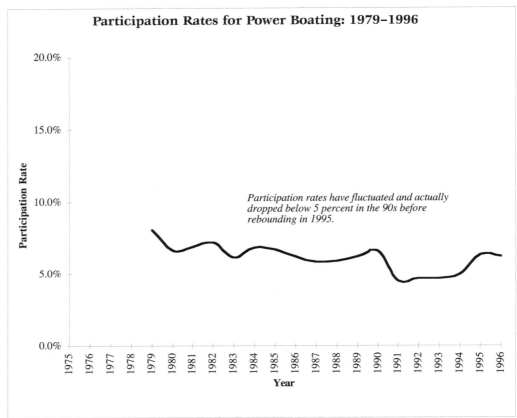

Participation Rates for Power Boating: 1979–1996

Participation rates have fluctuated and actually dropped below 5 percent in the 90s before rebounding in 1995.

Source: Simmons Market Research Bureau. *Study of Media and Markets*. New York, NY.

Table 7-80

Established markets: Midwest fishing on lakes remains a core market. The more upscale family market is also at least stable and possibly growing. On the whole, stability is probable for most market segments.

Low markets: Those with low incomes and in areas without access to appropriate water remain low markets.

Projections

Two factors suggest that the recent upturn may be a sign of some growth. They are increases in discretionary income and the movement of the "Boomer" cohort into life periods in which purchase of leisure toys becomes possible. There may be markets from former delayed gratification. The long-term stability, however, indicates that any such growth is not likely to be at more than a relatively low 2 to 4 percent rate and will plateau again in less than ten years. Jet skis may siphon off some of the market for those under age 30.

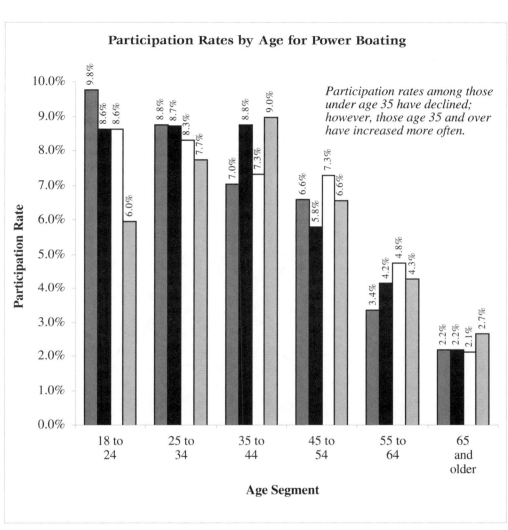

Participation Rates by Age for Power Boating

Participation rates among those under age 35 have declined; however, those age 35 and over have increased more often.

Source: Simmons Market Research Bureau. *Study of Media and Markets.* New York, NY.

Table 7-81

Sailing

Sailing can be on small and inexpensive "singlehanders" and on large yachts and competition boats. The two major markets are for smaller "day sailers" and for 20- to 30-foot sailboats with cabins. Regular sailors may be in competition formats as well as taking weekend and vacation cruises. Trend data date from 1979.

General Trends

The overall trend is one of a fluctuating decline around a 3.5 percent average rate from 1979 through 1986, falling to 2 to 2.5 percent from 1988 through 1992, and then a small increase to 2.8 percent until 1996. The 1996 rate drops to 2.4 percent. Sailing has had a long-term but irregular decline. 20 to 25 percent are frequent and about 70 percent, probably renters, infrequent. Further, it is a niche activity with only about 5 million participants and 50 to 70 million participation days with yearly fluctuations that may partly reflect weather patterns. The NSG surveys indicate a similar fluctuation with a drop after 1990 to about 4 million sailors of whom 25-30 percent sail 20 or more days a year. Despite economic growth, sailing has not kept pace. The luxury tax may have affected big boat sales (see Table 7-82).

Participation Rates for Sailing: 1979–1996

Participation rates have remained steady. Sailing has a narrow niche market.

Source: **Simmons Market Research Bureau.** *Study of Media and Markets.* **New York, NY.**

Table 7-82

Market Identification

Gender rates are 3.2 percent male to 2.5 percent female. The age decline is gradual: 3.5 percent age 18 to 34, 2.4 percent 35 to 54, and then 1.5 percent average 55 and older. College graduates sail at a 40 percent higher rate than those with some college, who in turn have double the rate of high school graduates. High income rates are over double those of moderate income households. Sailing is twice as high among singles. Rates are highest in the Northeast and West followed by the Midwest and South. The profiles partly depend on the type of sailing. Younger single sailors are more often in competition and those with children at home more often cruising. Costs are moderate for some sailing, but those cruising the seacoasts and Great Lakes commonly have substantial discretionary income to cover the boat, upkeep, and storage costs (see Table 7-83).

Growth markets: If there is any growth, it is most likely among the midlife adults who can now afford substantial leisure toys. This market is often for couples who have launched their children.

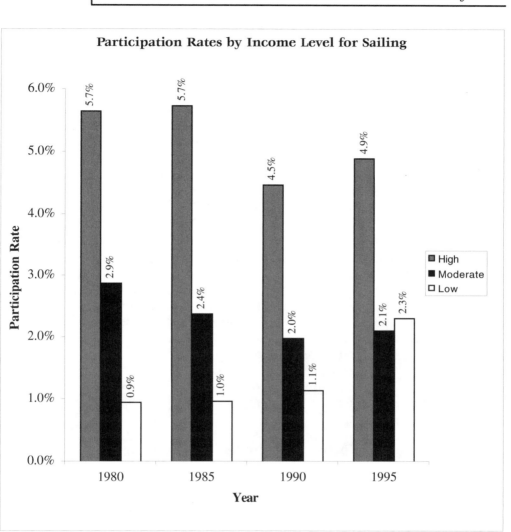

Participation Rates by Income Level for Sailing

Source: Simmons Market Research Bureau. *1980, 1985, 1990, 1995. Study of Media and Markets.* New York, NY.

Table 7-83

Established markets: The stable markets, usually declining somewhat, are upper income adults for larger sailboats and younger adults with college education for smaller boats. Sailing markets are marked more by income, education, and location than age. **Low markets:** Low income adults and those distant from lakes and shores are small markets. Also, sailing is seldom begun as a new activity in later life.

Projections

Any marked growth is unlikely after years of gradual decline. The only likely alternative is for a modest increase among "Boomer" midlife adults with higher education and incomes. More active water sports such as sailboarding will probably continue to erode the youth market. A decline in family sailing could erode the base long-term.

Jet Skiing

There are no long-term trend data for this relatively new activity. The market may be similar to that for water skiing. SMRB have collected data only since 1995.

General Trends

With data from only 1995 and 1996, no trend is evident. The prior growth of this water activity based on a new technology was rapid to a 3.8 percent level in 1995 and 3.7 percent in 1996. This yields 7 million jet skiers and 90 million participation days. The segmented market, along with some restrictions on use near swimmers and on protected lakes, suggests an activity that has a period of rapid growth and then peaks early. Despite promotion and media attention, that peak may have been reached. Further, less than 20 percent are frequent users and over 70 percent occasional. There is a large rental market at resorts, producing much of the occasional use.

Market Identification

Gender rates are 4.2 percent for males and 3.4 percent for females. Age is a powerful factor in market segmentation. The rate of 8 percent for those 18 to 24 drops to 5.4 percent age 25 to 34, 4.2 percent age 35 to 44, 3 percent age 45 to 54, and 1 percent age 55 to 64. Jet skiing is clearly a youth-based activity. The cost of the device is also a significant factor, with over 7 percent participation at high income levels and 2.7 percent for moderate incomes. The education factor is confounded by the high youth participation. Singles, of course, jet ski at twice the rate of the married. Regionally the West is highest at 6 percent followed by the Midwest and South at about 3.4 percent and the Northeast at 2.7 percent. The modal jet skier is a late teen or early 20s male living in the West and from a high-income family. That is a highly segmented market (see Table 7-84).

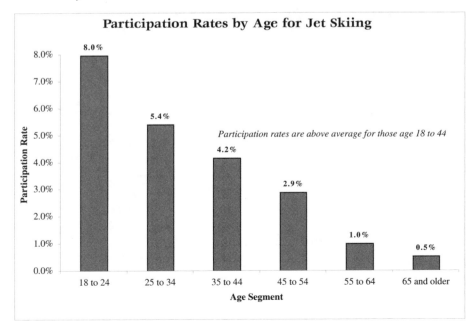

Source: Simmons Market Research Bureau. 1995. *Study of Media and Markets*. New York, NY.

Table 7-84

130

Growth markets: Some growth may be possible in areas of the Midwest and South with sizable water resources. Restrictions on use near beaches and at fishing lakes are a limitation in these regions. Anticipated growth may be limited by area and speed limit restrictions.

Established markets: Jet skiing is likely to remain predominantly a youth activity. The high percentage of occasional users, over 70 percent suggests that ownership is concentrated and limited by cost to higher-income households.

Low markets: Jet skiing will not become a general activity. The market is limited by age, cost, and locale as well as seasonality.

Projections

If the market has not already peaked, it is probably near its height. On the growth side, there is the excitement of the activity that requires relatively little learning or practice. On the down side there is the segmented market and its limitations. Growth beyond 10 million skiers, of whom 2 to 3 million would be from households that own the device, is not probable. This technology-driven activity may be a segment of the motorized and speed-based younger recreation market.

Waterskiing

This older activity is similar to jet skiing in some of its appeal and in its requirement of a watercraft with some power. It is different in that the boat is less specialized and that the activity is somewhat more skill-based. Data are available since 1979.

General Trends

The trend indicates some fluctuating decline since 1979. The 5.6 percent level of 1979 dropped to 4.5 to 4.9 percent for the next six years, then dropped again to about 4 percent from 1986 through 1990. Then there was a third decline to 3.2 percent in 1991, a small increase to 3.7 percent in 1992 and 1993, 4.25 in 1994, a jump to 5 percent in 1995, and back to 4.5 percent in 1996. Overall, the long-term gradual decline may have stopped and even reversed slightly. In 1996 there were 8.6 million waterskiers and over 80 million participation days. Only 12 percent water ski frequently and 75 percent infrequently. This suggests that a very small part of the total market is composed of boat and equipment owners. The NSG data including children and youth indicates 10.5 million water skiers in 1990 falling to 8 million by 1993 and 6.5 million in 1997, a falling trend without the small rebound of the SMS data. Again, about 30 percent ski even 10 days a year. Some rebound may be related to the use of jet skis for towing (see Table 7-85).

Market Identification

Even in the peak year of 1995, males outnumbered females with a 6.4 percent rate versus 3.6 percent. Age is the major factor: A 10 percent rate for age 18 to 24 falls to 7.5 percent for 25 to 34, 5.6 percent age 35 to 44, 2.6 percent age 45 to 54, 1.4 percent age 55 to 64, and 1 percent 65 and older. Singles water ski at almost twice the rate of the married. High income families double the rate for those from moderate income households. Education is confounded by the high proportion of student and college-age skiers. Water skiing is strongest in the West, 7 percent, followed by the South at 4.9 percent, Midwest at 4.7 percent, and Northeast at 3.2 percent. Again, these rates are from the peak year of 1995. The modal water skier is a young male with access to a sizable body of water and from an upper income household (see Table 7-86).

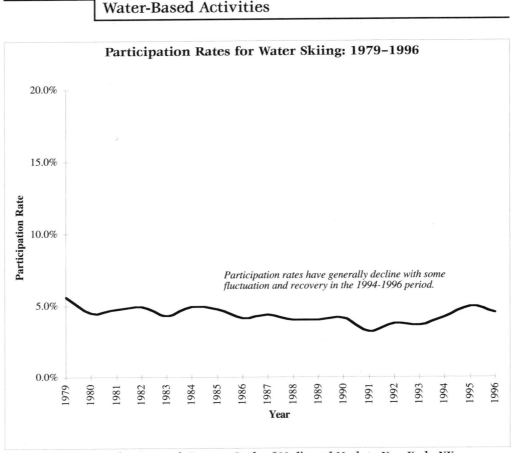

Participation Rates for Water Skiing: 1979–1996

Participation rates have generally decline with some fluctuation and recovery in the 1994-1996 period.

Source: Simmons Market Research Bureau. *Study of Media and Markets*. New York, NY.

Table 7-85

Growth markets: No major growth is likely. Further, jet ski competition has cut into the same segmented market even though jet skis can be used to pull water skiers. Any growth will probably be from households with increasing incomes and teens in residence (see Table 7-86).

Established markets: Access to water is the first requirement. The established market is composed of such households with adequate discretionary income and school-age children.

Low markets: The high percentage of occasional water skiers suggests that the market for those who own the power boat and equipment is quite narrow as specified above. Age and access to water limit markets.

Projections

The youth-segmented niche market, a declining youth age cohort, and the costs indicate that growth in unlikely without a major shift in income distribution. Further, many bodies of water are restricted for higher-speed boating with area, speed, and wake limits. The long-tern trend may well revert to the gradual decline of the 1980s.

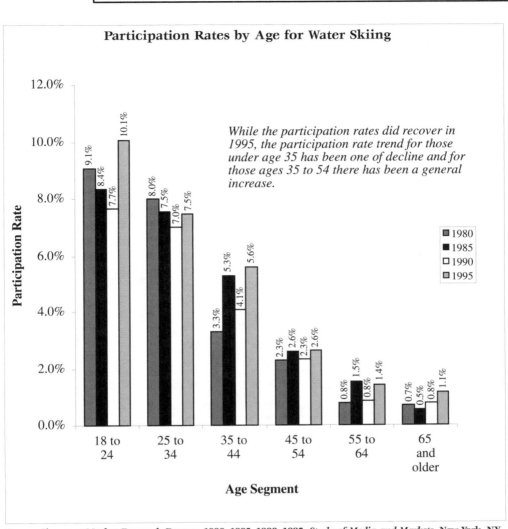

Participation Rates by Age for Water Skiing

While the participation rates did recover in 1995, the participation rate trend for those under age 35 has been one of decline and for those ages 35 to 54 there has been a general increase.

Source: Simmons Market Research Bureau. 1980, 1985, 1990, 1995. *Study of Media and Markets*. New York, NY.

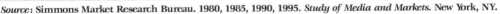

Table 7-86

Skin/Scuba Diving and Snorkeling

The distinctions among several kinds of underwater swimming present some problems in categorization. The SMRB data combine "skin diving" and surface snorkeling while the NSG surveys separate snorkeling and scuba diving, which will be presented separately. SMRB trend data begin in 1979.

General Trends

This is a growth niche activity with a long period of stability from 1979 through 1991 at about a 1.7 percent rate followed by a jump to 2.8 percent in 1992, 3.5 percent in 1993, almost 5 percent in 1995, and then 3.9 percent in 1996. Even if the 1995 figure is an aberration, there is a pattern of growth in the 1990s. In 1996 there were 7.5 million in this combined activity and almost 90 million participation days. Only 15-20 percent, however, were frequent and 70 percent infrequent. The NSG surveys including children and youth show 5.4 million engaged in snorkeling alone in 1991, 3 years of stability, and then some growth to 6.3 million in 1997, of whom just over 20% snorkeled 20 or more days a year. Overall, the activity has had moderate growth in the mid-1990s, but remains a niche activity. The NSG data show similar growth for scuba diving with 2 million divers in 1991 rising to 2.4 million in 1993-96 and 2.3 million in 1997. About 40 percent of open water scuba divers participated 10 or more days a year. The skill and licensing requirements of open water scuba diving raise the proportion of regular and committed divers. The occasional market includes vacation snorkeling and diving, often at resorts supporting such activity (see Table 7-87).

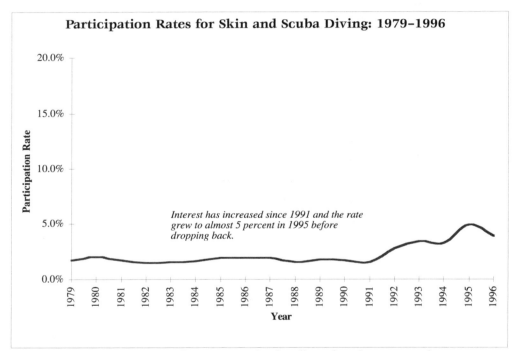

Participation Rates for Skin and Scuba Diving: 1979–1996

Interest has increased since 1991 and the rate grew to almost 5 percent in 1995 before dropping back.

Source: **Simmons Market Research Bureau.** *Study of Media and Markets.* **New York, NY.**

Table 7-87

Market Identification

For the combined category of SMRD data, there is a gender difference, in the peak year of 1995 6.1 percent male to 3.8 percent female. The age pattern is at about 7 percent age 18 to 34, just over 5 percent age 35 to 54, and 2 percent or less 55 and over. Singles dive at a 50 percent higher level than the married, high income at twice the rate of moderate, and those with college education 60 percent higher than high school graduates. The activity is most common in the West at 6.7 percent with rates about 4.5 percent in the remainder of the country. Combining scuba and skin diving and snorkeling probably lessens the market segmentation. The bias toward upper-income participants who can afford access to the special environments, however, remains clear (see Table 7-88).

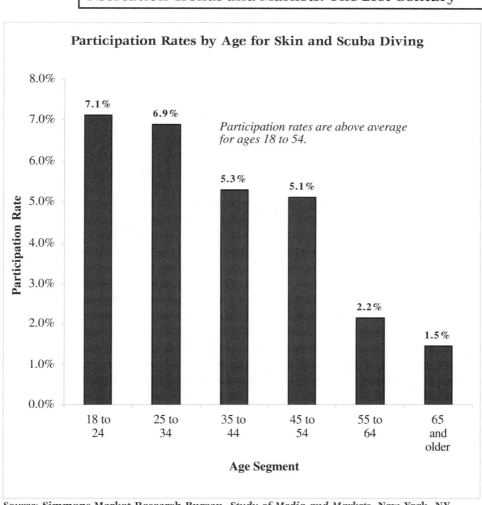

Participation Rates by Age for Skin and Scuba Diving

Participation rates are above average for ages 18 to 54.

Source: Simmons Market Research Bureau. *Study of Media and Markets.* New York, NY.

Table 7-88

Growth markets: Such diving and swimming seems to be more resource-related than segmented by age. Growth, then, is most probable among those who can afford to live or vacation in the special environments. Current growth is highest in the West and among those with high incomes. The skill requirements for licensed scuba diving make it a very specialized niche activity.

Established markets: Upper-income adults with a history in the combined activities retain participation well into midlife. The frequency rates, however, suggest that this is a vacation activity for most except the core of committed scuba divers.

Low markets: All those without access to the diving and snorkeling environments are low markets. This is, of course, most of the population.

Projection

There may be some continued growth as targeted above. In general, however, this is a niche set of activities that cannot become more inclusive. Occasional participation is related to resort areas that rent equipment and often provide some instruction. One growth factor would be the development of "underwater parks" for scuba divers in coastal and Great Lake areas, but this is primarily for skilled divers. A reduction in skilled swimming would erode the market. There is no indication of more than continuing modest growth in the more general markets.

Swimming

Swimming includes a vast variety of styles and behaviors as well as venues. People swim in pools, rivers, lakes, and oceans. At the shore they may sun, eat, drink, flirt, and occasionally dip in the water. In pools, teens gather for social exchange and exhibition, adults swim laps, parents play with children and talk while watching, children and youth practice for team competition, and many play water games. All this is called "swimming." As a consequence, this category of activity is very general and inclusive. In managing a pool or community program, however, this broad market has to be segmented, specified, and measured. This is a mass market with seasonal appeal and, where resources exist, a small year-round market.

General Trends

The overall adult trend for swimming is one of gradual decline of about 1 percent a year with a possible recent rebound. The rate held at about 31 percent from 1979 through 1985 and then began a gradual decline to 27 percent in 1988, 24 percent in 1990 and 1993, followed by a rise to 32 percent in 1995 and 31 percent in 1996. This latest rate yields 60 million swimmers and 1,156 million participation days. About 35 percent of the total swim frequently and 45 percent infrequently. The NSG surveys including children and youth indicates a gradual decline since 1990 from 67 million swimmers to 60 million in 1996 and 97. Of these 5 percent swam more than 110 days a year. 95 percent, then, were not year-round competition or lap swimmers (see Table 7-89).

Market Identification

As stated in the introduction, generic swimming is so inclusive that targeted marketing has to specify the form and venue. There is no gender difference. In 1995 40+ percent participation rates do not drop to 28 percent until age 45 and then to 19 percent age 55 to 64 and 8 percent age 65 and older. There are education and income differences that are not dramatic. Those with college education swim at 30 percent higher rates than high school graduates and those with high incomes 35 percent more than moderate. Those from low income households are only half as likely to swim as from those with high incomes. Income can screen participants from access to pools and beaches. This analysis is for adults only and omits the higher rates of swimming by children and youth, even though the totals are dropping according to the NSG surveys (see Table 7-90).

Growth markets: Even the recent upturn is not keeping pace with population trends. The greatest growth is from low-income households, perhaps reflecting some change in provisions and recruiting programs. Greater retention of the "Baby Boomers" is the most likely market for possible growth with some increases already located for older adults.

Established markets: This inclusive activity has wide appeal in both pool and beach forms. The core market, however, is that, children and youth for public pools and beaches and the family market for private pools and beaches.

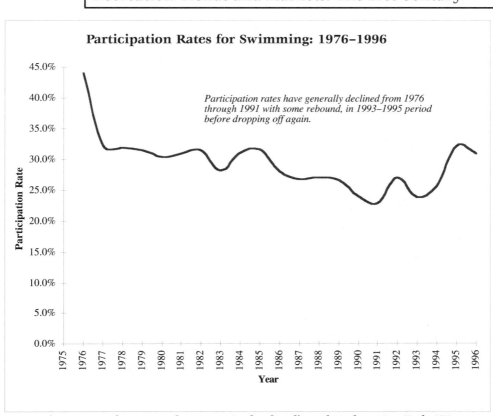

Participation Rates for Swimming: 1976–1996

Participation rates have generally declined from 1976 through 1991 with some rebound, in 1993–1995 period before dropping off again.

Source: **Simmons Market Research Bureau.** *Study of Media and Markets.* **New York, NY.**

Table 7-89

Low markets: Despite water aerobics and the persistence of some older swimmers, in general the low markets are the old and the poor. Special programs, however, can increase these low rates in specific locations.

Projections

It is likely that the decline may have ended, especially if communities replace older pool facilities and increase access to low-income children and youth. The key, however, is among the large "boomer" population segment as they move into later life. There are signs of increased rates of swimming that, if they persist, can counter the reduced market of children and youth. Water parks may attract some additional interest in swimming. Most probable is stability at or near the rebound rate with some shift to older swimmers.

Surfing

Surfing, unlike swimming, is a niche activity with specific locations. Dedicated surfers, however, travel to those locations at least on vacations. Trend data are available only since 1991.

General Trends

Surfing is a niche activity that has grown somewhat in the 1990s from a very small base. The 1991 rate of 0.8 percent has about doubled with a high of 2.2 percent in 1994

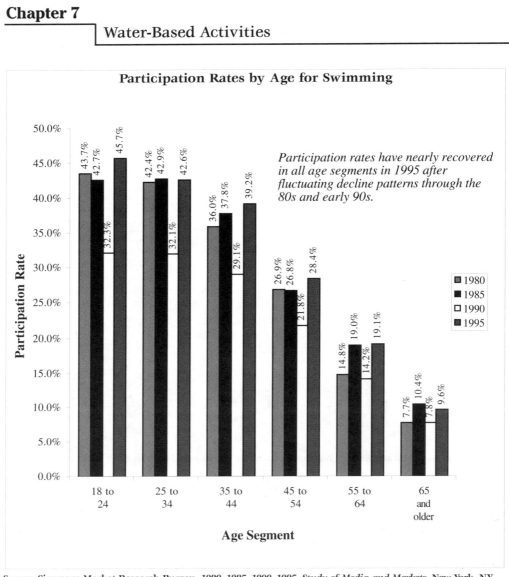

Participation Rates by Age for Swimming

Participation rates have nearly recovered in all age segments in 1995 after fluctuating decline patterns through the 80s and early 90s.

Source: Simmons Market Research Bureau. *1980, 1985, 1990, 1995. Study of Media and Markets*. New York, NY.

Table 7-90

and a most recent 1.5 percent in 1996. In general, only about 2 percent of the adult population ever surfs. This yields about 3 million surfers age 18 and over and 60 million participation days. Of these, about 40 percent are frequent and 30 to 50 percent infrequent. Surfing seems to be divided between the committed and those who do a little, perhaps on vacations. Wet suit technology and board improvements have extended the season for frequent participants (see Table 7-91).

Market Identification

In 1995 there was little gender difference, 2 percent male to 1.7 percent female. The rate of 2+ percent is steady to age 45 and then drops to 1.6 percent age 45 to 54, 1 percent age 55 to 64, and a surprising increase to 1.6 percent for those 65 and older. These figures suggest that many surfers do not fit the image of bronzed young males

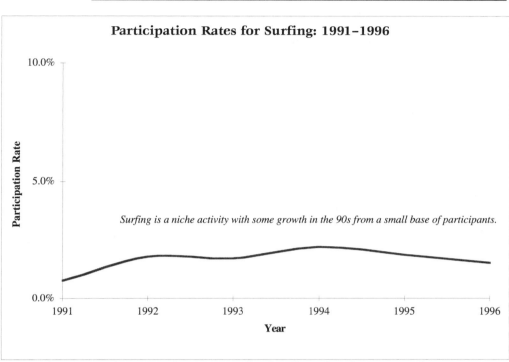

Participation Rates for Surfing: 1991–1996

Surfing is a niche activity with some growth in the 90s from a small base of participants.

Source: **Simmons Market Research Bureau.** *Study of Media and Markets.* **New York, NY.**

Table 7-91

running high surfs in Hawaiian competitions. The more inclusive types of boogie boards and body surfing are included in the survey reports. Education level does not discriminate and income only slightly. There are, of course. 30 percent more singles than the married. Surfing would appear to be divided between the "big wave" elite and the more inclusive "play in the wave" participants.

Growth markets: Growth is most probable among the occasional vacation surfers who travel to coastal resorts with moderate waves and equipment. There may also be carryover from the growing sport of snowboarding with seasonal rhythms (see Table 7-92).

Established markets: The core remains the young surfers on the West coast and in Hawaii. The secondary market is those who vacation there and in other coastal locations.

Low markets: Those who lack access to surfing conditions are, of course, a low market, that is, inland regions and many coastal areas as well.

Projections

Overall participation may increase slightly related to resort vacations. The core of "big wave" surfers, however, will not grow unless snowboarding brings in a modest number of crossover surfers.

Windsurfing

This is another niche activity. The sport has changed from the more sedate "board sailing" to "windsurfing" with more manuverable boards and extreme conditions. SMRB data are available for only 1995-96, but NSG totals are available from 1991.

139

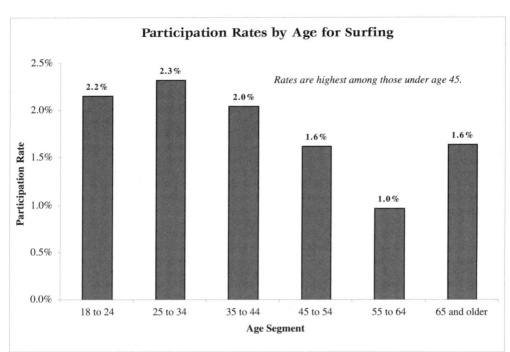

Participation Rates by Age for Surfing

Rates are highest among those under age 45.

Source: **Simmons Market Research Bureau. 1995.** *Study of Media and Markets.* **New York, NY.**

Table 7-92

General Trends

The SMS data are inconsistent, with a 1.3 percent rate for 1995 and 0.7 percent for 1996. This gives a range of adult participants from 1.3 million to 2.3 million and 28 to 50 million participation days. About 35 percent are frequent. The more inclusive NSG figures are more useful. They indicate a trend of stability or slight decline from 1991 beginning with an 0.8 percent participation rate falling to 0.5 percent in 1995, 0.7 percent in 1996, and 0.5 percent in 1997. Of these, 20-30 percent wind surfed 20 or more days a year. In general, this seems to be a stable, highly specialized, niche activity.

Market Identification

Wind surfers may be either male or female. Age is a factor with 1995 rates of 1.8 percent age 18 to 34, 1.3 percent age 35 to 54, and 0.5 percent age 55 and older. Education and income do not discriminate, probably due to student windsurfers. The single rate is twice that of the married. Windsurfing is most common in the West followed by the Northeast and South with the Midwest trailing 50 percent behind the West. This activity is relatively strenuous and skill-based for those who do it regularly (see Table 7-93).

Growth and established markets: The lack of trend data does not permit market specification based on growth patterns. The market is skewed toward the young from households with discretionary income and access to bodies of water. It is, therefore, an age-graded and localized market. Again, however, there are those who try the activity at vacation venues with rented or loaned equipment.

140

Low markets: Most of the overall recreation market. Any activity requiring costly equipment, access to a special resource, and acquiring skill will remain a niche activity, whatever its intrinsic appeal.

Projections

The NSG data indicate relative stability. There are no countertrends to alter this except for the aging of the population. Overall, a small but gradual decline led by demographics would have to be countered by the appeal of the activity in order to maintain current rates.

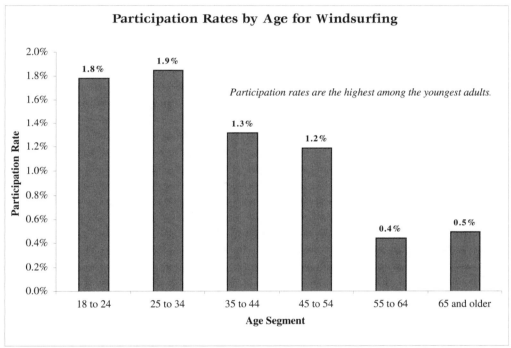

Source: **Simmons Market Research Bureau.** *Study of Media and Markets.* **New York, NY.**

Table 7-93

Chapter 8

Winter Activities

For the most part, the activities in this section are outdoor. They require snow or ice in all cases. Ice skating is both indoor and outdoor as is the team sport of ice hockey. Figure skating is indoor, but in the North there is considerable skating on frozen lakes and ponds. One problem with trend analysis for activities that require snow or ice is that there are fluctuations from year to year and region to region. There have been winters when there has not been enough snow for skiing, especially in the Northeast and upper Midwest. In the West, some seasons have been limited by too much snow. The trend analysis here includes both the actual participation figures and a two-point moving average that smooths out year by year fluctuations. Some even suggest that global warming is moving the line for reliable winter activities gradually northward. In any case, winter activities are seasonal, regional, and often uncertain.

Ice Skating

As suggested, ice skating includes casual skating in rinks and outdoors, figure skating as a small niche activity, and even speed skating in selected locales such as Milwaukee, Wisconsin; Northbrook, Champaign, and Glen Ellyn, Illinois; and Nutley, New Jersey. Adult trend data are available since 1979 for the generic category.

General Trends

A decline in ice skating in the 1980s turned to a rebound in the early 1990s. For adults, rates of 4.4 percent in 1979 and 5 percent in 1980 gradually declined to 2.5 percent in 1985 followed by rates of about 3 percent in 1989–1990. The overall rate grew to 3.5 percent from 1992 to 1994 and then to 4 percent in 1995–1996. Some suggest an "Olympics effect" for skating due to TV exposure. These current rates produce 8 million skaters and 70 million participation days. Only 10 percent of skaters are frequent, however, with 80 percent skating infrequently or casually. There is a core market of committed skaters, many in figure or speed skating or hockey, and a wider market who skate a few times when the local ice is good. The NSG surveys including children and youth indicate a similar trend with 6.5 million skaters in 1990 growing to 7.8 million in 1994, 7.1 in 1995, 8.4 in 1996, and 7.9 in 1997. About 15 percent skated 20 or more days a year. Some yearly fluctuation is probably due to weather. There also appears to be an "Olympics effect" with a temporary increase every four years (see Table 8-94).

Market Identification

Figure skating is predominately female and ice hockey male. Speed skating and casual skating include both genders as indicated by the overall rate in which a slight male bias has changed to female, 4.5 percent female to 3.9 percent male in 1995. Skating is youth and young adult oriented with a 7.3 percent rate for those 18 to 24, 6.6 percent 25 to 34, 5.3 percent 35 to 44, 2 percent 45 to 54, 1.4 percent 55 to 64, and 0.7 percent 65 and older. NSG data indicate even higher rates for youth. Those with college education skate at twice the rate of high school graduates, those from high-income families at twice the rate of moderate, and singles double the rate of married.

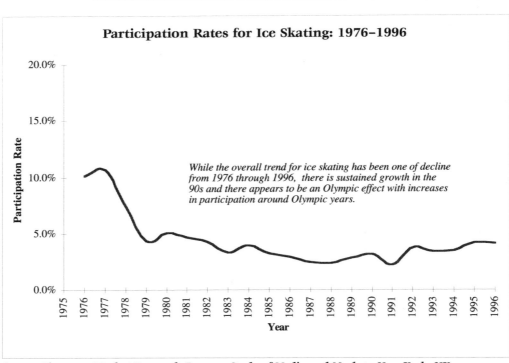

Participation Rates for Ice Skating: 1976–1996

While the overall trend for ice skating has been one of decline from 1976 through 1996, there is sustained growth in the 90s and there appears to be an Olympic effect with increases in participation around Olympic years.

Source: Simmons Market Research Bureau. *Study of Media and Markets*. New York, NY.

Table 8-94

Rates are highest in the Northeast at 6.4 percent followed by the West at 5.2 percent, the Midwest at 4.5 percent and the South at 2.1 percent. The modal skater is now a single young female from an upper income family. Again, however, the types of skating distinguish market segments. Overall, casual skaters outnumber regulars at least 5 to 1 (see Table 8-95).

Growth markets: Supply does create some demand in this activity. New indoor rinks or good outdoor conditions increase the local rate of skating. There is more growth among females than males. Most recent growth has been in the West. Due to the costs of indoor ice, growth among regular skaters will continue to be limited.

Established markets: This is a market divided between occasional skaters where winter ice is available and those committed to a particular ice sport such as figure skating, hockey, and speed skating. Growth in the first depends on weather and fluctuates. Growth in the second is stimulated by TV and enabled by supply.

Low markets: Other than regions and communities without seasonal ice, the low markets are related to the cost of access to indoor rinks and to the "fear of falling" among older adults.

Projections

The rebound in the mid-1990s is partly related to the interest stimulated by the Olympics and TV programming. Such trends tend to be temporary. The continuation of such trends depends on the increase in facilities and supporting sponsorships. Such growth is most common in the Northeast and West and is highly localized. Again,

144

costs of facilities, ice time, and equipment are limiting. The probability is that the rebound has peaked and there will be longer-term stability of what remains a targeted activity with limited resources and appeal.

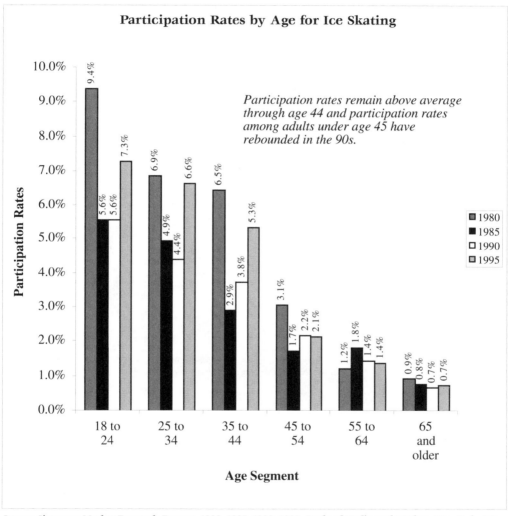

Participation Rates by Age for Ice Skating

Participation rates remain above average through age 44 and participation rates among adults under age 45 have rebounded in the 90s.

Legend: 1980, 1985, 1990, 1995

Source: Simmons Market Research Bureau. 1980, 1985, 1990, 1995. *Study of Media and Markets*. New York, NY.

Table 8-95

Skiing—Cross-Country

Data are available since 1980 for this niche activity. Nordic skiing is clearly distinguished from Alpine skiing by equipment as well as terrain. It was promoted as a more accessible alternative to downhill skiing in the 1980s, but never attained a wide base of participation. It is a niche activity often related to higher levels of education.

| Winter Activities

General Trends

Cross-country or "Nordic" skiing is quite weather-dependent so that there will be some year-to-year fluctuation. Allowing for that, adult participation is essentially level from 1980 through 1996. The rate was 2.4 percent in 1980 and rose as high as 2.8 percent in 1986 and as low as 2.1 percent in other years to end back at 2.3 percent in 1996. This yields about 4 million Nordic skiers and an average of 34 to 42 million participation days, a figure with wide fluctuation from year to year. The activity is weather dependent. Snowmaking is usually limited to downhill venues. About 10 percent of Nordic skiers are frequent and 75 percent occasional or infrequent. The NSG surveys show some decline from 5 million in 1990 to 3.4 million in 1995 and 1996 and 2.5 million in 1997. According to the NSG surveys, 25 to 30 percent skied 10 or more days a year. Overall, cross-country skiing is a static or slightly declining sport with weather-related fluctuations. Unreliable snow conditions are an endemic problem (see Table 8-96).

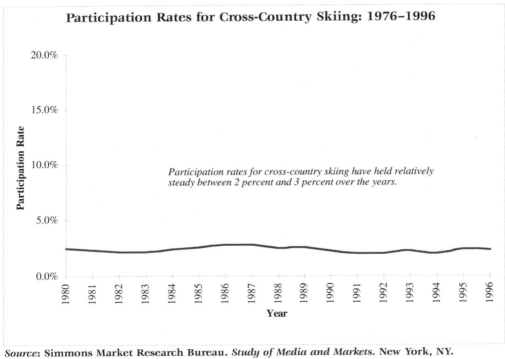

Participation Rates for Cross-Country Skiing: 1976–1996

Participation rates for cross-country skiing have held relatively steady between 2 percent and 3 percent over the years.

Source: **Simmons Market Research Bureau.** *Study of Media and Markets.* **New York, NY.**

Table 8-96

Market Identification

There is a small gender tilt toward females, a 2.6 percent rate to 2.1 percent male. There is essentially no age-related decline up to age 65. This unusual pattern makes Nordic skiing a lifetime activity for the small niche of participants. College graduates double the rates of those with some college, and high school graduates and those with high incomes ski at twice the rate of moderate income skiers. Singles and the married are not markedly different. Nordic skiing is most common in the Northeast, at 3.4 percent followed in 1995 by the Midwest and West at 2.8 percent and the South at 1.2 percent. Regional differences also vary from year to year. In some years the Midwest and West have exceeded the Northeast. Nordic skiing can be a family sport that includes school-age children living at home, as indicated by rates for this type of household (see Table 8-97).

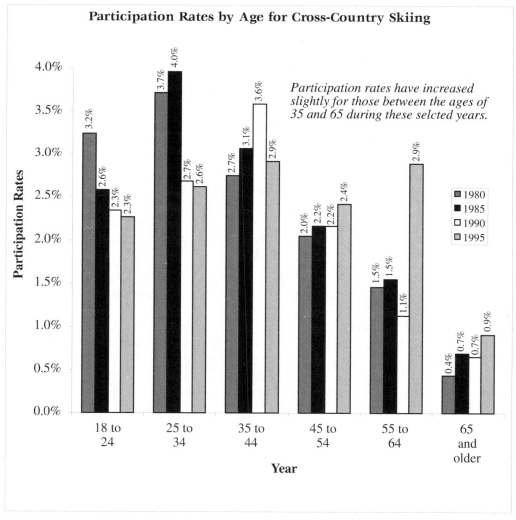

Participation Rates by Age for Cross-Country Skiing

Participation rates have increased slightly for those between the ages of 35 and 65 during these selected years.

Source: Simmons Market Research Bureau. 1980, 1985, 1990, 1995. Study of Media and Markets. New York, NY.

Table 8-97

Growth markets: This is not a growth activity. There are signs, however, of the female fitness market increasing slightly along with skiers age 55 and older and the married. There may be a slight shift as younger skiers age and continue the activity. Any growth will probably be among the midlife cohort.

Established markets: The core is small. Over 70 percent ski less than five times a year. The young adult market, especially male, is declining slightly. This suggests an activity that will barely hold onto its base of participation.

Low markets: The general population is a low market for this niche activity except in areas where there is wide access to trails and rental equipment.

Projections

Despite its promotion as an aerobic and nature-based activity, Nordic skiing has not increased the niche market it captured 20 years ago. The lower rates for young adults suggests a likely gradual decline unless it is offset by midlife adults with higher rates of maintaining participation and access to more trails. Overall, this niche activity will either stabilize or continue a slow gradual decline. One counter possibility is multi-sport winter resorts that provide trails.

Skiing—Downhill

Downhill or "Alpine" skiing has a long history and is supported by a wide variety of resources. There are the very upscale resorts in the Rocky Mountains and other premier locales and modest rope tows on hills in city parks. The cost of equipment and travel to the top venues has made this an income-related activity despite various lower-cost and easy-access modes of sliding down snow-covered hills. Trend data are available from the 1970s. Downhill skiing has limited participation, but remains a substantial recreation activity despite its relative absence in large areas of the country. For some flatlanders, it is a once-or twice-a-year special trip. It also weather-related with yearly fluctuations based in snow conditions. Some of the skiing market may be diluted by snowboarding.

General Trends

From 1980 through 1994, the adult rate of downhill skiing remained flat at about 4 percent. In 1995 and 1996 there was an increase to 5.5 percent. This latter rate produced 10.5 million skiers and 80 million participation days. On average, 10 percent of Alpine skiers ski frequently in a given year and 80 percent infrequently. It is possible, however, to be a serious skier and only manage one trip to the slopes if the mountains are distant. A large proportion of the market is at a distance from the resource requiring overnight travel. The NSG surveys indicate a decline from 11.4 million skiers in 1990 to 9.2 million in 1993 and then a rebound to 10.2 in 1995, 11.5 in 1996, and 12 million skiers in 1997. Of these about 15 percent ski more than 20 days a year. Overall, the skiing market was relatively stable for two decades with a recent upturn. About 80 percent of the total market is occasional (see Table 8-98).

Market Identification

Gender is somewhat skewed toward males, 6.5 percent to 4.9 percent participation rates. Alpine skiing has a strong age distribution: 9 percent age 18 to 34, 6.2 percent age 35 to 44, 3.7 percent age 45 to 54, 2.9 percent 55 to 64, and less than 1 percent age 65 and older. It is an upscale activity. College graduates ski at over three times as those with some college and over twice the rate of high school graduates. For most years, high income skiers are up to twice the participation rate of moderate, but in 1995 an increase in moderate-income skiers produced almost equal rates. Singles ski at double the rate of the married. Skiing is most common in the West, 11% in 1995,

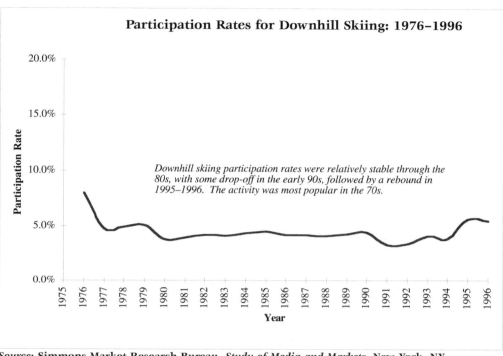

Participation Rates for Downhill Skiing: 1976–1996

Downhill skiing participation rates were relatively stable through the 80s, with some drop-off in the early 90s, followed by a rebound in 1995–1996. The activity was most popular in the 70s.

Source: **Simmons Market Research Bureau.** *Study of Media and Markets.* **New York, NY.**

Table 8-98

followed by 6.3 percent in the Northeast, 4.4 percent in the Midwest, and 2.8 percent in the South. The modal skier is a young male from an upper-income household living in the West. There is a major proportion of downhill skiers, however, who make trips once or twice a year to ski areas and who continue skiing well into midlife. A segment of even frequent and moderate skiers concentrate their participation in short periods of time including long weekends as well as week-long trips (see Table 8-99).

Growth markets: Growth rates have been higher for women, older skiers, and, most recently, those with moderate incomes. Growth is not so much targeted narrowly, but is among those categories that have had somewhat lower rates of participation including the family market. That is, skiing is becoming somewhat less exclusive, perhaps partly due to some less costly and more accessible venues.

Established markets: Alpine skiing remains, however, an upscale activity due to the multiple costs of equipment, access, travel, and style costs. There is a significant income-based family market, despite the bias toward young singles with access to ski runs and discretionary income. One question is the impact of snowboarding on the youth segment of the market. This activity draws primarily younger participants who may take up skiing at lower rates than previous cohorts.

Low markets: Except for a few public and low-cost venues in the West and Northern tier states, cost restricts the downhill skiing market more than age or gender.

Projections

The long-term gradual stability or even slight decline seems to be reversed. The recent upturn suggests a broadening of the market. Increasing the supply of destination

149

resorts and regional facilities may have increased the demand with greater accessibility and promotion efforts. This may be offset, however, by competition in the younger market from snowboarding. Any growth will come from midlife affluent adults, including those with children, and will be dependent on economic growth and increased significant discretionary income. Technology improvements have largely had their impact and are now more marketing strategies.

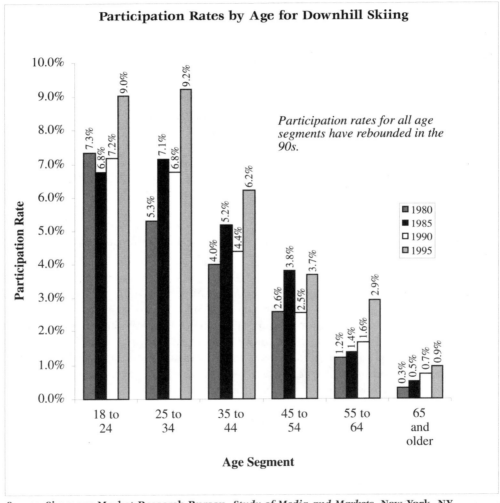

Participation Rates by Age for Downhill Skiing

Participation rates for all age segments have rebounded in the 90s.

Source: **Simmons Market Research Bureau.** *Study of Media and Markets.* **New York, NY.**

Table 8-99

Snowboarding

Snowboarding is a niche growth activity. It can take place on regular ski slopes, competing or even conflicting with traditional Alpine skiing. It can also be adapted to smaller hills, which may be available in or near communities without nearby mountains. Ten years ago less than 5 percent of ski areas permitted snowboarding. Now 95 percent have adapted to this activity.

General Trends

Trend data are available only since 1993. The adult rate has increased from 1.8 percent in 1993 to 2.3 percent in 1995. Of these, 30 percent are frequent. The change rate is +13 percent a year. NSG data including children and youth indicates growth from 1.5 million participants in 1990 to 2.1 in 1994 to 2.5 in 1997. Of these, 25 percent snowboarded 10 or more days a year. The overall trend is clearly one of growth of this new activity based on a new device and a traditional resource, the ski run, and new areas such as half pipes and bowls (see Table 8-100).

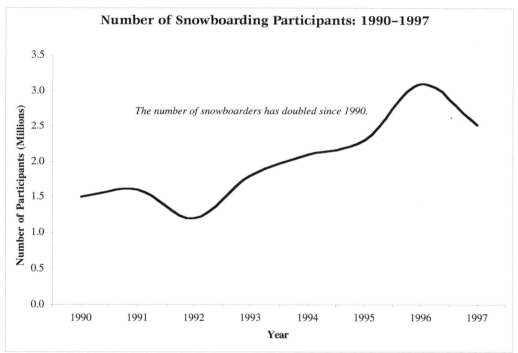

Number of Snowboarding Participants: 1990–1997

The number of snowboarders has doubled since 1990.

Source: **SGRnet. National Sporting Goods Association. Princeton, NJ. (www.sgrnet.com).**

Table 8-100

Market Identification

Snowboarders tend to be male, 75 percent, but with the female participation growing. They are young with the highest rates age 12 to 17 with a 40 percent drop for age 18 to 24, another 25 percent decline for age 25 to 34, half that rate for 35 to 44, and few participants age 45 and older. It is more common in the West and upper Midwest. The activity is less skewed toward upper incomes than Alpine skiing due to less costly equipment and a wider set of venues.

Growth markets: There is growth among females and in the young adult age categories. In general, the growth indicates a broadening of the market from the initial young male core. The evolving market is primarily composed of young adults.

Projections

It is always difficult to forecast when a growth activity with a small base will peak. One issue with snowboarding is how its space conflicts with traditional skiing will be accommodated at major ski resources. Separated runs are costly for a niche market, but may be necessary to satisfy the larger ski market. The segmented nature of the market suggests a growth cycle of less than 10 years with short-term trends of a declining rate of growth likely. This is an activity often introduced to adults by youth rather than vice versa. Olympic exposure may also have an impact for this activity, with lower costs and wider access than traditional skiing.

Snowshoeing

This is a traditional niche activity generally limited to the Northern tier of states. NSG surveys indicate a very small base of participation with some growth. The 0.4 percent rate in 1992 was followed by 0.6 percent in 1995 and 0.7 percent in 1997. Of these, 15 to 20 percent snow shoed 20 or more days a year. Adult males outnumber females 2 to 1. There is no significant age decline up to age 55. It is most popular in the Northeast and upper Midwest. This activity could have some continued gradual growth in the older age segments due to the aging of the population, but remains a regional niche activity. In selected areas, it may become more related to exercise walking. Some snowshoeing may also be related to snow conditions and cross-country skiing. Although a limited niche activity, there may be localized growth due to media exposure and the more inclusive age appeal.

Snowmobiling

This activity has a fairly long history since its inception in the 1970s. Two markets have been identified: the farm use market in heavy snow regions and the recreational market. The first of those who use the device for winter work is smaller, but relatively steady. The recreational second market of trail riders and ice fishers probably provides most of the variation. Trend data is available from 1979.

General Trends

The has been a steady state adult activity since 1979. The 2.4 percent 1979 rate has fluctuated: 2.6 percent in 1981, 2.2 percent in 1984 and 1986, about 2 percent from 1987 through 1994, 2.4 percent in 1995, and back to 2.1 percent in 1996. This fluctuation may reflect snow conditions more than any change in the market. There are about 4 million snowmobilers and 50 million participation days. In most years as few as 10 percent of the participants were frequent and other years the percentage was as high as 18 percent, probably due to variations in snow conditions. The infrequent percentage fluctuated between 60 and 80 percent. The NSG survey in 1997 found 3.4 million participants of whom 20 percent snowmobiled 20 or more days (see Table 8-101).

Market Identification

Again, there is a core of adult farm or transportation use that may confound the recreational use figures somewhat. The gender bias is small, in 1995 2.6 percent male to 2.2 percent female. The age decline is steady but gradual: 3.5 percent age 18 to 24, 3.7 percent 25 to 34, 2.7 percent 35 to 44, 1.4 percent 45 to 64, and less than 1 percent 65 and older. There is no education differentiation, but high income participation is 40

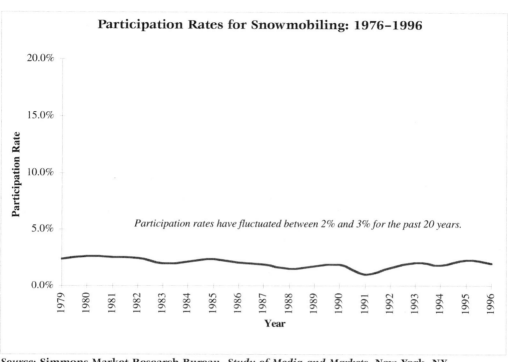

Participation Rates for Snowmobiling: 1976–1996

Participation rates have fluctuated between 2% and 3% for the past 20 years.

Source: **Simmons Market Research Bureau.** *Study of Media and Markets.* **New York, NY.**

Table 8-101

percent higher than moderate and low. Some analysis suggests that there is a high-end market of households with multiple machines and trailers who drive to resort areas for trail riding and a moderate-income market of localized use in snowbelt regions. There are more singles than the married, but households with children have higher rates than those without. Snowmobiling is regional: 4.2 percent in the Midwest, 3.3 percent in the Northeast, 1.7 percent in the West, and 1 percent in the South. In general, snowmobiling is an adult activity located primarily in the Northern tier of states (see Table 8-102).

Growth markets: With no overall growth, growth segments are difficult to identify. If any, the modest growth market is households with young children. This suggests that this may be more a family or group activity than a high-power activity for much of the market.

Established markets: Rural male adults in the upper Midwest are the core market.

Low markets: The failure to attract more youth and young adults suggest a stable market as identified with no indications of real growth outside such segments.

Projections

There are no indications of growth. Year to year changes seem to be resource rather than market-related. Some years premier snowmobile races are held in the mud. On the other hand, there is a persistent market in the snow regions, especially among those with access to back country and trails. Technology improvements may be balanced by restrictions in some areas on sound pollution and ground damage.

153

Winter Activities

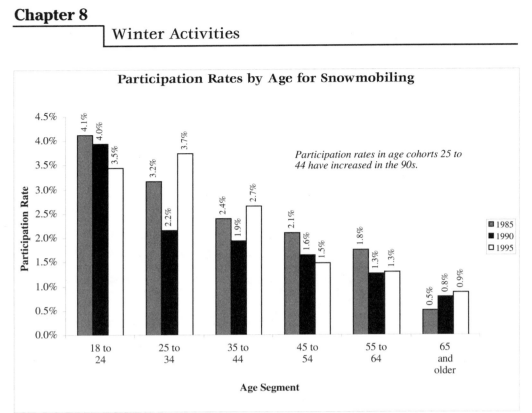

Participation Rates by Age for Snowmobiling

Participation rates in age cohorts 25 to 44 have increased in the 90s.

Legend: 1985, 1990, 1995

Age Segment	1985	1990	1995
18 to 24	4.1%	4.0%	3.5%
25 to 34	3.2%	2.2%	3.7%
35 to 44	2.4%	1.9%	2.7%
45 to 54	2.1%	1.6%	1.5%
55 to 64	1.8%	1.3%	1.3%
65 and older	0.5%	0.8%	0.9%

Source: Simmons Market Research Bureau. 1985, 1990, 1995. *Study of Media and Markets.* New York, NY.

Table 8-102

Chapter 9

Travel Activities

The most common travel, over 75 percent of overnight trips, is by car. The tourism industry has been reluctant to separate business and recreational travel. What is recognized, however, is that recreational aims and activities are a major part of the total travel market. People travel to ski, visit museums, attend concerts, watch football and soccer playoffs, scuba, sail, lie on the beach, backpack, and so on. Therefore, the preceding activity analysis is important to assessing travel markets. However, the major forms of travel are also markets in their own right. The trend analysis offered here is somewhat different from most of the travel data gathered for the industry in that it is based on household survey data rather than destination or transportation usage. Most of the data gathered from airlines, hotel and resort chains, and other suppliers is valuable because it is specific to the type of travel. Our trend analysis is more generic, but presents a picture of general likelihood to travel, an element that often precedes choices of destinations and carriers.

Domestic Travel

As already suggested, most domestic overnight travel is by car. Domestic travel includes overnight trips of over 100 miles, whatever the purposes. It is often to visit family and friends or combines such visiting with particular recreation destinations. Often recreational activities made possible by resources during the trip or at the destinations are central to the choices. Midwesterners drive west to camp. They fly to the mountains to ski or to the keys to scuba. Recreational tourists also increasingly are taking "mini-vacations" over long weekends to have a break more than once a year. Business travelers may combine recreation and business activities in a single trip. This generic category with trend data available from 1979 includes this variety of modes of travel.

General Trends

Adult domestic travel of over 100 miles declined somewhat from 62 percent in 1979 to about 50 percent from 1985 through 1993 and then rebounded back to 64 percent in 1995 and 1996. Almost 125 million adults took such a trip in 1995 and 1996. Travel volume data from SMRB are not easily accessible (see Table 9-103).

Market Identification

The inclusive nature of the category makes market specification difficult. Overall, the rates hold steady except that those with high incomes travel at double the rate of those with low incomes. Growth, however, has been strongest in the older age categories and among those with some college education. There has also been higher growth among two-person households, often those who have launched their children. The core growth travel market, previously the targeted young adults, is evolving to an older adult market with more flexible schedules and discretionary income.

Projections

The rebound since 1993 has been steady but gradual. With the key market segment of older adults growing and the industry responding to this market, continued growth in domestic travel is probable. This growth can continue until the "Boomers" reach their 70s and begin to stay closer to home.

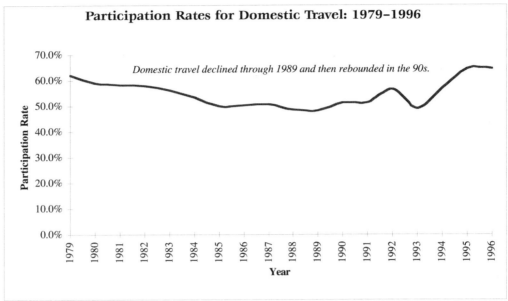

Source: Simmons Market Research Bureau. *Study of Media and Markets*. New York, NY.

Table 9-103

International Travel

International travel is somewhat more market-specific than domestic travel due to generally higher costs. Canada is still the most common "foreign" destination, however. Other international travel is most often by air with attendant costs. Some such travel combines business and leisure purposes that may be difficult to disentangle. The SMRB surveys asked about international travel over a three-year period outside the contiguous 48 states and not for military purposes. The trends, then, are three-point moving averages.

General Trends

This type of travel also had a decline to the mid-1990s and then a rebound. The 1979 19 percent rate fell to about 15 percent from 1983 through 1990 and then began a gradual rise to 22 percent in 1995 and 23.5 percent in 1996. In 1996 there were 45 million international travelers (see Table 9-104).

Market Identification

The more costly international travel is skewed toward upscale markets. There is no significant gender difference or age-related decline through the 55 to 64 category. It may be assumed that the "active old" market remains important. Those with college education, however, travel out of the country at three times the rate of high school graduates. Those from high income households engage in international travel at three times the rate of moderate and four-and-a-half times the rate of low income travelers.

156

Those without children living at home, at both ends of the age spectrum, do significantly more international traveling. The modal international traveler is a high-income college-educated adult without child rearing responsibilities. Growth, then, is most evident among the 18 to 34 and 65 and over age categories, especially those from two-person households.

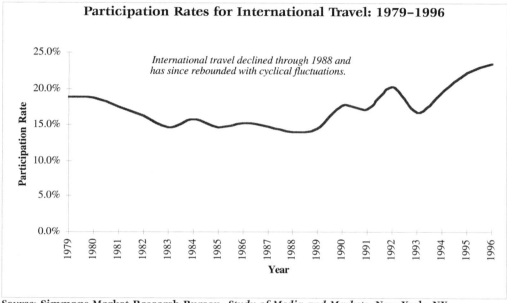

Participation Rates for International Travel: 1979–1996

International travel declined through 1988 and has since rebounded with cyclical fluctuations.

Source: **Simmons Market Research Bureau.** *Study of Media and Markets.* **New York, NY.**

Table 9-104

Projections

The strong dollar has been a factor in recent international travel growth, a factor that may change. In general, however, the large "Boomer" cohort is entering that post-launching period with discretionary income that supports such travel. Barring major economic changes or political crises, continued gradual growth can be expected for the first quarter of the 21st century.

Visiting Theme Parks

Some theme park attendance reflects travel of over 100 miles. However, those theme parks, other than Disney, that have been most successful are located in urban areas where they can attract repeat business. This is, then, only partly a travel-based activity. It could also fit under the "day trips" category.

General Trends

This activity has had fluctuating growth since 1980. The rate of 11.5 percent from 1980 through 1983 fell to 9 percent from 1985 through 1988, and then jumped to about 20 percent for three years, fell again to under 16 percent in 1992, and then grew to 24 percent in 1994 and 28 percent in 1995 and 27.5 percent in 1996. This yields 53 million adults going to theme parks. Volume data are not available (see Table 9-105).

Travel Activities

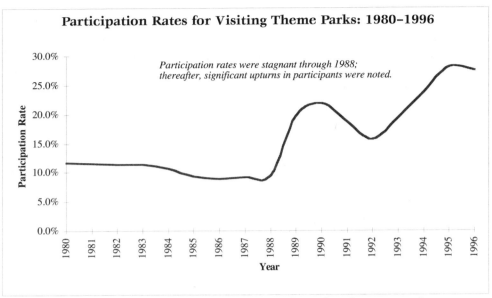

Participation Rates for Visiting Theme Parks: 1980–1996

Participation rates were stagnant through 1988; thereafter, significant upturns in participants were noted.

Source: **Simmons Market Research Bureau.** *Study of Media and Markets.* **New York, NY.**

Table 9-105

Market Identification

Theme parks are, of course, oriented toward children, youth, and families. Despite efforts at broader programming, households with children living at home are the core market. Many theme parks are trying to broaden their markets with a greater variety of shows and other entertainment. There is no gender bias. Age, however, is significant with rates of 27 + percent dropping to 18 percent age 45 to 54, 16 percent 55 to 64, and 9 percent 65 and older. Education is not significant. High income rates are 25 percent higher than moderate and may reflect trips to the major and more costly parks. Low income rates were much lower until the mid-90s rebound when they increased significantly. The highest growth rates have been among singles, those under 35, those from larger households, and those with low incomes. There seems to be some element of supply creating demand, especially by less costly local theme parks and parks with more specialized themes.

Projections

With growth highest in larger households and that population segment shrinking, the recent growth in theme park attendance may have peaked. A counter trend would be a more localized and diversified set of theme parks that are less costly to attend. There may also be some growth from the teen children of the "Boomers," also a local and regional market. For destination theme parks, population shifts suggest that the growth cycle will probably level off in the next decade. Newer types of parks such as water, sports, historical, and wildlife parks may widen the market somewhat.

Cruise Ship Vacations

Supply and promotion factors have made this a growth activity. The industry is projecting significant growth in the next decade and building new mega-ships to meet the expected demand. Reliable data on cruise ships as "destination resorts" are available only since 1990. Many cruises provide gambling venues on the ships, in special ports, or both.

General Trends

A 4.3 percent adult participation rate in 1990 increased to 5.4 percent in 1993, 6.4 percent in 1994, and 7.5 percent in 1995, falling slightly to 7 percent in 1996. About 13 to 14 million adults took cruises in 1995 or 1996. This is still a small part of the total travel market, but is entirely recreational and vacation-based (see Table 9-106).

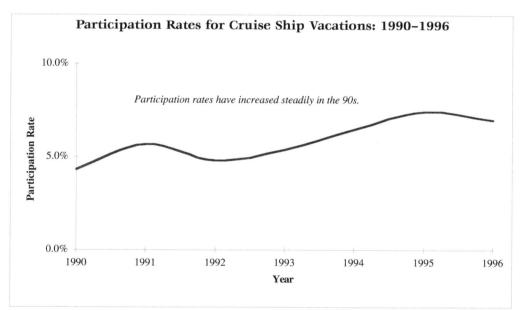

Participation Rates for Cruise Ship Vacations: 1990–1996

Participation rates have increased steadily in the 90s.

Source: **Simmons Market Research Bureau.** *Study of Media and Markets.* **New York, NY.**

Table 9-106

Market Identification

The cruise market is more female than male, in 1995 8.2 percent to 6.7 percent. The age rate remains fairly steady from 18 through age 44 at about 6 percent, rises to 8 percent age 45 to 54, and then jumps to 11.5 percent age 55 to 64 and 10 percent 65 and older. This is one of the rare activities in which participation increases with age. The aging population is the main target for expansion. The married slightly exceed the single or divorced/widowed rate. Those with high incomes take cruises at double the rate of moderate, and those with college education double the rate of high school graduates. Adults in the Northeast cruise at a slightly higher rate than the rest of the country. Those who have no children living at home takes cruises at over twice the rate of residential parents. The growth has been overall among these markets. The modal cruise traveler is 55 or older without children at home and significant discretionary income. The married market is still central despite the substantial numbers of older-age singles.

Chapter 9

Travel Activities

Projections

The major market segments of the population, adults over 55 with upper-level incomes is growing. On this basis, continued gradual growth is likely. Whether or not the projected increase in supply will increase the demand substantially or just retire older ships is problematic. This activity, like all others, has a saturation point. Keys are repeat business and the saturation of popular destinations. Terrorism and accidents may also be dampening factors. On the other hand, new ships can be both more comfortable and cost-efficient.

Chapter 10

Home and Local Activities

The main focus in this book is on those activities that are the basis for recognized markets. Recreation businesses are different in that they are based on participation in activities that no one has to do. Further, there are always alternative activities for available time. Therefore, patterns and histories of engagement, availability and quality of resources, cultural values and socialization, and personal negotiations among alternatives are significant for decisions. The kind of material in this book is a useful background in understanding choices. It is also useful to have a picture of alternatives. The relatively brief analyses that follow are intended to give a fuller view of the vast panoply of possibilities for leisure and recreation.

Most of the activities in this section take place in the home or local area. They include both engaging activities and entertainment. Most leisure takes place in and around the home. The major use of time is, of course, watching television. This may be a priority choice or it may be residual, what people do when nothing else is possible or attractive. There are also many other home-based activities that draw considerable participation. Along with activities in the residence and yard, there are other activities in the community that at least punctuate the overall leisure interest and investment pattern. This section introduces many of those activities primarily for comparison purposes. A basic picture of trends and the magnitude of participation is especially interesting when compared with some of the niche activities in previous analyses. Gardening and gambling are far more common than jet skiing and surfing. The spectrum of activities pursued as leisure is almost limitless. Not included here are television watching, which is measured in a variety of ways, attending sports events of various types, and many other activities not included in our data sources.

Bird Watching

Bird watching can take place in the yard or even from a window. There are also organized bird watching programs and special trips to prime sites. Bird watchers may be in a kind of competitive event to identify species in particular locales, or just enjoy the activity in the backyard feeder. Trend data are available only for 1994 through 1996.

General Trends

There was an increase in adult bird watching from 5.6 percent in 1994 to 7.9 percent in 1995 and 7.6 percent in 1996. That yields 14.5 million participants. Sales trends of feeders and seed also indicate some growth (see Table 10-107).

Market Identification

The gender ratio is in favor of females, in 1995 9.2 to 6.6 percent. Bird watching is an activity for older persons with a rate that increases with age from 4 to 5 percent ages 18 to 34 to 8 to 9 percent ages 35 to 54, and 11 percent age 55 and older. It is not biased by region, income, or education levels. It is a general activity with the special feature of its appeal and access to older adults.

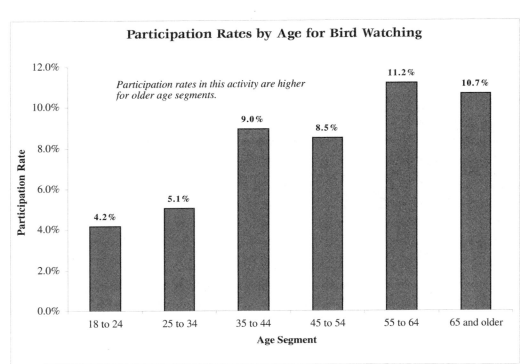

Participation Rates by Age for Bird Watching

Participation rates in this activity are higher for older age segments.

Age Segment	Participation Rate
18 to 24	4.2%
25 to 34	5.1%
35 to 44	9.0%
45 to 54	8.5%
55 to 64	11.2%
65 and older	10.7%

Source: **Simmons Market Research Bureau.** *Study of Media and Markets.* **New York, NY.**

Table 10-107

Projections

As the population ages and interest in nature increases, bird watching will continue to grow gradually. This is also a niche activity for older adults with environmental interests.

Indoor Gardening and Plants

This activity may be quite simple, a few plants in pots, or involve complex apparatus and high levels of knowledge. Trend data are available from 1979.

General Trends

The overall trend has been one of gradual decline. The adult rate fell from 32 percent in 1979 to about 20 percent from 1988 through 1990, 23 percent 1991 through 1994, and then a slight rise to 27 percent in 1995 and 26 percent in 1996. There are about 50 million indoor gardeners (see Table 10-108).

Market Identification

This is a gendered activity, with females double the male rate of participation. The 30 percent participation rate is consistent from age 25 through 64 and then drops to 23 percent for 65 and older. Those with college education have 50 percent higher rates than those with only high school education. There is no income or regional bias. This is an activity for all ages of women and a significant number of men. Where growth exists, there are no differentiating factors, indicating a very generalized activity.

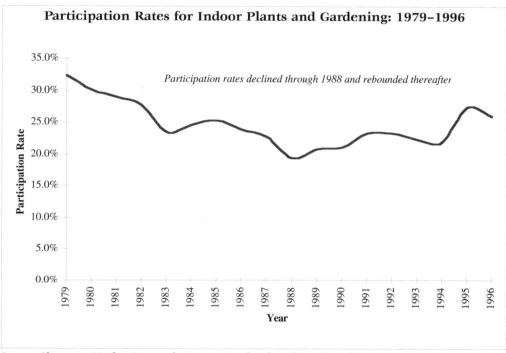

Participation Rates for Indoor Plants and Gardening: 1979–1996

Participation rates declined through 1988 and rebounded thereafter

Source: **Simmons Market Research Bureau.** *Study of Media and Markets.* **New York, NY.**

Table 10-108

Projections

Gradual growth is probable due to the aging of the population and the easy access and low cost of the activity.

Outdoor Flower Gardening

No differentiation is made here between small border flower beds and elaborate gardens. Trend data are available for this general and inclusive activity since 1989.

General Trends

Despite some fluctuation, there has been recent growth in outdoor flower gardening. An overall adult rate of 27 percent jumped to 38 percent in 1995 and dropped back to 35 percent in 1996. There are 65 to 70 million flower gardeners. This is a general activity with wide participation (see Table 10-109).

Market Identification

Females outnumber males with 1995 rates of 44.5 percent to 31 percent. Again, there is little age gradation except for a jump up from 34 percent to 44 percent after age 34 and a decline among the frail elderly. Flower gardening is somewhat biased toward those with college education and higher incomes, with a 30 percent difference in participation rates. Flower gardening is least common in the South, with a rate about 10 to 15 percent lower than the rest of the country. Overall, this is a general and inclusive activity without the common age decline.

163

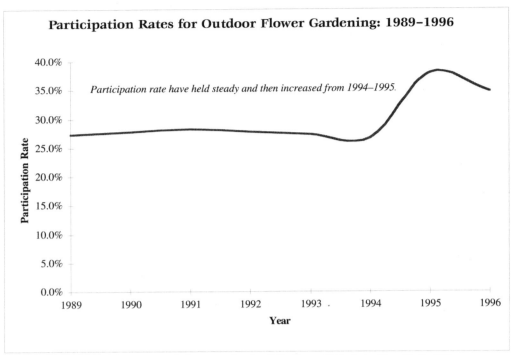

Participation Rates for Outdoor Flower Gardening: 1989–1996

Participation rate have held steady and then increased from 1994–1995.

Source: **Simmons Market Research Bureau.** *Study of Media and Markets.* **New York, NY.**

Table 10-109

Projections

Growth includes all age segments. Gradual growth is probable for flower gardening as the population ages. Those who have launched their children may have more time for gardens.

Outdoor Vegetable Gardening

Adult trend data begin in 1989.

General Trends

Like flower gardening, there is a pattern of overall growth despite some fluctuation. The 18 percent rate in 1989 dropped slightly in 1994 to 16.5 percent and then rose to 23.7 percent in 1995 and 21.4 percent in 1996. This yields about 40 million vegetable gardeners, about two-thirds the rate of flower gardening (see Table 10-110).

Market Identification

Gender rates are almost equal. Vegetable gardening actually increases with age from 20 percent age 25 to 34 to 29 percent through age 64 and 25 percent age 65 and older. There is no education or income bias. Participation in the activity is most common in the Midwest, 35 percent, followed by the South at 27 percent, the West at 18 percent, and the Northeast at 10 percent. This differs from flower gardening in greater male participation and the regional differences.

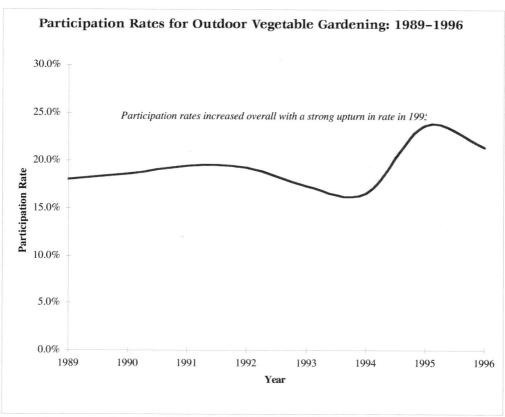

Participation Rates for Outdoor Vegetable Gardening: 1989–1996

Participation rates increased overall with a strong upturn in rate in 199

Source: **Simmons Market Research Bureau. *Study of Media and Markets*. New York, NY.**

Table 10-110

Projections

Continued gradual growth as the population ages is probable. Growth is greatest among those over 35 and outside the Northeast. Empty nesters and early retirees are a potential growth market.

Music

Listening to Music

There are countless ways to listen to music. It takes place in the home, car, concert hall, and through portable devices. It includes rap and rock, classical and country, pop and romantic. It is often a secondary activity that accompanies other engagement or social contexts. Despite the fact that most adults do it, data are available only for 1994–96. Simmons data do not distinguish between primary and secondary listening of portable and car players.

General Trends

Just over 50 percent of the adult population report listening to music. That comprises about 100 million listeners (see Table 10-111).

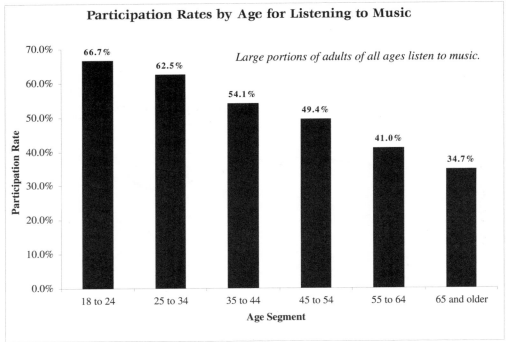

Participation Rates by Age for Listening to Music

Large portions of adults of all ages listen to music.

18 to 24	66.7%
25 to 34	62.5%
35 to 44	54.1%
45 to 54	49.4%
55 to 64	41.0%
65 and older	34.7%

Source: **Simmons Market Research Bureau. 1995.** *Study of Media and Markets.* **New York, NY.**

Table 10-111

Market Identification

Targeting markets requires specifying the various modes of listening to music. Radio "narrowcasting" illustrates how markets are identified by age, culture, style, and even "taste cultures." As a very general category of activity, there are few distinguishing factors. Females listen slightly more than males. There is a gradual age decline from teens to retirees beginning at over 67 percent and dropping slowly to 35 percent for age 65 and older. Those with college education and high incomes listen most. The South has slightly lower rates of listening than the rest of the country. Useful market segmentation, however, requires specification of the types of music and media.

Projection

The wide variety of media instruments and the relatively low cost of many make this an inclusive activity that will at least retain its participation levels. New listening formats and lowered costs of equipment will sustain the overall music listening market.

Playing a Musical Instrument

Musical instruments may be played alone or in groups. School contexts are organized, but most communities offer adult opportunities. Playing involves practice as well as performance. Data are available from 1985.

General Trends

Rates for adults have been fluctuating but with overall stability at about a 7 percent rate from 1985 through 1994. 1995 and 1996 show an increase to 8.8 percent. A crucial factor is the financial support of music in the schools, where a high proportion of introductory learning takes place. There are about 17 million playing musical instruments (see Table 10-112).

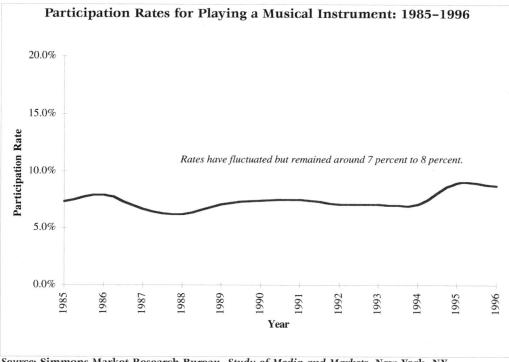

Participation Rates for Playing a Musical Instrument: 1985–1996

Rates have fluctuated but remained around 7 percent to 8 percent.

Source: Simmons Market Research Bureau. *Study of Media and Markets*. New York, NY.

Table 10-112

Market Identification

There are no significant gender differences. The 15 percent rate for age 18 to 24 drops to just under 10 percent for ages 25 to 44, 7.7 percent age 45 to 54, 5.7 percent 55 to 64, and 5 percent 65 and older. College graduates play at 3 times the rate of those with only high school education and singles at double the rate of the married. Rates for those with high incomes are 10.8 percent, moderate 8.5 percent, and low 5.8 percent. Playing is 50 percent higher in the West than the rest of the country. In general, the longer one plays in school the greater the likelihood of later adult engagement.

Projections

Continued gradual growth may be projected based on rising rates of college education. A negative factor, however, could be the discontinuation of music programs in poorly-funded primary and secondary schools. The future of skill-based committed activity is a larger issue that is relevant for activities such as playing musical instruments.

167

Attending Concerts—Country Music

Trend data are limited, beginning in 1993.

General Trends

There are indications that country music concerts may have peaked in the mid-1990s and are currently declining. The 5.3 percent rate of 1993 has declined to 4.5 percent in 1995 and 1996. Such short-term changes may, however, be fluctuations rather than a trend. About 9 million adults attend country music concerts (see Table 10-113).

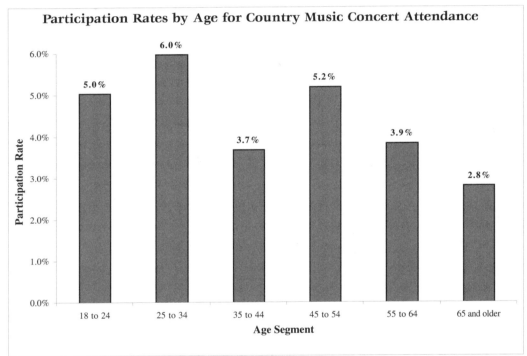

Participation Rates by Age for Country Music Concert Attendance

Source: Simmons Market Research Bureau. 1995. *Study of Media and Markets*. New York, NY.

Table 10-113

Market Identification

Females attend somewhat more than males, 5 percent to 4 percent. Age rates are relatively consistent to age 65, suggesting that the market may be aging. Those who have attended college but not completed a degree attend more than college or high school graduates. Income does not discriminate. Rates are highest in the Midwest and significantly lower in the Northeast. Country music is a classic mid-America activity by almost all segmentation elements.

Projections

Growth seems unlikely as the population ages and education levels rise. Rapid decline, however, is also unlikely. The retention of a core following in the short-term is probable.

Concerts—Pop and Rock

Data are available for adults from 1985 through 1996. The constantly-changing styles of such music and the tastes of each youth cohort shift so quickly that more precise specification of styles and formats is difficult. The data here do not include the age groups with highest devotion to non-concert media for pop and rock, teens under age 18, whose tastes change rapidly from rock to rap to hip hop, and so on (see Table 10-114).

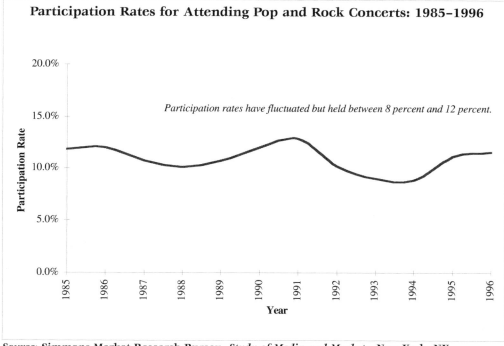

Participation Rates for Attending Pop and Rock Concerts: 1985–1996

Participation rates have fluctuated but held between 8 percent and 12 percent.

Source: Simmons Market Research Bureau. *Study of Media and Markets*. New York, NY.

Table 10-114

General Trends

Overall, there is a fluctuating decline beginning at a 12 percent rate in 1985 and 1986, fluctuating between 10 and 12 percent, with rates of 9 percent in 1993 and 94, 11 percent in 1995, and 11.5 percent in 1996. This trend suggests a slight recent increase. There are about 21 million adults age 18 and over who attend rock and pop concerts .

Market Identification

Gender differences are minor. Age is the major factor with a 24.6 percent rate age 18 to 24, 15.8 percent age 25 to 34, 11.7 percent 35 to 44, 8 percent 45 to 54, 2.7 percent 55 to 64, and 1.5 percent 65 and older. Because of the youth factor, education level is highest for those with some college. Singles attend concerts at three times the rate of the married. Rates are highest in the West and lowest in the South. The income distribution is also skewed by student participation with high income households highest, low income second, and moderate income households slightly lowest. This is a youth and even student based market with some residual interest that may reflect the marketing of older performers and groups on the concert circuit. There are significant taste differences within the overall market.

Projections

An aging population does not bode well for such concerts. The long-term projection would be for fluctuating gradual decline. Some core markets, however, are likely to remain even as specific styles change.

Concerts—Classical Music

Data are available from 1985. Classical concerts include amateur as well as professional performances and venues from the great concert halls to high school gyms and local churches.

General Trends

There has been a growth in attendance from 1985 that seems to have peaked in the mid-90s and may be declining somewhat. The rate of about 4.7 percent was relatively consistent to 1991 when it rose to 5.6 percent, 5.8 percent in 1993, and then dropped to 5.4 percent in 1994 and 5 percent in 1996. This yields about 9.5 million concert-goers (see Table 10-115).

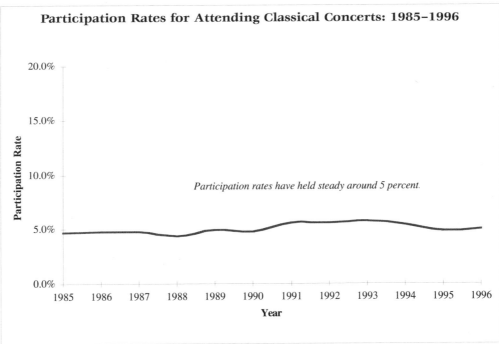

Participation Rates for Attending Classical Concerts: 1985–1996

Participation rates have held steady around 5 percent.

Source: Simmons Market Research Bureau. *Study of Media and Markets*. New York, NY.

Table 10-115

Market Identification

Females somewhat outnumber males, 5.3 percent to 4.3 percent. The age pattern is one of an increase by age categories that may reflect cohort interest more than age-related factors. The 4.2 percent rate for age 18 to 24 rises to 5 percent age 35 to 44, 5.5 percent 45 to 64, and 6.4 percent 65 and older. College graduates attend at almost double the rates of those who have attended college and four times the rate of high school graduates. High incomes attend at double the rates of those with moderate levels. Rates are highest in the Northeast and West with the South lowest. Classical music interest is clearly education-related. The contradiction is that cohorts with only some college education but not degrees attend more often. This may reflect the supply in college and university communities.

Projections

The long-term projection is for gradual declines in classical concert attendance as the core audience ages and is succeeded by cohorts with lower rates of commitment. "Boomers" will, however, have the income to attend if they renew interests gained in their education experiences.

Day Trips

There has been considerable attention given to overnight travel labeled "tourism" due to its major position in the world economy. However, most travel is domestic, 85 percent by car according to the National Travel Data Center. Further, there are many kinds of day trips taken by families and other groups that tend to fall between the tourism research cracks. They are not major trips, and are not related to a particular sport or resource-based activity. Yet, they are a common element of the overall mix and rhythm of leisure. Here we will summarize data on such activities in a way that is not fully representative of their personal, family, social, and cultural significance.

Visiting Art Museums

Trends since 1991 show fluctuating growth for adults. About 10 to 11 percent of the population visited art museums from 1991 through 1994 followed by an increase to 15.6 percent in 1995 and 13.2 percent in 1996. This yields over 25 million adult visitors. The gender bias is slight, a rate of 17 percent female to 14.2 percent male. Rates by age are consistent to age 55 when there is a 30 percent drop. Those with college education visit at three times the rate of others and high income rates are double moderate. Museum visiting is highest in the Northeast and West. The rising education levels of each adult age cohort indicates that a continued gradual growth in art museum visiting is probable. The recent trend toward special promotions and touring exhibits may also be a factor in the increase (see Table 10-116).

Visiting Other Museums

Data from 1991 indicate a pattern of fluctuating growth from 12.8 percent in 1991 to about 11 percent in 1993 and 94 and a jump to 18 percent in 1995 and 15.8 percent in 1996. "Other" museums would include natural history, scientific, children's, and other institutions. There are about 30 million museum visitors. There is no gender difference and little decline with age prior to age 65. Education is a major factor with college graduates visiting at a 50 percent higher rate than those with some college and three times the rate of high school graduates. Those with high incomes visit at 40 percent higher rates than moderate. Rates are about the same regionally except for the almost 50 percent lower rate in the South. This would seem to be an activity with a long-term growth potential related to education and income levels. Rates are highest in households with children as well as the educational and income resources (see Table 10-117).

171

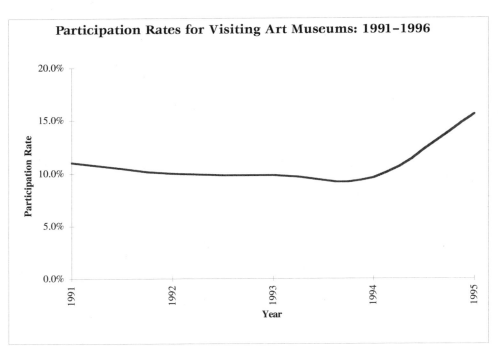

Source: Simmons Market Research Bureau. *Study of Media and Markets*. New York, NY.

Table 10-116

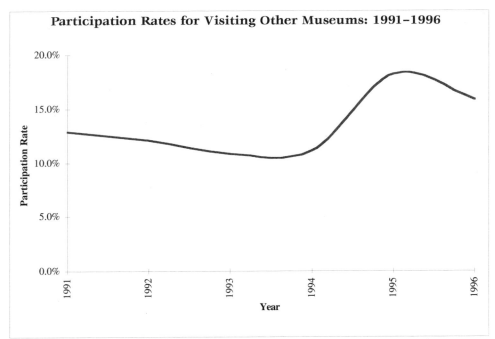

Source: Simmons Market Research Bureau. *Study of Media and Markets*. New York, NY.

Table 10-117

Going to a Beach or Lake

This might be termed the "picnic" activity although many visits do not involve eating. Most people go in groups. The rates since 1994 are substantial despite fluctuations that may be partly weather-related. The 1994–96 yearly rates were 28 percent, 37 percent, and 35 percent. About 65 to 70 million adults make such day trips each year. This is a general activity with little significant market segmentation except for higher rates in households with children at home. Those with higher education or higher incomes make such trips at a 35 percent higher rate. There is an age-related decline from 45 percent to 35 percent at age 45 and a continued decline to 24 percent age 55 to 64 and 14 percent 65 and older. This is a classic family activity. Locally it is related to access to attractive water. The pattern may be more one of fluctuation at a high level than a long-term growth or loss pattern. There may be some decline as "Boomers" children leave home and then a rebound as they have children (see Table 10-118).

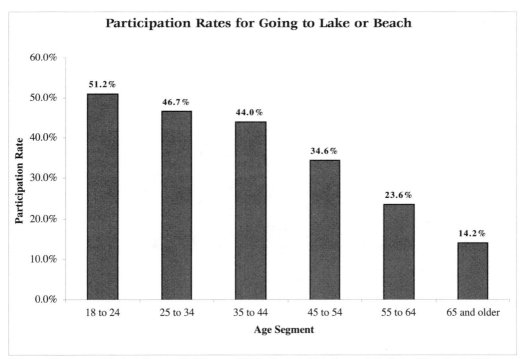

Source: **Simmons Market Research Bureau. 1995.** *Study of Media and Markets.* **New York, NY.**

Table 10-118

Visiting State Fairs

The overall rates since 1990 have increased from about 8 percent to 10 percent in 1995 and 9.7 percent in 1996. About 19 million adults visited state fairs. There is little gender and age difference up to age 65. Nor do education and income prove to be strong indices. The regional rates are 12 percent in the West, 11 percent in the Northeast and Midwest, and 7.4 percent in the South. The married and single attend at about the same rates. The main negative factor, urbanization, appears to have had less impact than might be expected, perhaps due to the location and diverse programming of state fairs. The growth categories are supported by demographic trends. Continued strong marketing should support state fairs, with some possibility of modest broad-based growth. Note that state fairs are only partly agricultural and include auto and horse races, rock and pop concerts, and a variety of entertainment activities with more segmented markets (see Table 10-119).

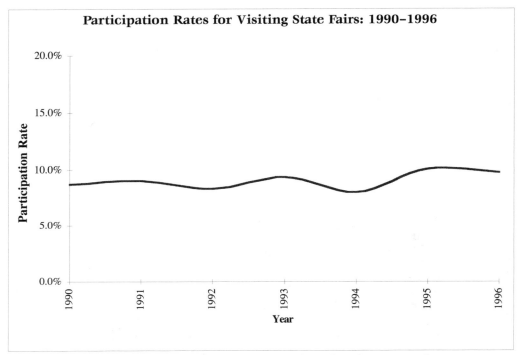

Participation Rates for Visiting State Fairs: 1990–1996

Source: **Simmons Market Research Bureau.** *Study of Media and Markets.* **New York, NY.**

Table 10-119

Visit Zoos

Adult attendance in this classic child-oriented activity from 1991 has risen from 15 percent to almost 19.7 percent in 1995 and 16.8 percent in 1996. About 30 to 35 million adults visit zoos in a year. There is a slight female rate bias, 20 percent participation to 19 percent for males. The highest ages are the parental years, and visitors come with households with children at twice the rate of those without. College education doubles the rate, and high income households visit at a 30 percent higher rate than moderate. This is a general group activity with a child focus. Of course, grand-parents bring children, too. Long-term growth is based on marketing the special attractions of the current zoos that do much more than display animals and birds. A general stability is more probable and will be based on fertility rates. A decline as "Boomer" children age and then a rebound as they have children is probable (see Table 10-120).

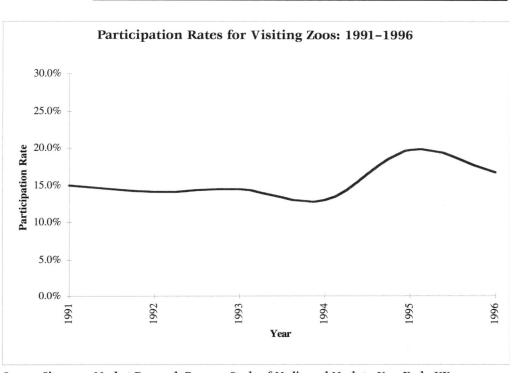

Participation Rates for Visiting Zoos: 1991–1996

Source: **Simmons Market Research Bureau.** *Study of Media and Markets.* **New York, NY.**

Table 10-120

Local Entertainment

Many activities that are not strictly recreation are done primarily as leisure. This includes shopping and eating out. Other events are more related to the entertainment value of the venue, including a variety of performances. This set of activities includes both kinds of local activities. The summaries are based on a fuller data set than is presented here to provide comparative analysis.

Dining Out (not fast food)

While eating out on trips and for business purposes is a part of the mix, a high proportion of dining out is leisure. Such events are social for families, groups of friends, and those with romantic aims. Especially if fast food meals are excluded, social aims rather than just avoiding cooking at home become part of the meanings of the event.

With only three years of data, the growth trend is not well established. The adult rate increased from 42 percent in 1994 to 55 percent in 1995 and 1996. About 105 million adults dined out each of those years. There are stylistic and cost differences related to income. The rate for those with high incomes is 30 percent higher than moderate-income households. Those with college education dine out 40 percent more than high school graduates. Marital status and having children at home are not segmenting factors. Regional differences are minor. Dining out is a broad-based general activity. Most adults do it. Those with higher incomes do it frequently. The restaurant trade is sensitive to income and offers a range of price levels. Barring an economic

175

recession, the projection for the future would be for continued growth, especially as the "Boomers" have more discretionary income and have launched their children. Households with time pressures and higher discretionary incomes remain a key market (see Table 10-121).

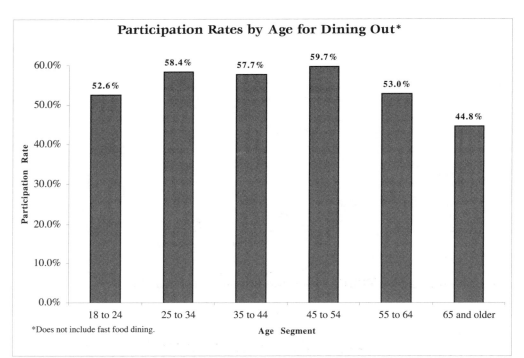

Source: Simmons Market Research Bureau. *Study of Media and Markets*. New York, NY.

Table 10-121

Going to Bars and Night Clubs

Like dining out, this is a growth activity for the three years of adult trend data. The 18 percent rate of 1994 increased to 22.5 percent in 1995 and 1996. About 43 million adults visit bars and night clubs. Male rates exceed female 25 percent to 20 percent. Age is a major factor with a rate of over 36 percent for age 18 to 34 falling to 22 percent for age 35 to 44, 16 percent for age 45 to 54, and 7 percent for age 55 and older. Those with college education go out 40 percent more than those without. The student factor is strong with singles doubling the rate of the married. Income is less of a factor and regional differences are small. The modal bar or night club visitor is a single young adult, but there are other market segments related to social class and other identifying factors and to the style of the establishment. The young adult market is not growing. Continued growth is likely to be segmented by social identity and the social aims of various market segments. Legal restrictions on age and smoking may be a dampening market factor (see 10-122).

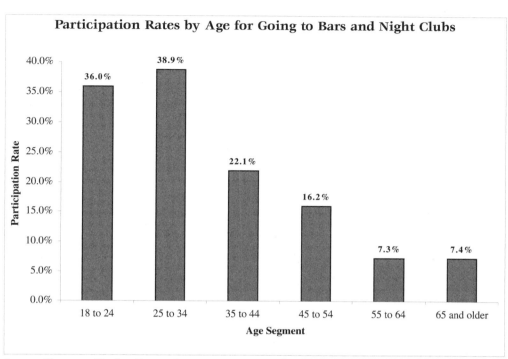

Participation Rates by Age for Going to Bars and Night Clubs

Source: **Simmons Market Research Bureau. 1995.** *Study of Media and Markets*. **New York, NY.**

Table 10-122

Going Dancing

Trend data since 1989 indicate a fluctuating pattern with modest growth. This cyclical activity is difficult to predict due to fads in styles. The growth segments are young adults, especially singles, and seniors. It is a market divided by styles. A 16 percent rate in 1989–90 fell to 15.5 percent in 1994 and rose to 17.1 percent in 1996. About 33 million adults went dancing that year. Females danced more than males, 18 percent to 16 percent. The age distribution is one of decline up to 65. It is 31 percent for age 18 to 24, 24 percent 25 to 34, 15 percent 35 to 44, 13 percent 45 to 54, 8.5 percent 55 to 64, and then 9 percent 65 and older. Singles outnumber the married over 2 to 1. Those with some college, including students, went dancing at twice the rate of high school graduates. Income is also a factor, 21 percent for high income and 15 percent moderate. Again, there are many styles of dancing that segment the markets. Disco, ballroom, swing, country western, and folk tend to draw different markets. The growth, however, is at each end, younger singles and the retired. The young market is not a growing population segment so that major growth is unlikely. The senior market, often nostalgic and still limited, may well grow further (see Table 10-123).

Movies (theater)

The trend since 1982 of adults who have gone to a motion picture theater in the last 90 days is one of fluctuating decline followed by a recent rebound. The 1982 42 percent rate fell to 31 percent in 1988 and 1989 and then began a rebound to 38.5 percent in 1992 and 93, 45 percent in 1994, 53 percent in 1995, and 47 percent in 1996.

177

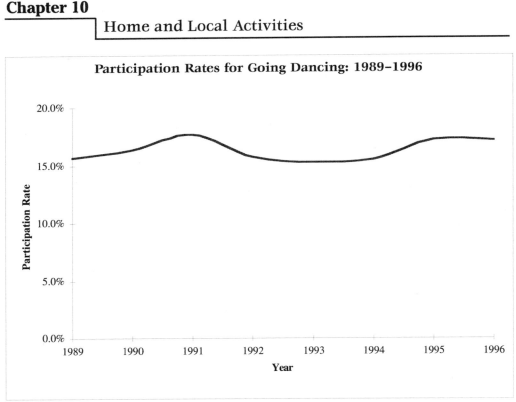

Participation Rates for Going Dancing: 1989–1996

Source: **Simmons Market Research Bureau.** *Study of Media and Markets.* **New York, NY.**

Table 10-123

About 90 million adults went to movies in a 90-day period. The major market of teens under 18 is not represented in these data. Aside from the youth segment, the market is fairly general. There is no gender difference. The post-student age decline is significant from 55 on. There is some bias toward those with college education and higher incomes. Rates are highest in the West. Singles go only 25 percent more than the married among adults 18 and older. Despite rising prices, this popular activity is increasing, partly in response to the supply of new multiplex theaters and, paradoxically, advertising on television. Promotion budgets of major films may be almost 50 percent of their total cost. Growth is not differentiated and suggests that the current higher rates will continue or even grow somewhat. Fluctuations may be related to quality and market mixes. New technologies of pay-at-home cable and satellite transmission may alter the theater market (see Table 10-124).

Theater (live)

This activity can include school and amateur productions as well as professional theater. As such, it is a community activity. The trend since 1988 is one of decline and then recycled growth. The 1982 17 percent rate declined gradually to under 11 percent in 1988 and 1989. Then there was gradual growth to 13.5 percent in 1993 and 1994, 16.7 percent in 1995, and 18 percent in 1996. That yielded almost 32 million theatergoers in 1995. The market for community and school theater is much more inclusive than that for professional theater in urban areas. Females go more than males, 19 percent to 14 percent. The age curve is reversed with a 14 percent rate for

178

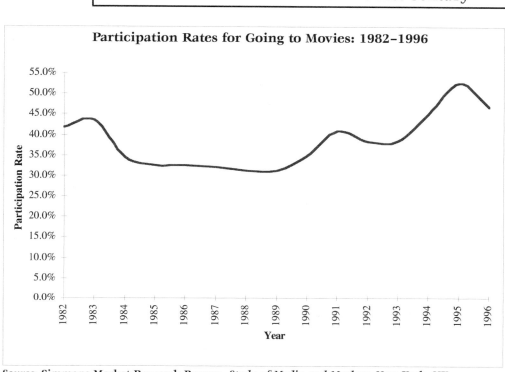

Participation Rates for Going to Movies: 1982–1996

Source: **Simmons Market Research Bureau.** *Study of Media and Markets.* **New York, NY.**

Table 10-124

age 18 to 34 increasing to 17 percent age 35 to 44, 21 percent age 45 to 54, 19.5 percent 55 to 64, and 15 percent 65 and older. College graduates attend at almost three times the rate of high school graduates. High income is a major factor. Rates are highest in the Northeast followed by the West, Midwest, and South in that order. Attendance at professional theater, a relatively costly event, tends to be an elite activity. However, community or school productions may have wider appeal. The positive factor in growth is the aging population who are most likely to attend live theater. The growth of community theater may also increase the supply. The niche market for more expensive professional theater, on the other hand, is limited and probably relatively stable (see Table 10-125).

Dance Performances

Trends since 1985 show an overall decline following a peak in 1988. The adult rate was 8 percent in 1985 and seems to have grown slightly to 10 percent or higher in 1987 and 1988. Since then a relatively steady overall rate of about 4 percent fluctuated somewhat with a high in 1993 and low in 1995. The gender ratio is over 2 to 1 female. Rates for those with college education are 50 percent higher than high school graduates. The same is true for high over moderate incomes. The age category of 18 to 24 is almost double those for older adults, but rates remain at over 3 percent up to age 65. Dance is a niche activity, most popular among those who dance or have danced when younger. The decline is general. The exceptions are families with daughters in dance programs and the core market of women with higher education levels. These are not growing market segments (see Table 10-126).

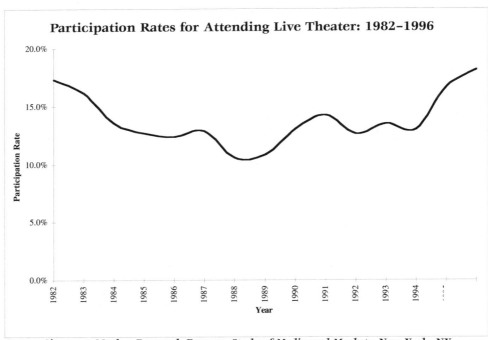

Source: Simmons Market Research Bureau. *Study of Media and Markets.* New York, NY.

Table 10-125

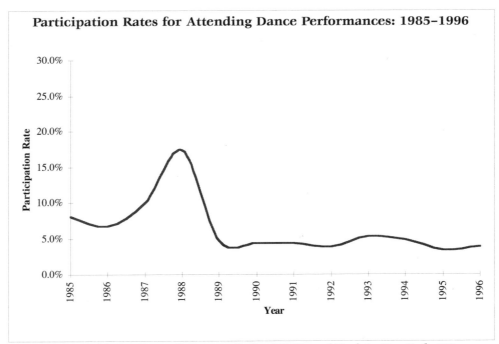

Source: Simmons Market Research Bureau. *Study of Media and Markets.* New York, NY.

Table 10-126

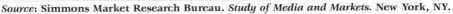

Comedy Clubs

The trend for this special activity peaked in 1995 after growth since 1989 and then has declined. The comedy club market grew from 5.2 percent in 1989 to a brief 7.3 percent peak in 1993 and then a return to 6 percent in 1994 and 5.4 percent in 1996. About 10 million adults attended comedy clubs that year. Female attendance slightly exceeded male, 6 percent to 5.6 percent. Those age 18 to 34 have 30 percent higher rates than those 35 to 44 and 60 percent higher than 45 to 54. Rates fall to 2 percent for age 55 to 64 and 1 percent for 65 and older. Singles go twice as often as the married. Those with some college education, often students, attend more than graduates and over twice as much as high school graduates. This specialized market is composed of young adults, often students, and most often single. The activity has some fad characteristics as well as a market segment that is not growing. Further decline to a niche plateau is probable (see Table 10-127).

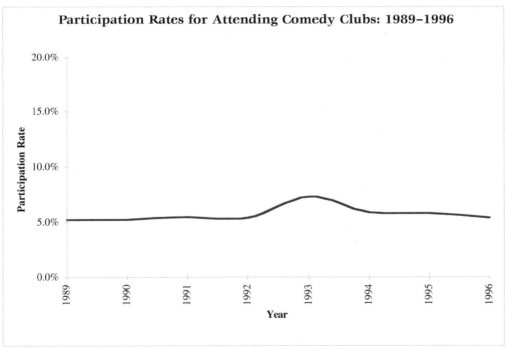

Source: **Simmons Market Research Bureau.** *Study of Media and Markets.* **New York, NY.**

Table 10-127

Crafts and Hobbies

There is trend data available on 10 crafts and hobbies. For the most part, these take place in the home. There are, however, workshops for ceramics, painting and sculpting, and photography. While some may be occasional, commitment to a skill most often produces a relatively high level of regular engagement. This engagement, often called "serious leisure," focuses on skill, a quality product, and long-term investment of time and money in the activity. The requirements for such activity are less

181

age-related than many activities, so they may benefit from the aging population. The overall trend figures, however, include occasional as well as committed participants. Not included here are a wide range of collecting activities that involve many adults and that may be lifelong.

Ceramics and Pottery

This niche activity has had a slight decline in the 1990s, from a 2.4 percent rate in 1991 to 2 percent in 1995 and 2.3 percent in 1996. There are in excess of 4 million potters and ceramic artists. Females outnumber males with a 2.8 percent rate to 1.1 percent for males. The 3 percent rate for those 18 to 24 is double the 1.5 percent rate of those age 45 to 64. Higher education is a strong factor, but not income. The activity is strongest in the West with the Midwest lowest. The young adult female population, most of whom are in the paid work force, is not a growing market segment. Further modest decline is probable unless "Boomers" return to the activity as they age.

Jewelry Making

The 1991–1996 trend is one of fluctuating participation at a low level: 1.5 percent in 1991, 1.8 percent in 1993, 1.2 percent in 1994, and 1.6 percent in 1996. There are about 3 million jewelry makers. They are almost 3 to 1 female. No other factors differentiate the market except region, with the West and Northeast almost twice the rate of the Midwest and South. This predominately female niche activity will likely remain a special interest market limited by the high proportion of women in the paid labor force.

Building Miniatures (models)

There has been some growth in this niche activity since 1991, from 2.9 percent to 3.5 percent in 1996. That rate yields about 6.5 million miniature builders. The market is mainly male, 5.7 percent to 1.3 percent female. There is an age factor with a 6.2 percent rate 18 to 24 dropping to 4 percent age 25 to 34, 3 percent age 35 to 54, and 2 percent 55 and older. There is a large component of single student-age builders. This small market may be segmented by types of models and miniatures. The data base is too limited to make any reliable projection. The aging of the society will not support sustained growth.

Model Railroads

Since 1991 this small niche activity has grown from a 1.2 percent rate to 1.4 percent with 2.6 million model railroaders. They are 2 to 1 male. The rate for age 35 to 44 is 2.3 percent and otherwise about 1.4 percent up to age 65. Education is not a factor, and higher income only moderately so. The activity is most common in the Northeast. Cost and space factors are likely to keep this activity limited in size and growth. Model railroading is likely to remain a niche market, but may have some growth from the small base as "Boomers" age.

Needlework

This activity has declined from 1979 from a high of 20 percent to about 11 percent from 1993 to 1996. There are now 21 million doing needlework that includes sewing as a hobby. The gender ration is 10 to 1 female. Needlework increases with age from 7 percent age 18 to 24 to 13 percent age 35 to 54 and 15.8 percent 65 and older. There are no education, income, or regional biases. It is a general activity for older women.

Despite the growth of this population segment, the probability for growth is unlikely as the aging cohorts of women enter later life with less and less sewing experience (see Table 10-128).

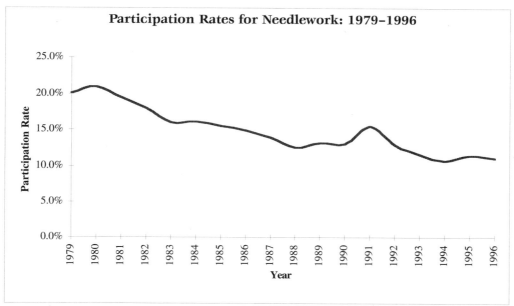

Participation Rates for Needlework: 1979–1996

Source: **Simmons Market Research Bureau.** *Study of Media and Markets.* **New York, NY.**

Table 10-128

Painting, Drawing, Sculpting

After years of decline from 1979, this composite arts activity has had a rebound. The rate fluctuated between 7.4 percent and 8.5 percent from 1980 to 1982, fell to an average of 6.5 percent from 1983 to through 1990, and rose to about 6.6 percent until 1995. The rebounding rate for 1995 was 9 percent and 8.7 percent in 1996. That produces 17 million doing these graphic and plastic arts. The gender rates favor females, 10.8 percent to 7.2 percent male. Those with college education do these arts at over twice the rate of those without. The age decline is gradual, but regular, starting at 15 percent for those 18 to 24, 11 percent for age 25 to 34, and 7 to 8 percent to age 65. The student segment is significant with singles outnumbering the married almost 2 to 1. The West has a considerably higher rate than the rest of the country. Higher education levels suggest further gradual growth, but the proportion of women in the paid work force throughout the adult life course is a deterring factor. Modest growth among older population segments may sustain continued, but limited, growth (see Table 10-129).

Photography

There has been overall growth since 1983 adding nearly 10 additional million participants. The 10.2 percent rate of 1983 held at about 11 percent through 1994 and then jumped to 13.8 percent for 1995 and 96. This rate yields over 26 million photographers. There is little gender difference. Rates by age do not drop from a 15 to 16 percent rate until age 55 and older with a 7.8 percent rate. College graduates, singles,

183

and those with high incomes do photography at a 30 percent higher level than others. Participation in the West is significantly higher than the rest of the country. The recent growth has been in all market segments in ways that broaden the market. With growth in older cohorts, the likelihood is that the moderate growth will continue, with the costs of equipment related to income. Demographic shifts support growth in this activity (see table10-130).

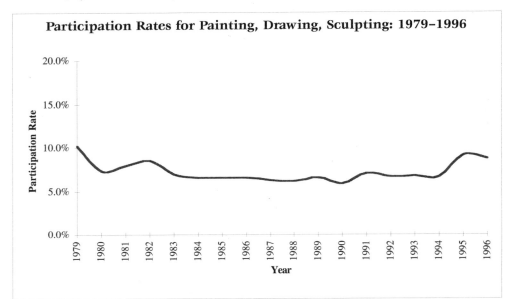

Participation Rates for Painting, Drawing, Sculpting: 1979–1996

Source: Simmons Market Research Bureau. *Study of Media and Markets*. New York, NY.

Table 10-129

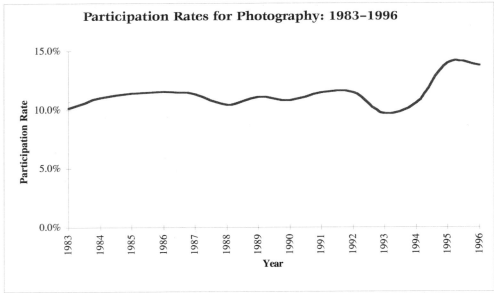

Participation Rates for Photography: 1983–1996

Source: Simmons Market Research Bureau. *Study of Media and Markets*. New York, NY.

Table 10-130

Quilting

Trend data on this ancient activity are only from 1993. Quilting seems to be a stable niche market with a rate of 3.8 percent of adults and 7.2 million participants. This is a female activity, 6.3 percent female to 1.1 percent male. Participation increases gradually with age through the 65 and older category. Rates are highest in moderate and low income levels. Quilting is least common in the Northeast. No trend is established in this activity for adult and older women, often of modest means. A sustained niche is the best that can be expected if younger women take up the activity as they move into later life (see Table 10-131).

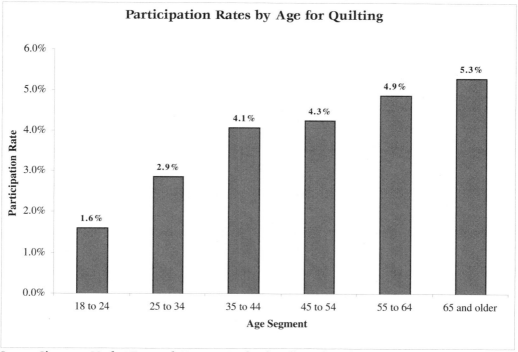

Source: **Simmons Market Research Bureau.** *Study of Media and Markets.* **New York, NY.**

Table 10-131

Woodworking

Since 1979, woodworking has had a fluctuating pattern without either growth or loss. The 9 percent rate of 1979 fell somewhat to 7 percent in 1988–89 and then rebounded back to 9 percent for two years, dropped as low as 6.4 percent in 1994, and then rose back to 8.7 percent in 1996. There are about 16 million woodworkers. This is a male activity by a 4 to 1 ratio. The rates are highest for adults age 35 to 64. Income and education do not segment the market. The married engage in woodworking at twice the rate of singles. Participation is highest in the Midwest and West. The fluctuation makes locating a long-term trend difficult, but the growth among older age cohorts suggest possible moderate future growth in an aging population (see Table 10-132).

185

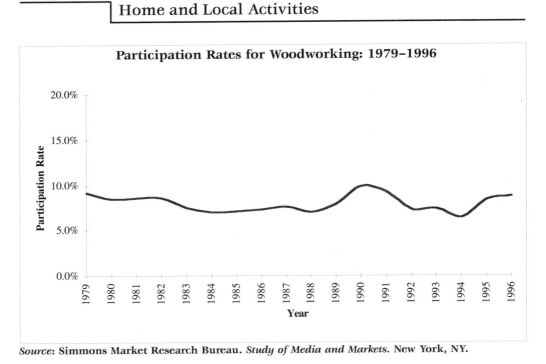

Participation Rates for Woodworking: 1979–1996

Source: Simmons Market Research Bureau. *Study of Media and Markets*. New York, NY.

Table 10-132

Furniture Refinishing

From 1992, the rate of about 6.5 percent has been fairly consistent yielding over 12 million furniture refinishers. The demographics show a small gender bias toward males, 7 percent to 5.8 percent. The 7 to 8 percent rate continues from age 25 through 54. Income, education, marital status, and region do not segment this undifferentiated market. This craft related to home enhancement may have small but steady growth. One question would be how much is related to special projects and how much an ongoing hobby activity continued from year to year. Aging may support some growth of the special project part of the market.

Personal Enrichment and Collecting

The general activity in this category is, of course, reading. There are, however, significant numbers of collectors. Only the most common forms are included here. There are collectors of almost every kind of artifact, often with national conventions, regional sales and exchange meetings, and at least one periodical. The total collecting participation would far outnumber the coin and stamp types for which trend data are available.

Reading Books

Considerable reading is of magazines and newspapers. The prediction that television would obliterate reading has not come to pass. Reading books is a growth activity with an inclusive market. The adult rate has grown from 32 percent in 1988 to 39 percent in 1992 and 47.5 percent in 1996. There are over 90 million adult book readers. Females read at somewhat higher rates than males, 45 percent to 32 percent. Except for those who did not graduate from high school or with low incomes, the market is broad and inclusive. Age is not a factor. The latest alleged threat to reading is the computer and the web as a source of information. Books, however, are portable and familiar. There is every reason to project continued growth in this market, especially among the growing older age cohorts. The older population with higher education levels may also respond to the development of mall chain book retailing and the convenience of on-line selection and ordering (see Table 10-133).

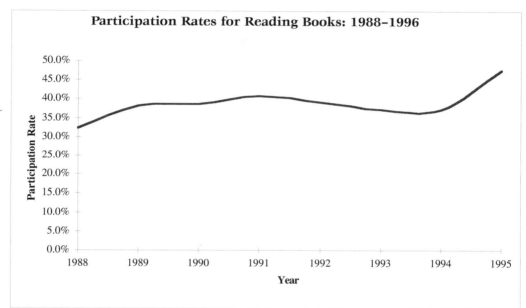

Participation Rates for Reading Books: 1988–1996

Source: **Simmons Market Research Bureau.** *Study of Media and Markets.* **New York, NY.**

Table 10-133

Adult Education

Adults take continuing education courses for many reasons. They may be seeking a new or improved work-related skill, gaining competence in a leisure activity, or just enjoying the learning experience and social interaction. The trend pattern since 1980 is fluctuating but steady with an 8 percent adult rate falling into the mid-6 percent range in some years and ending at 8 percent for 1995 and 1996. There are in excess of 15 million adults who take adult education courses. Gender rates are 50 percent higher for females. The strongest segmenting factor is previous education, with rates for those with some college education three times higher than for high school graduates. The age-related decline especially for those of retirement age seems to be reduced in the mid-1990s. There may be modest but steady growth from two sources: younger and midlife adults who seek marketable skills on a changing job market and the growing older adult segment with higher education levels than previous cohorts (see Table 10-134).

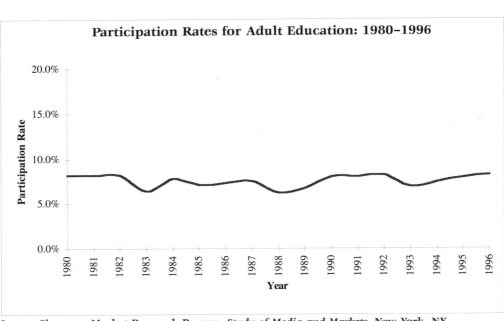

Participation Rates for Adult Education: 1980–1996

Source: Simmons Market Research Bureau. *Study of Media and Markets*. New York, NY.

Table 10-134

Antique Shopping

There has been fluctuating growth in the activity from 1989 beginning at a 9 percent adult rate and rising to 11.6 percent in 1995 and 96. There are 22 million adults who shop for antiques. They are 40 percent more likely to be female than male. There is no significant age drop until the 65 and older category. Antique shoppers are mostly likely to be married with college education and high or, at a 60 percent lower level of participation, moderate incomes. Participation is highest in the Midwest and, surprisingly, lower in the Northeast and South. Increases in the growing midlife age segments indicate a potential for continued moderate future growth and a sustained market (see Table 10-135).

Cooking for Fun

Since 1979, this popular home activity has been stable with a recent increase. The 1979–82 rate of 29 percent dropped gradually from 1983 to 1987, reached a low of 22 percent in 1988, grew to 26 percent and then jumped to 34 to 35 percent in 1995 and 1996. There are about 65 million pleasure cooks. Females cook for pleasure at a rate 25 percent higher than males. There is no significant age decrease up to the age 65 and older category. In fact, there are no strong demographic market segmentation factors. Growth has been in the young adult and retirement cohorts, indicating sustained growth patterns among most adult segments. Media attention and catalog promotions for equipment may also support the market (see Table 10-136).

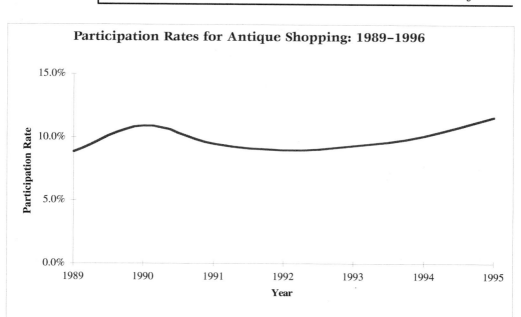

Participation Rates for Antique Shopping: 1989–1996

Source: Simmons Market Research Bureau. *Study of Media and Markets*. New York, NY.

Table 10-135

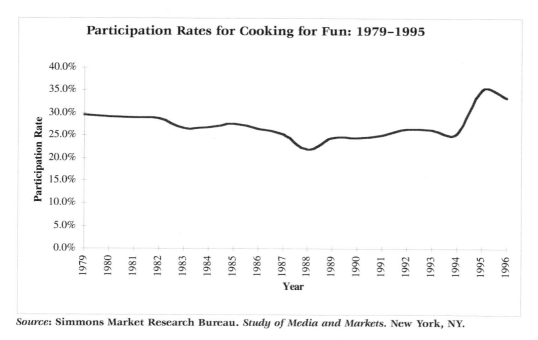

Participation Rates for Cooking for Fun: 1979–1995

Source: Simmons Market Research Bureau. *Study of Media and Markets*. New York, NY.

Table 10-136

Coin Collecting

The trend since 1979 had been one of decline followed by a recent upsurge in the mid-1990s. An adult rate of about 5 percent fell below 3 percent in 1988, leveled at 3 percent, and then jumped to 5.6 percent in 1995 and 6.8 percent in 1996. There are 11 to 13 million adult coin collectors. Males collect coins at a 40 percent higher rate than females. There are no other significant market segmenting factors. There is no clear explanation for the recent upsurge unless commercial enterprises are creating new markets with young adults and the retirement cohort providing the growth. There may be continued short-term growth, but it is not likely to be dramatic (see Table 10-137).

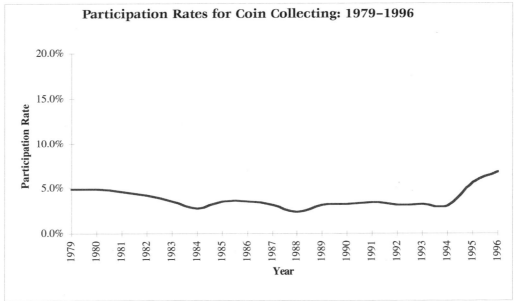

Participation Rates for Coin Collecting: 1979–1996

Source: **Simmons Market Research Bureau.** *Study of Media and Markets.* **New York, NY.**

Table 10-137

Stamp Collecting

This collecting activity also has a trend of decline from 1979 with a recent upsurge. A 2.8 percent adult rate in 1979 fell to a 2 percent level from 1983 through 1994 and then jumped to just over 4 percent in 1995 and 96. This pattern similar to coin collecting does raise the possibility that there was some change in the survey technique that produced the rise. The total of about 3.5 million stamp collectors was found to grow to 8 million in 1995 and 1996. Prior to 1995 the stamp collecting market was almost evenly divided by gender. College graduates and those with high incomes collect at somewhat higher rates. If the recent growth is related to overall promotion and special popular stamps, it may not last. Postal service promotions, however, may be producing a larger market and possible market spikes. Increases are in all market categories of age and income (see Table 10-138).

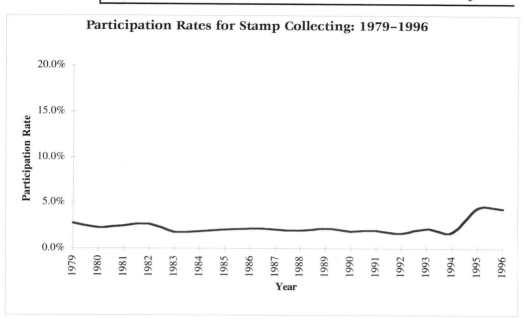

Participation Rates for Stamp Collecting: 1979–1996

Source: **Simmons Market Research Bureau.** *Study of Media and Markets.* **New York, NY.**

Table 10-138

Games and Gambling

The proliferation of legalized gambling has produced a rapidly rising trend from 1985 through 1996. More recent reports on riverboats and casinos suggest that the market, at least in many areas, may be saturated. Of course, some of the reported growth is the movement of previously illegal forms of gambling into legal contexts and varieties. Illegal gambling has not disappeared, however, and should be added to the official reports here. For example, to what extent have state-run lotteries supplanted the old "numbers" racket and how much of the old form continues? Card and other games may also be forms of gambling or may be played just for the competitive and social experience. There are, for example, "low stakes" games of poker that may be more a social than a gambling experience. The survey reports that follow cannot distinguish such styles of games and gambling, only that such activity occurs. However, they do give a general view of their importance in adult leisure.

Casino Gambling

The trend since 1985 has been one of growth. A 13 percent adult rate for 1979 and 1980 grew to about 14 percent from 1988 through 1991, over 17 percent for 1993 and 1994, and 28 percent in 1996. These rates yielded 25 million casino gamblers in 1990, 32 million in 1993, and 53 million in 1995. One question is the extent to which the upsurge in 1995 and 1996 reflects survey methods or increased opportunity and promotion. In any case, gambling is a general and inclusive activity. Most casino gambling is at the machines rather than tables despite some regional differences. There are no gender differences or significant declines with age. In fact, other than a lower rate in the South, casino gambling has strong participation at all education and income levels due to growth in the lower segments. Clearly, supply has increased demand. This a growth activity driven by the addition of casinos in the West, Midwest and Northeast. Opportunity increases demand, especially when casinos are opened near major urban populations. Gambling can be more a regular activity rather than one requiring overnight trips. The growth pattern is across the board. The only reasons to predict an approaching peak to this growth are the fact that every growth activity eventually saturates the markets, historical study has found a cycle of gambling growth and decline in the United States, and, some localized instances of oversupply and the failure of riverboats and casinos. Conversely, the growth in the older population suggests a continuing supply of "respectable" legal gamblers (see Tables 10-139 and 10-140).

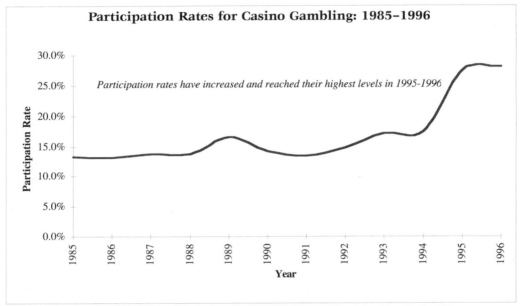

Participation Rates for Casino Gambling: 1985–1996

Participation rates have increased and reached their highest levels in 1995-1996

Source: **Simmons Market Research Bureau.** *Study of Media and Markets.* **New York, NY.**

Table 10-139

State Lotteries

This form of gambling also has a pattern of growth reflecting supply and promotion factors. The 25 percent adult rate in 1985 grew to 45 percent in 1990, 48 percent in 1993, and 57 percent in 1995 and 1996. There are signs, however, that the growth is leveling off. The 80 million lottery players in 1990 grew to 110 million in 1996. Lottery gambling also has inclusive demographics. Males gamble only 10 percent more than females. There is a steady rate by age up to a 20 percent decline for those age 65 and older. The Northeast has the highest rates and the South the lowest, reflecting the supply and promotion factor. This form of gambling doubled in a decade, but may be approaching market saturation. Further significant growth may depend more on innovative forms of lotteries and their promotion than increased interest. When over half the adult population plays and opportunities are available in supermarkets and convenience stores, gambling in all its forms seems to have become the largest single "recreation" activity outside the home (see Tables 10-141 and 10-142).

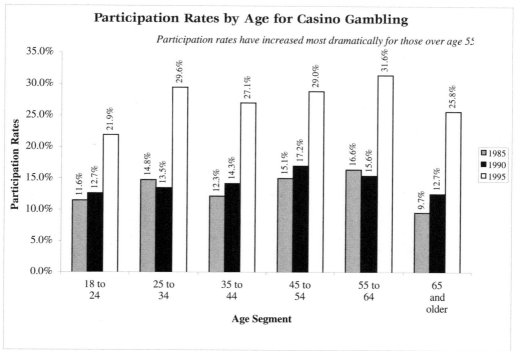

Source: Simmons Market Research Bureau. *Study of Media and Markets*. New York, NY.

Table 10-140

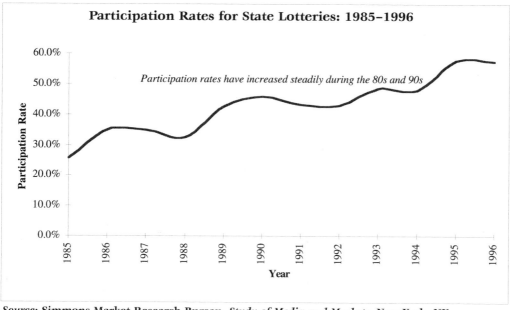

Source: Simmons Market Research Bureau. *Study of Media and Markets*. New York, NY.

Table 10-141

193

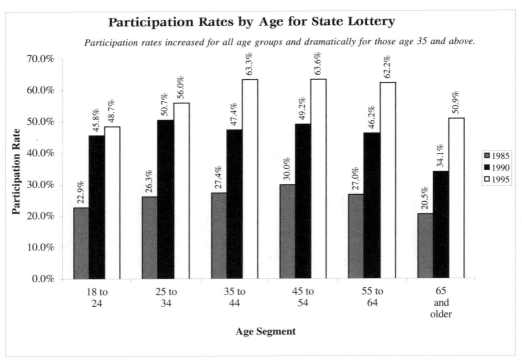

Participation Rates by Age for State Lottery

Participation rates increased for all age groups and dramatically for those age 35 and above.

Source: **Simmons Market Research Bureau.** *Study of Media and Markets.* **New York, NY.**

Table 10-142

Board Games

Since 1985, board games have undergone a major decline in participation followed by a rebound. A 22 percent rate in 1985 fell to 19 percent in 1989, about 21 percent in 1991 and 1992, another fall to 19 percent in 1993 and 1994, and then a rebound to 26 percent in 1995 and almost 28 percent in 1996. The 35 million participants of 1990 increased to 50 million in 1995. Females play over 30 percent more than males. Rates remain relatively steady to age 45 at about 24 percent, drop to 19 percent for 45 to 54, 11 percent 55 to 64, and 6 percent for 65 and older. Those with higher education levels and incomes play significantly more. The highest rates are in households with school-age children living at home. The greatest growth has been in the young adult and retiree age groups. The impact of computer games may reduce the more recent growth cycle. Overall, board games appear to have a secure family market, but one that is unlikely to continue to grow significantly as computer-adept children and youth enter their adult years. A possible exception would be the adaptation of some board games to internet play (see Table 10-143).

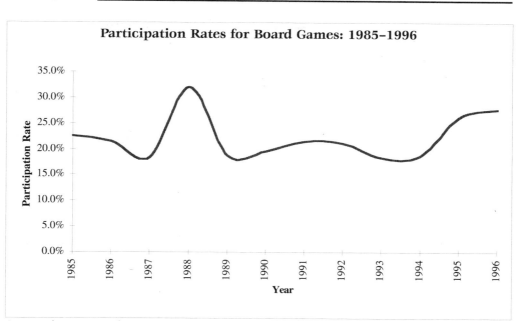

Participation Rates for Board Games: 1985–1996

Source: **Simmons Market Research Bureau.** *Study of Media and Markets.* **New York, NY.**

Table 10-143

Card Games

A trend of decline since 1984 seems to have been reversed in 1995 and 1996, if the widespread increases in the SMS surveys are accurate. A 28 percent adult rate in 1985 fell to 23 percent in 1988, leveled at 25 percent through 1992, fell again to 21 percent in 1993 and 1994, and then surged to 27 percent in 1995 and 33 percent in 1996. The 40 million participants of 1988 grew to 51 million in 1995 and 64 million in 1996. Card games, of course, include games such as contract bridge with a female bias and poker with a male bias. Some card games are customarily linked to gambling. The market segments differ according to the game. In general, females play cards 15 percent more than males. Ages 25 through 44 have the highest rates at 28 to 29 percent with a decline to 23 percent for age 45 to 54, 18 percent for 55 to 64, and 17 percent for 65 and older. Other segmentation is not strong except for lower rates by those who did not finish high school and with low incomes. Card playing as a general activity includes many different forms including gambling and venues from homes to casinos. The increases are highest among young adults age 18 to 24. The recent growth is driven by this young adult market so may continue at a decreasing rate. Questions involve the introduction of younger generations by older ones and internet forms of card games (see Table 10-144).

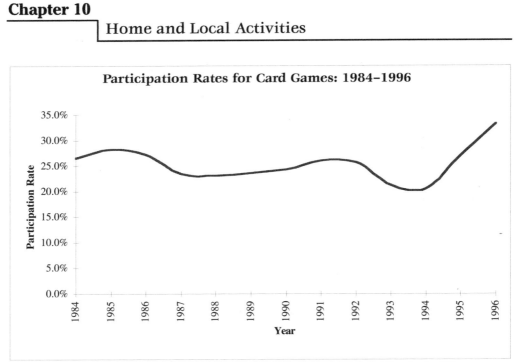

Participation Rates for Card Games: 1984–1996

Source: Simmons Market Research Bureau. *Study of Media and Markets*. New York, NY.

Table 10-144

Index

Recreation Trends and Markets: The 21st Century

Index